YANKEE
LEGENDS

YANKEE
LEGENDS

PIVOTAL MOMENTS,
PLAYERS & PERSONALITIES

MARK NEWMAN

1-30-19

Published by Blue River Press
Indianapolis, Indiana
www.brpressbooks.com

Distributed by Cardinal Publishers Group
A Tom Doherty Company, Inc.
www.cardinalpub.com

ISBN: 978-1-68157-131-7

Cover Design: Keith Lowe
Book Design: Glen M. Edelstein
Editor: Dani McCormick
All photographs courtesy of the Bain Collection at the Library of Congress unless otherwise noted.

Printed in the United States of America

10 9 8 7 6 5 4 3 2 1   18 19 20 21 22 23 24 25 26 27

INTRODUCTION

It was one of those Norman Rockwell mornings in March of 2018 as I drove past homes with luminescent snow piled high on rooves, on my way to the frigid hamlet of Cooperstown and the site where Babe Ruth and 10 other immortals were first enshrined in 1939. I parked next to a heap of the white stuff and arrived at the office entrance of the National Baseball Hall of Fame and Museum on Main Street. I brushed some snow off my coat and stepped in from the cold.

Jeff Idelson, the Hall of Fame's longtime president and previously a faithful publicist for the Yankees of George Steinbrenner, was there, and I began to fill him in a bit on the book that I was about to begin researching there for the next few days.

"It's about Yankee legends, so I thought I would start where so many are enshrined," I told Jeff.

"'Yankee legends.' That's redundant, isn't it?" he replied.

I have thought about those words through the entire exercise of writing this book. As a Hall of Fame voting member of the Baseball Writers' Association of America, I have spent long hours thinking about what merits induction into the Hall of Fame of all halls of fame. I have sat on the benches in the middle of the Gallery room like so many fans, alone with one's thoughts while contemplating the bronze plaques on the surrounding walls. You know, those thoughts that take you back to that particular inductee's own golden age of domination on the field, and your own memories of watching them and sharing priceless ballpark time with family members.

Now, however, I was looking at those plaques in a different light. I began counting my steps, counting the plaques, studying their arrangements, even their facial features, and whether they looked straight ahead or to the side. By my count, fully 16 of the 20 alcoves or walls featured New York Yankee representation on this day.

A record nine players and 12 individuals overall were inducted just from the 1932 Yankees. The players, with election year in parenthesis, include: Earle Combs (1970), Bill Dickey (1954), Lou Gehrig (1939), Lefty Gomez (1972), Tony Lazzeri (1991), Herb Pennock (1948), Red Ruffing (1967), Ruth (1936, three years before induction) and Joe Sewell (1977). Those 1932 Yankees are also represented in Cooperstown by Manager Joe McCarthy (1957), General Manager Ed Barrow (1953), and Owner Jacob Ruppert (2012).

Such an infinitesimal number of aspiring ballplayers go on to the professional ranks, to the Majors, and then to Cooperstown. Yet league-wide, the proportion of Yankee inductees to others remains remarkably high.

"The museum is for fans of all players and all teams, and the experience is filled with artifacts and stories that talk about the game as it's unfolded over the centuries," Idelson said. "But the Yankees have been the most successful franchise in baseball history by their number of championships, and to build championship teams, you have to have legendary players that step up. Some do it for a short period of time, some make a career out of it. The fact that the Yankees have so much real estate in Cooperstown, in the plaque gallery and the museum, is a testament to their continuous winning."

With Mariano Rivera (2019) and Derek Jeter (2020) on the verge of expected first-ballot election in back-to-back years—and sure to threaten or surpass Induction Week attendance records due to Yankee fans' easy access and unbridled passion—this was a particularly auspicious time to undertake a Yankee Legends book that approaches the subject from a Cooperstown-centric perspective. That was the peg for this project.

"Every year, fans from all thirty teams and teams that no longer exist come to Cooperstown," Idelson continued. "Being located in New York state, in some ways, perhaps was a bit fortuitous given the winning ways of the Yankees for all those years. If this museum were located anywhere else in the country, it would have the same flavor, because you can't deny the number of ways that the Yankees have impacted baseball history, but given that Cooperstown is within driving distance of Yankee Stadium assures that every Yankee fan can make it to Cooperstown if he or she wants."

Yankee fans have just about everything a baseball fan could want, with 27 titles entering the 2019 season and usually the best personnel and a shot at a postseason. They also have far, far more books devoted to their organization than any other, including the squad up in Boston.

During a Midwest book tour while promoting *Diamonds from the Dugout* in January 2018, I met with the Blue River Press team at their headquarters, and that is when Tom Doherty suggested a new project on team legends, starting with the Yankees. My first reaction was one of apprehension, maybe incertitude. That is some big ground to cover. I decided to approach it like a recording artist doing a cover of an over-covered song . . . maybe a holiday hit. And in my case, it was going to start and finish in Cooperstown, where hallowed Yankees live on.

In no way is this book meant to be a ranking of the top 50 Yankees or anything of the sort. There are plenty of those. These are 50 essays of *pivotal* points in franchise history, with lots of extras. Every topic was approached with the word "pivotal" in mind. For instance, Yogi Berra and Jorge Posada becoming catchers, or Whitey Ford perfecting the slider and Mo the cutter.

The list of essays is reasoned yet arbitrary, and many Yankee fans no doubt would substitute their own favorites here and there. That is one thing that sets this franchise apart from any other: There are so many stars from the field and front office who would be obvious inclusions in other teams' books but have to fight for space in this kind of account. Ruth's Called Shot is deconstructed and debated for time immemorial, yet it was not really all that pivotal, and in all those many thick folders of Ruth clips that I perused in the Hall's Giamatti Research Center, there were none that could shed light on it to prove he did or didn't call that 1932 World Series homer at Wrigley Field. Teammates, his wife, opponents, and other witnesses were divided on whether he called it, and that is just the way it will remain for all time.

There were more than enough pivotal moments to study instead. As I sauntered through the Gallery that snowy day, I started as always with the Ruth wall, and then worked my way to the main entrance. Suddenly, it seemed surprising to see a wall or alcove that did *not* include Yankee representation. I exited the Gallery, headed for the library, and stopped at the "Voices of the Game" exhibit that lets you hear famous broadcast calls.

There was Bob Wolff's call of Don Larsen's 1956 World Series perfect game. "Man, what a thrill this is!" Wolff said to his listeners.

I looked at Grantland Rice's last Underwood, and I thought about Wolff's words and how Idelson had greeted me. I covered Yankee World Series, I was there for their last All-Star Game and last regular season game in 2008, I got soaked in the 2009 champagne celebration and watched Jeter wave in the parade. I played high school ball in Indiana against Don Mattingly and shared in our pride over his ascension to Donnie Baseball status. Just watching ordinary day and night games in the Bronx, grabbing garlic fries and sitting high or low, I enjoyed those times with family. But man, what a thrill this is to write a book about Yankee legends.

MARIANO RIVERA

It is no coincidence that Mariano Rivera and Derek Jeter appear in consecutive order on these pages. Each of their Major League debuts with the Yankees occurred on a West Coast swing in May of 1995—the former in Anaheim on the 23rd and the latter up in Seattle just six days later. Each brought the house down with triumphal farewell tours: the former in 2013 with 1 1/3 perfect innings of relief and an unforgettable removal by his "Core Four" friends, and the latter in 2014 with a scripted walk-off single in trademark opposite-field fashion. Then came their Monument Park dedications in 2016 and 2017, respectively.

Now comes the inevitable bliss for Yankee fans: back-to-back inductions of those greats into the Hall of Fame. I am not going out on a limb in saying that both will have my own vote on the first ballot. Rivera will be an obvious pick for the Class of 2019 and Jeter will be an obvious pick for the Class of 2020. Record-breaking attendance totals are realistic possibilities in both cases, for two men who not only personified Yankee success on a team and individual scale, but also for two humanitarians who projected only dignity, consistent professionalism, durability and idol status exemplified by all those 42 and 2 jerseys that graced two versions of the Stadium.

"When you have players who transcend the game by also being popular to fans, their popularity skyrockets come Induction day," Hall of Fame president Jeff Idelson said. "When you think about the great Yankees of all-time, nobody connected better with fans than Mariano and Jeter. That's why it is expected that attendance in Cooperstown would reach historic levels for Mariano and for Derek, if they are elected. It is the chance to say 'thank you' for a career well done.

"When you have made yourself accessible for an entire career, it is inviting for a fan to want to come up and have that opportunity. Popularity does matter, it really does. Being at the top of your game is one thing, but the accessibility and how you treat the fans is what drives attendance numbers through the roof on Induction Sundays."

Rivera converted a record 652 saves, clearly establishing himself as the best reliever in baseball history and in all likelihood owning an unbreakable record given the subsequent devaluation of the save statistic. His glory could be measured far beyond saves as well. He compiled the best ERA+ (205) in MLB history, and thanks to his final appearance, the lowest ERA (2.21) of any pitcher in the live-ball era (since 1920). His 1.000 WHIP was the lowest in the live-ball era and third in MLB history for any pitcher with at least 1,000 career innings pitched. He appeared in more games (1,115) than anyone in AL history, and was selected to 13 All-Star Games, claiming the MVP title in the 2013 swan-song game at Citi Field.

The postseason credentials are especially staggering in looking back. It is the kind of immortal-like success rate one often associates with Babe Ruth, Lou Gehrig, Joe DiMaggio et al. He belongs in the same breath as them. Rivera won five rings. He compiled a gaudy 0.70 postseason ERA in 141 innings, and was named MVP of the 1999 World Series against Atlanta. In 96 postseason appearances, he gave up more one earned run *once*.

"You have to put him with Ruth, Gehrig and Mantle," Yankee Hall of Famer Reggie Jackson said during Rivera's farewell tour. "Joe DiMaggio didn't play long enough. . . . [Rivera] is the measuring stick for relievers, for greatness, for clutch performance. He is the measuring stick for the Yankees organization."

The pivotal moment in Rivera's evolution toward such immortality was a one-two punch of fate: his rookie-season switch from starter to reliever, and, to a greater extent, the discovery and institutionalization of his signature cutter pitch.

RETIRED NUMBERS

Since Lou Gehrig became the first baseball player to have his jersey number (4) retired, the Yankees have made the ritual a fact of life for generations. They have retired numbers for 23 legends, including one through 10 and an astounding five catchers alone. Eight and 42 have been retired twice, the latter because Major League Baseball retired Jackie Robinson's number league-wide in 1997. Next!

NUMBER	NAME	POSITION	YEAR RETIRED
1	Billy Martin	MGR	1986
2	Derek Jeter	SS	2017
3	Babe Ruth	RF	1948
4	Lou Gehrig	1B	1939
5	Joe DiMaggio	CF	1952
6	Joe Torre	MGR	2014
7	Mickey Mantle	CF	1969
8	Yogi Berra	C	1972
8	Bill Dickey	C	1972
9	Roger Maris	RF	1984
10	Phil Rizzuto	SS	1985
15	Thurman Munson	C	1980
16	Whitey Ford	LHP	1974
20	Jorge Posada	C	2015
23	Don Mattingly	1B	1997
32	Elston Howard	C	1984
37	Casey Stengel	MGR	1970
42	Mariano Rivera	RHP	2013
42	Jackie Robinson	2B	1997
44	Reggie Jackson	RF	1993
46	Andy Pettitte	LHP	2015
47	Ron Guidry	LHP	2003
51	Bernie Williams	CF	2015

"A gift from God," Rivera called it, to anyone who would ask.

Rivera's arm slot varied less than two degrees on any type of pitch, making it nearly impossible for batters to gauge what kind of pitch was coming. His four-seam fastball was thrown on a vertical axis and typically rotated at about 1,500 rpm. By adjusting his grip by just a stitch of two and altering his fingertip pressure, that four-seamer turned into a cutter, released on a tilted axis and typically rotating at up to 1,600 rpm. The faster the spin, the greater the curve. That slight change in his delivery amounted to about eight more inches of break, an enormous increase, and what mattered most is that the increased break happened in the last 10 feet of the ball's path. That made it impossible to read and get a barrel on it.

Ted Williams said hitting a fastball was the hardest thing to do in sports, and one could amend that statement to specifically include a Mariano Rivera cutter. The difficulty was magnified when considering that a hitter would see his pitch on a limited basis, late in Yankee games. Many other pitchers tried to emulate it and none could master it. The true beauty of Rivera's cutter was that he invented it and took it into retirement with him, his strength and his alone.

It all began one day in 1997 while playing catch before a game with Ramiro Mendoza, his longtime setup man.

"All of a sudden the ball just started cutting," Rivera said. "It was natural. I was gripping the ball all kinds of ways. Different ways and the ball was doing the same thing, cutting. I'm thinking, 'Why is this ball moving?'

"Mendoza got upset with me. He yelled, 'Throw the ball straight.' I said, 'Man, I'm trying. It just won't go that way.'"

Rivera had blown away batters with his four-seamer in the 1996 title season, mixing in a slider—standard reliever formula. In 1997, he said, the ball just "started moving. In games and on the side. Everywhere. I wasn't throwing it with an off-set grip, the way a lot of guys do. It was my same four-seam grip.

"I remember at first worrying about what happened to my four-seamer. I remember working with [pitching coach] Mel Stottlemyre trying to straighten it out. And it kept cutting. Finally, Mel said, 'You know, leave it like that.' And I did. I was able to throw it harder than other guys because it was such a natural release. Just grab it with my four-seam grip and throw that sucker down the middle and let it move. That's how it started. "

HOF ARTIFACT INVENTORY

Game-used equipment in the Baseball Hall of Fame:

MARIANO RIVERA

B-154.2013	Yankees cap worn by Mariano Rivera during his final All-Star Game in 2013. He was named MVP, pitching a perfect eighth inning in the American League's 3-0 victory over the National League.
B-178.2013	Baseball signed by on Aug. 6, 2013, while in Chicago with the Yankees. Rivera announced that 2013 would be his final season and asked all the teams to have some fans available for a meet and greet as part of his Farewell Tour. Donors of the ball were selected by the White Sox to be at the Chicago event.
B-186.2008	Yankees home jersey worn in the 2008 All-Star Game played at Yankee Stadium. Black armband was added in memory of Bobby Murcer.
B-203.2006	Cap worn on July 16, 2006, when he recorded his 400th career save.
B-223.2009	Baseball signed by Andy Pettitte and Rivera on May 29, 2009, when Pettitte was credited with the win and Rivera picked up the save. This was the 58th career win/save combination for the teammates.
B-365.2009	Cap worn during the 2009 World Series, where he earned his fifth ring. Rivera pitched 5 1/3 innings and allowed three hits and no runs, recording two saves.
B-368.2000	Cap worn during the 2000 World Series, where he finished off a three-peat with a Game 5 save in the Subway Series against the Mets.
B-382.99	Shoes worn during the 1999 World Series. Rivera was named Series MVP.
B-170.2011	Bat used by Toronto's Brett Lawrie on Sept. 17, 2011, batting against Rivera in the bottom of the ninth. Lawrie's broken bat ground out to first base was the second out of the inning. Rivera got the next batter to fly out and record his 601st career save, tying Trevor Hoffman's record.

Rivera was originally scouted by Herb Raybourn in Panama in 1988. Raybourn was a light-hitting, good defensive shortstop at the time, and left uninterested. "I saw that he could run, he had a good arm and he had good hands, but I didn't think he could be a major league shortstop," Raybourn said. "So I passed on him."

A couple years later, Rivera called Raybourn again and told him he had begun pitching. Raybourn returned for a second look. "I said the Mariano Rivera I knew was a shortstop," Raybourn said. "They told me that he was a pitcher now." After witnessing only nine pitches, Raybourn and the Yankees were sold. They signed him as an amateur free agent on February 17, 1990.

On May 23, 1995, the Mariano Rivera era officially began. He debuted on that aforementioned road trip against the then-California Angels, and went on to make 10 starts in 19 appearances for manager Buck Showalter—struggling to a 5.51 ERA in 67 innings. He took the loss in a September 5 start against Seattle—the team that would end the Yankees' playoff hopes a month later—and Showalter had used him exclusively out of the bullpen for the remainder of the season.

Rivera would never start another game in the Majors, becoming the greatest closer instead.

He was a key reason for the beginning of the Yankees dynasty in 1996. That season, Rivera served as a multi-inning right-hander and struck out 130 batters in 107 2/3 innings. That 10.9 strikeout-per-nine-inning rate would be the highest mark of his career. Incumbent closer John Wetteland became a free agent and signed with the Texas Rangers following that World Series celebration, opening the door for Rivera to take over the role. Mo saved 43 games in 1997 with a 1.88 ERA and never gave up the role for the next 17 seasons.

A top-10 Hall of Fame voting percentage would have seemed only natural, given how he owned his position in a way no other recent—or near-future—player has owned his. Alas, in this age, there are some BBWAA voters who see such first-ballot lock status as a way to instead use that vote to help a fringe candidate either reach 75 percent or merely stay on the ballot. Whatever the final numbers, Rivera enters Cooperstown with a memory of a final out and a businesslike congratulatory greeting from Monument Park neighbor Jorge Posada.

"I get the ball, I throw the ball, and then I take a shower," Rivera said. That became typical of his famous humility and stoic, calm-and-collected nature—a characteristic of confidence and consistency that helped define the successful run of Joe Torre teams in the Bronx.

Rivera threw the final pitch of the World Series in four consecutive years, 1998 – 2001. The first three were clinchers, and the fourth was the bloop single given up to Luis Gonzalez with a drawn-in infield, a blown save that ended Game Seven of the unforgettable post-9/11 series against Arizona. That was a rare hiccup for Rivera, along with the 2004 AL Championship Series against Boston. You can remember them so easily because they stuck out like sore thumbs. And yet it was Rivera's ability to forget them so easily that made him a legend.

He commanded utmost respect of opponents throughout his career, with the farewell tour in 2013 bringing it all to the surface. The Minnesota Twins gave him a rocking chair of broken bats; a typical result of a signature Mariano cutter in on a batter's hands. For Rivera, though, that last go-round was all about the fans. He made a special point at each series of having conversations with ballpark employees of varying roles, thanking them for being there—an astounding and unprecedented gesture in the Majors. It was so typical of his nature, though. When he was allowed to continue to wear his signature number 42 as Jackie Robinson's number was retired throughout the Majors, Rachel Robinson said Mo was the perfect person to carry on her late husband's legacy.

The AL Reliever of the Year Award has been annually awarded in Rivera's name since 2014, with the NL version awarded in Trevor Hoffman's name. They are the only people ever to reach 600 saves, and the opposing closers from the 1998 World

Series. I thought it also was fitting that Hoffman was inducted into the Hall of Fame in 2018, meaning the probability that they would go in as back-to-back inductees. So in April of 2017, as Hoffman sat in the Hall's Gallery rotunda answering media questions following his own Hall orientation tour, I asked what he thought about that subject.

"Yeah, I'm going to go out on a limb and say [Rivera] is probably going to be a first-ballot Hall of Famer," Hoffman replied with a hearty laugh. "Having had the opportunity to get to see him now on an annual basis with the World Series, he exudes class. Getting to see it first-hand rather than through television or excerpts on a radio, I obviously know his talents as a player, but the man is equally as great off the field. He has been a great ambassador for the game and he'll be a welcome addition here."

In 2015, after Yoga Berra died, the *Times* wrote that Whitey Ford had inherited the mantle of "greatest living Yankee." But was it true? Going by wins above replacement at Baseball Reference, Ford is second (53.9) to Rivera (56.6) on the Yankees' all-time list. Maybe it depends on how one defines "greatest." Is it rings? Is it stats? Is it how much a player truly owned his position? Is it a less quantifiable measure of respect by today's total Yankee fan base, based on sweet memories of youth? Perhaps it will be one of these next two Hall of Fame inductees, headed to Cooperstown in consecutive summers. It will be a generational argument, with plenty of love to go around for the legends. In any case, it is truly amazing that a relief pitcher with a freak pitch accumulated more bWAR than any other pitcher in Yankees annals.

DEREK JETER

Walk-off, Flip, Dive, Mr. November, 3000.

If you can identify with that personal ranking of Derek Jeter's five greatest moments, then you probably also have been counting down the days to the summer of 2020 and a Hall of Fame induction for the ages. That is my own order, and yours may have some variation of the moments or an occasional substitute. There is a temptation here to rank a more everyday visual in the number one slot, such as the mere sight of seeing number two in ready mode at shortstop any random inning on his last Opening Day at the Stadium. But these are the biggest individual moments for the unmatched icon of a generation in baseball, and thus sacrosanct in any presentation of a top five.

"The thing that means the most to me is being remembered as a Yankee," Jeter said that day at the start of Spring Training in 2014, when he announced it would be his final season. "I have to thank the Steinbrenner family for giving me the opportunity to live my dream."

The opportunity came in 1992, when the Yankees drafted Jeter with the sixth overall selection out of Kalamazoo Central High School in Michigan. He had earned a scholarship to the University of Michigan, where a girlfriend was going to attend, and the Yankees front office had been concerned he would go there. "No," scout Dick Groch assured them, "the only place he's going is to Cooperstown." Indeed, Jeter was a Yankee fan since his boyhood days when he would visit his grandmother over in New Jersey, and he looked up to big Dave Winfield back then and literally dreamed of playing in pinstripes.

Now here he was, getting his pro career underway with the Yankees of the Gulf Coast League after that summer's draft, playing 47 games and then reporting to Greensboro, N.C., for 11 more games in the Class A South Atlantic League. Among the priceless memories of September 2014, when Jeter departed from the stage in one of the most classic ways possible, was the collection of memories that would come out in drips and drabs. Sweeny Murti unearthed many of the best ones for CBS New York, as he asked baseball lifers for their first impressions of Jeter and included hilarious recollections from Core Four cohorts.

"It was 1992, and I heard that our first-rounder was coming to the Greensboro Hornets," Jorge Posada said. "It was the beginning of August and they brought him up just to see how he was going to do. And when I saw him walk in, it wasn't pretty.

"We were on the field, I think he got there a little late. He comes out and he's got ankle braces on, big old high-top Nikes, his hat is kind of tilted up. Skinny, skinny—I mean he's skinny now, imagine him twenty pounds less. Super skinny, and I'm like 'This is our first-rounder, seriously?' You know I'm, like, hating on the guy a little bit.

"He goes out there [in the game] makes a play in the hole, shows a big arm, [on another play] makes a spin move behind second base, and then hit a home run to left-center. So he really shut me up [laughs]."

Andy Pettitte had a similar refrain: "It was his first game, or first couple games, in Greensboro, and I was having a real good year. He gets called up . . . playing shortstop, and he made a couple of errors in that game. And I'm thinking, 'What is this?' I think he did hit a home run in that game, but I kind of joke around saying my first impressions were, 'Who is this kid they put behind me, ruining my games for me?' I kind of give him a hard time about that."

DEREK JETER'S TOP 5 MOMENTS

Many people have ranked Derek Jeter's greatest moments, and the order varies widely based on personal thrills and one's own connection with those events. Here is my own rundown:

1. Walk-off single in final home game. Just when it looked like Jeter had already batted for the last time at home, David Robertson became the first pitcher in Major League history who was actually appreciated by his fans for blowing a save. He gave up three runs to Baltimore in the top of the ninth to tie the score at 5-5, and that meant another at-bat for Jeter. After a sacrifice bunt by Brett Gardner, Jeter faced Evan Meek and delivered a classic opposite-field stroke that scored pinch-runner Antoan Richardson from second with the winning run.

2. The Flip. Facing elimination down 2-0 to the Athletics in the 2001 ALDS, the Yankees had a 1-0 lead in the bottom of the seventh inning in Oakland. Terrence Long hit a double to right field off Mike Mussina and Jeremy Giambi tried to score from first. Shane Spencer made a poor throw from right that sailed way up the first base line, but Jeter came all the way from shortstop to field the throw and made a miraculous backhanded flip to Jorge Posada that nabbed Giambi at home and ended the threat. The Yankees held that lead and took the series in five games. It marked the first time an AL team won a Division Series after losing the first two games at home.

3. Diving into the stands against Boston. It was July 1, 2004 at Yankee Stadium, with the scored tied at 3-3 in the top of the 12th inning. Trot Nixon hit a shallow blooper toward the third-base side with two runners in scoring position and two outs. Jeter ran full steam from shortstop to catch it and his momentum carried him into foul territory and eventually caused him to dive into the seats as the low side wall could not stop him. He was forced to leave the game after emerging with facial cuts and bruises, but the Yankees eventually won the game in 14 innings. The rivalry was at its peak back then, and this play symbolized the spirit of it.

4. Mr. November. The 2001 World Series was played in a new time in America, amid heightened security measures after an unspeakable tragedy. There was tension about a large crowd gathering in Yankee Stadium, while work continued down at Ground Zero. After Arizona took the first two games at home, the Yankees won Game 3 and then went into the 10th inning tied at 1-1. As the clock struck midnight, the large scoreboard read: "Attention Fans, Welcome to NOVEMBER BASEBALL." It was the first official Major League game ever played in that month. Jeter came up with two out and hit a full-count pitch from Byung-Hyun Kim over the wall in right to tie the series. Reggie Jackson had been Mr. October, and a fan held up a sign that called Jeter "Mr. November." The name stuck.

5. 3,000th hit. Jeter entered play on July 9, 2011 with 2,998 career hits. After singling in the first inning, he yanked a 3-2 offering from David Price into the left field seats at Yankee Stadium in the third inning to join the exclusive club. Jeter became the 28th player in MLB history to reach the milestone, and for good measure, he added three more hits that day for a historic 5-for-5 afternoon.

Honorable mentions: Home run on the first pitch of Game 4 in the Subway Series at Shea Stadium, leading toward a third straight ring and a World Series MVP award; the home run caught by fan Jeffrey Maier in Game 1 of the 1996 ALCS against Baltimore; and the single in 2009 that gave Jeter 2,722 hits, breaking Lou Gehrig's 70-year record for most Yankee hits.

Those stories are priceless, in part because they say so much about how a nucleus bonded and grew up together to form a dynasty. Jeter was likeable. Oh, fans "hated" him at outposts throughout baseball, in the days when the Yankees' payroll was dwarfing all-comers. Think back to MLB's 2009 series of "I Live For This" television spots, and the one starring Jeter. Narrating his own highlight reel, he said: "I also enjoy going on the road, people booin' us and hatin' us." But that's a different kind of hate. It gradually came with an underlying respect from people all over. Two examples in particular come to mind:

One was his 14th and final All-Star Game in 2014 at Minnesota. Jeter led off the bottom of the first with a double (scoring on Mike Trout's triple), and then singled his next time up. The ovation reminded me of another All-Star Game I had covered, the 1989 NBA event in Houston, where Kareem Abdul-Jabbar received a standing ovation and then was willed by fans to return to the game later to set the all-time All-Star scoring record. Jeter's All-Star finale was similarly impactful, because he led off for the AL with a double (scoring on Mike Trout's triple) and then singled.

The other was the most telling gesture of all. At Fenway Park, where the rivalry had raged throughout his career, Red Sox and traveling Yankee fans expressed their appreciation. He drove in a run with an infield single in his final at-bat, and after Joe Girardi removed him for a pinch-runner, Jeter was showered with love and took an extra curtain call. In Boston.

"It always feels good any time the fans respect how you play," Jeter said for the first of those stories. "It's never something you think about, but you definitely take it as a huge compliment."

That quote is from one of my MLB.com stories about

Most Popular Jerseys, a regular ranking from MLB and the MLB Players Association. Jeter's career overlapped mine with MLB in nearly two decades, and one of my occasional duties was to write about those digital sales trends. The number two pinstriped jersey was undisputed king. It was maybe the best metric of popularity within the game, moreso than All-Star balloting. We started doing this at the beginning of the 2011 season, and here were the players who topped each list through his farewell season:

2014 Postseason: Derek Jeter
2014 All-Star Week: Derek Jeter
2014 Opening Day: David Ortiz
2013 Postseason: Mariano Rivera
2013 All-Star Week: Derek Jeter
2012 Postseason: Derek Jeter
2012 Opening Day: Derek Jeter
2011 Opening Day: Derek Jeter

The only exceptions on that list were the number 42 jerseys that fans bought en masse in the final months of Rivera's final 2013 season, followed immediately by Big Papi sales as part of an overall boom in Red Sox sales following their 2013 World Series title. Other than that, Jeter owned the list. He honestly invented it. The game of baseball developed around him, the face. When we at MLB Advanced Media presented the first live stream of an MLB game on August 26, 2002, it was of course a Yankees home game against Texas, and I would frequently quote Jeter about how important it was that the new technology kept his fans closer to the game. Anything big in baseball business usually revolved around him in some way.

His mere importance to the game and his widespread popularity only made some fans try harder to find weakness in his contributions on the field. He was not Omar Vizquel in the field, but he is No. 10 all-time among shortstops in WAR (72.4 on Baseball Reference), and the only two in that top 10 not in the

Hall are Alex Rodriguez (number two) and Bill Dahlen (number seven).

"He's a special young man, not only the baseball part of the game, but he's just been a great role model for all the young kids," said Joe Torre, a second father figure to Jeter during their years together. "To do that in New York, especially as a single player where there are a lot of distractions that can certainly cut into what you do, I think he's been tremendous."

When Jeter made his debut with the Yankees in 1996, the only single-digit numbers not yet retired by the Yankees were two and six. He and Torre would take care of that, but first the matter of an everyday shortstop had to be finalized, and that was the pivotal moment in Jeter's Yankee career.

Derek Jeter at bat against the Orioles in 2008.
Courtesy of Keith Allison

HOF ARTIFACT INVENTORY

Game-used equipment in the Baseball Hall of Fame:

DEREK JETER

B-318.96	Yankees jersey 1996 WS; AL Rookie of the Year.
B-436.98	Spikes worn during 1998 WS.
B-362.2000	Batting helmet, 2000 WS, MVP.
B-136.2011	Batting helmet, 3000th hit, 7/9/2011.
B-137.2011	Batting gloves, 3000th hit.
B-110.2014	2014 A-S Game cap.
B-326.97	Bat, AL Division Series, 9/30/97.
B-438.98	Bat, 1998 WS.
B-254.2000	Bat, 2000 All-Star Game, MVP.
B-120.2006	USA jersey from 2006 WBC.
B-232.2008	Bat used during the final home stand of the New York Yankees' 2008 season, the last season in the original Yankee Stadium.
B-325.2009	Batting gloves worn September 11, 2009 when he recorded his 2,722nd career hit at Yankee Stadium, passing the previous record set for hits at Yankee Stadium held by Lou Gehrig.
B-362.2009	Bat used during 2009 WS, Game 6.
B-231.2008	Spikes worn when he recorded the hit that broke Lou Gehrig's record for career hits at Yankee Stadium on September 16, 2008.
B-154.2014	Glove used by Derek Jeter of the New York Yankees during his career spanning from 1995 to 2014.

That career began inauspiciously. On May 29, 1995, Jeter made his Major League debut and batted ninth and played shortstop. He was 0-for-5, including a two-out strikeout swinging with pinch-runner Gerald Williams stranded on third in the top of the 11th. The Yankees would lose that game in 12. The next day, he struck out his first time up to make it an 0-for-6 start, but his next at-bat was a leadoff single off Tim Belcher and he later scored, on his way to a 2-for-3 outing.

"First hit's probably the one that stands out the most," Jeter said when I asked him during the 2009 AL Championship Series to share his favorite hit. (His first response, more characteristically, was actually: "Next one you're gonna get.") Jeter continued: "Anytime you get your first anything, it's better. Relief. I went oh-for-five my first game. So I think anytime you get the first. You at least got *something* to show for it."

Jeter batted .250 with 11 strikeouts in those 15 games as a 1995 call-up, and then was brought along to the classic Game Five loss at Seattle in that subsequent AL Division Series, not as an active postseason player but just so he could experience the intensity while on the bench. He went to 1996 Spring Training with the expectation of being the Yankees' everyday shortstop, but he continued to scuffle in Florida and that expectation was now in question.

Not only was it in question, but the Yankees came perilously close to making a trade that would have completely changed the course of club history—and not for the better. This is another reason I wanted to begin this book with Rivera and Jeter one-two, in addition to their Cooperstown pecking order. When you talk about pivotal moments in Yankees history, a trade that almost happened looms among the franchise's five most critical junctures.

In addition to Jeter's spring struggles, infielders Tony Fernandez and Pat Kelly were injured. Some people in Steinbrenner's inner circle were unsure if they could rely on the rookie. Seattle wanted to trade shortstop Felix Fermin to New York, and they wanted either Rivera or Bob Wickman. The Boss was considering it and needed serious input. Gene Michael, Bob Watson, Brian Cashman and Torre convened in the manager's office for lively debate.

"It was a fight to convince The Boss to stand down and not force us to do a deal none of us were recommending," Cashman recalled in 2013. "And it wasn't because we knew what we had in Mo or Wickman, it was we had committed to go with young Jeter. Thankfully, we didn't do that deal. . . . We wound up keeping both Wickman and Mariano. Life of the Yankees could have changed drastically if a mistake is made there."

Rivera flourished as John Wetteland's setup man in 1996 and then saved 43 games after replacing him the next year. Jeter was the Opening Day shortstop in 1996 and he hit his first career homer that day off Dennis Martinez in the fifth inning of a 7 − 1 Yankee victory in Cleveland. "He played like he had been there ten years," Paul O'Neill said of Jeter.

He not only proved himself at shortstop as a rookie, but he won AL Rookie of the Year. Best no-trade ever?

"I was told Derek Jeter would be my shortstop and I told the press that," Torre said. "I happened to be watching TV and I heard Derek respond to pretty much the same question . . . and he said 'I'm going to get an opportunity to be the shortstop.' And that struck me. Here's a twenty-one year-old kid with so much presence at that time. And then in Spring Training, he never was flashy, he didn't do very much. But he never seemed to change, he just seemed to be the same guy."

Jeter would go on to amass 996 hits over his first five full seasons and was a major part of the Yankees four world championships during that span. He would appear in no fewer than 148 games at shortstop in any of those five seasons. He emerged as part of a three-headed AL elite shortstop, one might say: Jeter, A-Rod and Nomar Garciaparra. While the other two would move around, Jeter would never play at any spot other than Yankee shortstop, and not until the final game of his career would his team ever be out of contention.

Jeter finished high on several all-time MLB lists with 3,465 hits (6th), 1,923 runs (11th), 4,717 times on base (12th), 544 doubles (34th), 4,921 total bases (23rd), 2,674 games at short (2nd), 12,602 plate appearances (10th) and 11,195 at-bats (7th). He set Yankee records for games played, at bats, plate appearances, doubles, hits, stolen bases, hit by pitch and times reaching base. Passing Lou Gehrig's Yankee hit records was just one of many remarkable achievements.

The same Steinbrenner who had to be convinced to keep his young shortstop named him the 11th captain of the Yankees on June 3, 2003. "He represents all that is good about a leader," Steinbrenner said. "I'm a great believer in history, and I look at all the other leaders down through Yankee history, and Jeter is right there with them." Both of them were right there on the VISA commercial as well, making light of Jeter's reputation as arguably New York's most eligible bachelor.

That was a relevant status, too. Jeter was adored for his looks as well as consistent professionalism and his ability to come through so many times on the big stage, like those two plays in the 2001 postseason alone: The Flip in Game Three of the ALDS against Oakland, and his "Mr. November" home run to end Game Five of the thrilling post-9/11 series against Arizona.

Whole families would coo. Jeter was also one of the reasons for the proliferation of female-fitting and kids' jerseys that you could now easily order online. It was little wonder that number two was seen everywhere you looked at Yankee Stadium, and for a long time.

That number two jersey was finally retired along with his Monument Park plaque unveiling on Mother's Day in 2017. The ceremony was the most watched event (non-game) in YES Network history. His 2020 induction could break another record, as so many of those same Jeter fans have just a short drive up the Thruway and then over to Glimmerglass.

Jeter could have slipped into the night like so many Major League greats, just waiting for the Hall's call. He did the opposite. He took an aggressive step into the publishing world, and then joined an ownership group that bought the Miami Marlins, with him in the CEO role. He even raised a family. I thought life had completely moved on, but before writing this I went back to watch that 2014 black-and-white Gatorade farewell video, where he hops out of the car on his way to Yankee Stadium and hangs out with fans on his way to the finale. I watched his last at-bat at Yankee Stadium again and tried to keep it together after his game-winner.

Nope, still too soon. Number two defined a generation for us. Like the woman's sign read on his final day at Fenway, "Don't cry because it's over, smile because it happened."

New York Highlanders

By the turn of the twentieth century, baseball was riding a wave of popularity as a national pastime and New York had the most popular team in America. But that team was not the Yankees. The early Yankees were, as sportswriter George Vecsey phrased it, "Second-rate, second-class, second division, secondhand," that itinerant of a franchise drudged in the shadow of a more glamorous outfit in the very same borough of Manhattan, the New York Giants. New York also was home to the Dodgers, who had some success in the late 1800s.

The Yankees franchise began as a result of the Baltimore Orioles failing. A previous Orioles franchise was among the dominant National League teams in the 1890s but was disbanded when the NL contracted from twelve teams to eight. When the American League was formed in 1901, a new Orioles franchise was created. They were owned in part by manager John McGraw, who starred as a player for the old NL Orioles.

McGraw's volatile personality clashed with the mission of AL president Ban Johnson, who, among other things, discouraged raging at umpires to incite fan violence. McGraw had been secretly looking for ways to manage a team in New York for some time, and midway through the 1902 season he bolted to manage the Giants and took key players with him.

Johnson took control of the Orioles franchise, but its survival was in jeopardy. Before the 1903 season, he found of pair of suitable (read: powerful and shady) owners in Frank Farrell and Big Bill Devery, who would pay the $18,000 purchase price and run the team as a New York franchise. Whether the Orioles "moved" or the New York team was a "startup" is semantics. Bottom line, Johnson's fast-growing AL now was in the country's largest city, and today's Yankees consider their history as beginning with the 1903 season, not Baltimore.

Where to play? The venue eventually known as Hilltop Park was constructed in just seven weeks on land where New York Presbyterian Hospital stands today in Washington Heights. The new team became known as the Highlanders, after the Gordon Highlanders, a British military unit, and also due to the physical location. But newspapers took to the patriotic term Yankees, and especially the condensed "Yanks" for headline space.

After 10 years in Hilltop Park, the Highlanders moved into the Polo Grounds and officially made the "Yankees" name official. Colonel Jacob Ruppert would come onto the scene and create a winning tradition unlike any other. In those seasons under the official "Highlanders" name, the team had only finished above fourth place in the AL (out of eight) three times.

The Highlanders on Opening Day at Hilltop Park in 1908.

The 1904 season had been the Highlanders' best by record, finishing 92 – 59 and just a game and a half behind the Boston Americans. Spitballer Jack Chesbro set of one of baseball's enduring unbreakable records that year, winning 41 games on the way to the Hall of Fame. "Happy Jack" was another big reason Manhattanites came out to see the new AL team.

"Luck is just a matter of hustling," he said in 1904. "I'm lucky because I get out and hustle. Any man with any ability at all can be one of the lucky ones if he digs into the work."

No matter how much Chesbro and the Highlanders worked that year, they were not going to meet the Giants if they had overtaken Boston. The Giants, the NL's best, had made it abundantly clear that they were not going to play the AL champion. McGraw hated Johnson, and Boston had already further legitimized Johnson's new league by defeating Pittsburgh in what the Giants considered an "exhibition series" in 1903. So 1904 and 1994 are the only skipped years in the World Series era, and the Yankee franchise would wait until 1921 for its first World Series appearance and 1923 for its first championship.

Chris Chambliss

My friend and fellow author Mark Littell has been involved with historic moments more than once as a player, including giving up Pete Rose's 3,631st career hit to break Stan Musial's National League record. Here is a verbatim Facebook message that Littell sent me for this book regarding his memory of throwing one fateful pitch for Kansas City to Chris Chambliss at Yankee Stadium on the chilly night of October 14, 1976:

"The pitch was a FB . . . it was up and out of the zone. When it went up and the wind caught it . . . it started to drift. I didn't know either way. It went out around two feet. The stall was kind of disturbing. It was cold as hell. Call Buck [Martinez, his catcher] out and said, why don't we just get the Hell outta here. No fans touched me but they were on the mound before I hit the grass. U walked off."

That covered a lot of things that happened in a very short amount of time. It was the Game Five clincher in the American League Championship Series. George Brett's three-run homer off reliever Grant Jackson had wiped out a 6 – 3 Yankee lead in the eighth inning, and Littell had come out of the bullpen in the bottom of that inning to retire New York in order. Now he was back on the mound to start the ninth, facing Chambliss, the burly All-Star first baseman and cleanup hitter who was 10-for-21 so far in the series.

"Please do not . . . litter the field," P.A. announcer Bob Sheppard pleaded with the rowdy sellout crowd of 56,821, as

Little continued his warmups. There already had been multiple delays caused by bottles, beer cans, firecrackers and toilet paper being thrown by fans. "Please do not . . . throw bottles on the field. And the Yankees request good sportsmanship on the part of all."

Finally after a 10-minute wait, the grounds crew cleared enough of the debris from the field for the ninth to get underway. It was about 30 degrees. Chambliss stepped into the left side of the batter's box against the righty. He had already singled and doubled in the game. The Yankees were on the brink of returning to the World Series for the first time in 12 years, an unspeakable drought back then. Failure was not an option in the Bronx on this night, and hell was going to break loose if the Bombers returned to the biggest stage.

"Pretty easy for me, because I hit the home run that put the Yankees into the World Series in '76 for the first time in twelve years," Chambliss told me at an MLB Alumni event in Manhattan, when I asked him what hit had meant the most in his career. It was almost 40 years to the day when we relived it. "So that was obviously the biggest home run of my life.

"It was just a tight moment, because it was a game that went back and forth. We had a three-run lead, and it was the eighth inning when George Brett hit a home run and tied the game. So we come into the last of the ninth, and I was the first hitter, so it was really a tense moment. I happened to hit the first pitch, high fastball, and hit it out. It was a great moment."

Chambliss, batting with a slightly closed stance, turned on it fast and tomahawked it high into the air. It seemed to soar forever into the black sky, even though it barely cleared the right-field fence, in front of those cops and just beyond Hal McRae's attempt to leap and catch it. Chambliss took a moment to admire the blast but it soon became clear that he would need to get a move on.

Howard Cosell—a New Yorker not masking his pleasure with the outcome—screamed with satisfaction on the ABC broadcast: *"It's gone!!!"* Phil Rizzuto let out a classic *"Holy*

Cow!" to his audience. "With all that delay," the Scooter said on the air, "we told you Littell had to be a little upset."

Littell escaped into the KC clubhouse unmolested, he said. Chambliss barely made it around the bases. Touched second base with his hand. Knocked down once. Spun around. Helmet nearly stolen off his head. Cops trying to help him reach third. It was such a wild scene, unheard of by today's fans. Then barreling through anyone in his way, never able to touch home plate. Police tried to escort him through the chaos and finally into the dugout ahead of Willie Randolph.

"It was a little rough for me, because all of the fans came on the field right after I hit it," Chambliss said. "I had to make my way through a lot of fans and knock some people over and stuff. It was a wild run."

Teammate Graig Nettles coaxed Chambliss back out of the clubhouse to try to make it official and touch home plate. Chambliss was given an NYPD raincoat to throw on and escorted back out there to do just that, as home plate umpire Art Frantz was still waiting and had made no formal signal. Alas, there was no home plate. Fans had uprooted that, too. So Chambliss touched the hole where home plate once rested, and that was good enough for Frantz, making the Bronx Bombers' return to the biggest stage official.

I asked Chambliss, still burly and strong, if he had played football back in the day.

"I did, I played in college," said Chambliss, who had attended MiraCosta College in Oceanside, Calif.; Montclair State; and then UCLA. "I played end at first, but then I became a halfback later on. I was OK, I was OK."

OK enough that he romped 65 yards for a touchdown on his first carry as a running back after moving to that position his senior year. He was a strong football player, and that is what Chambliss looked like on that glorious night for the Yankees.

He has said that he still has the bat and ball from that moment, courtesy of the NYPD. No one knows where the helmet went, because fans stole it during his journey home.

"That was just a culmination of a great year," Chambliss said. "We went into that year into the new Yankee Stadium, because they refurbished the ballpark. Seventy-six was a special year, and it ended with that home run. We played the Reds and they wiped us out in the World Series, but again, that home run was really the highlight of my career."

Johnny Bench and the Big Red Machine swept New York in the World Series, but the Yankees were at least in the show that mattered again. It would start a three-year run of Fall Classics, and the Yankees would win the next two. George Steinbrenner had promised when he bought the team in 1973 that he would return them to winning ways, and on that cold night at Yankee Stadium while fans covered the field, he was inside the raucous clubhouse wiping champagne from his eyes. Chambliss had played a pivotal role in fulfilling that promise to fans.

He was traded to Atlanta after the 1979 in a six-player swap that brought catcher Rick Cerone to the Bronx. Looking back, it was an annual fact of life that Chambliss would face the Royals in the ALCS. It happened three straight autumns, and although he was 1-for-17 in the 1977 ALCS, he tormented them again by batting .400 in the 1978 ALCS. The highlight will always be the one that started that streak.

"I was just at the right place at the right time," Chambliss said. "It was just a great moment. The only lesson I got from it really was the fact that dreams come true. That's what that was, that was a dream."

Bucky Dent

The Yankees and Red Sox entered Game 163 of the 1978 season with 99 wins apiece. Kansas City had won 92 to win the AL West, and the Dodgers had won 95 in the NL. "It's a shame that this is not the World Series, that our series is not seven games and when we're finished with each other that the season then isn't over," Yankees owner George Steinbrenner told the Red Sox after that one-game playoff. "We are the two best teams in baseball. We said that on the field today. We won, but you didn't lose."

Carl Yastrzemski summed up the Red Sox response to that: "We have everything in the world to be proud of, what we don't have is the ring." Indeed, the Curse of the Bambino lived on that day, never to be reversed until a quarter-century later. The Yankees had somehow overcome Boston's 14-game lead in the AL East standings back on July 19. And the one Boston fans cursed the most on that day and for months to come was "Bucky Fuckin' Dent."

He was acquired from the White Sox right before the 1977 season for LaMarr Hoyt, minor leaguer Robert Polinsky and $200,000. The trade worked for both clubs, because Hoyt would become the 1983 AL Cy Young Award winner. Dent would win two rings and go down in history as the guy who screwed the Red Sox yet again.

The game was started by former Yankee Mike Torrez for Boston and eventual Cy Young Award winner Ron Guidry for New York on short rest. Yaz homered off Guidry in the second and the score remained 1 – 0 until AL MVP Jim Rice singled in a second run in the sixth. With Torrez still working on a shutout, Dent came up with two men on and two outs in the bottom of the seventh.

According to Jim Kaat, manager Bob Lemon wanted to pinch-hit but had no one available due to injuries and moves earlier in the game. So, it was up to the light-hitting (.243) Dent. Torrez missed low with the first pitch. Dent then fouled the second pitch off his left ankle and was in pain. Normally he wore a shin guard, but not this time. With the depleted bench, he had to stay in there. Then, Torrez left the 1 – 1 pitch right over the middle of the plate and Dent took the most important swing of his career. The ball sailed over the Green Monster as Yaz looked up in despair.

"When I hit the ball, I knew that I had hit it high enough to hit the wall", Dent said. "But there were shadows on the net behind the wall and I didn't see the ball land there. I didn't know I had hit a homer until I saw the umpire at first signaling home run with his hand. I couldn't believe it."

His legacy was sealed when Goose Gossage retired Yaz to end the game. The Yankees dispatched the Royals for a third consecutive year in the ALCS round and then successfully defended their world championship against the Dodgers.

When I covered the 2016 Thurman Munson Awards dinner in Manhattan, Graig Nettles was among the honorees and he recalled what Dent's homer meant at the time.

"When Bucky hit his home run in 1978, it set off a series of events," Nettles said. "If we don't get in the playoffs, we don't get in the World Series, and I don't get to show the world my defense, which I did in the World Series in 1978. Bucky started the whole thing."

Waite Hoyt

If the best thing to ever happen to the Yankees was the acquisition of Babe Ruth from the Red Sox for the 1920 season, then somewhere close behind it would be their acquisition of pitcher Waite Hoyt from the same Red Sox a year later. There are a couple of reasons for that.

One is simply his contribution to American history. Hoyt was the first Major Leaguer to go from a playing career on to a second career as a broadcast analyst, setting the stage for such others from Dizzy Dean to Phil Rizzuto to Joe Morgan to Bert Blyleven. In doing so, Hoyt would charm listeners with his yarns about Yankee clubs of the 1920s, and often about Ruth in particular. The gems would help fill Ruth biographies for years to come. Examples:

- "In St. Louis, Babe haunted a place operated by a rotund German woman," Hoyt said. "She cooked the most wonderful spareribs this side of Heaven, and the Babe could eat spareribs three meals a day. Many times when the Yankees had to hit the road out of St. Louis right after a game, Ruth would order twenty-five to thirty racks of spareribs from her to be delivered right to the train. The team used to occupy an entire sleeping car, so the Babe set up shop in the ladies' room, selling the ribs to the boys at a quarter a rack—plus all the home brew you could drink."

- "On the road, Babe never had the usual hotel room assigned to the other boys. The Yankee officials installed him in a sumptuous suite, as befitted the King of Diamonds. Immediately after games, Ruth retired to his suite. He changed to a red moray dressing gown and red Moroccan slippers. A long sixty cent cigar protruded from his lips, for all the world like the Admiration Cigar trademark. The king was in the throne room. His subjects were permitted audience. And the subjects came in droves. I have seen as many as two hundred and fifty people visit the Babe in a single night."

- "There's no doubt that Babe Ruth saved the game of baseball. He was not fat, and he did not have skinny legs. He had rather tapered ankles, but he had good-sized legs. He had a big chest and a small fanny, and he was not big around the waist. He did get fat the last two or three years he played. But he was not fat when he was in shape. It disgusts me to hear these fellows on the radio or in the papers say he was, from assumption . . . 'a fat drunk.' He was not a drunk."

We could spend many pages quoting Hoyt, in the same way that listeners hoped for rainouts so they could hear Hoyt tells stories on the radio. He was the Babe's best friend and saw plenty of that amazing inside world, and he shared these valuable insights only after his "uncanny" friend had left us much too young. Hoyt even had a Tudor home built in Larchmont, N.Y., just north of the city, that featured a special private entrance where Ruth could saunter in at any hour and hang out without fanfare.

But the other and more important reason why Hoyt's acquisition from the Red Sox looms so large in hindsight was his emergence as a "money pitcher." Those were the words of Taylor Spink, the legendary and influential publisher of *The Sporting News*, in April of 1942. When Spink wrote that description for the "Bible of Baseball"—exactly one half-century to the week before I joined that publication as an editor—it carried the same kind of weight that George Steinbrenner's "Mr. October" tag would do one day for Reggie Jackson. They were the same thing. Hoyt made his money in October, rising another level and playing a pivotal role in the Yankees' emergence as a club always expected to be in the World Series.

Hoyt pitched from 1918 – 38 for the Yankees and six other clubs, finishing with a 237 – 182 record and 3.59 ERA. He made his mark as a consistent force in the Yankees' rotation, averaging 18 wins and 253 innings per season over an eight-year stretch (1921 – 28) as the club won six pennants and three World Series titles. He was the ace of the greatest team in history, posting a 22 – 7 mark with a 2.63 ERA and 5.8 WAR for the 1927 club that went 110 – 44. Hoyt was elected to the Hall of Fame by the Veterans Committee in 1969.

Something to keep in mind as Andy Pettitte debate begins among voters, Hoyt's big difference-maker was no doubt his postseason value to his clubs. He was a three-time World Series champion (1923, 1927 and 1928), compiling a 1.83 ERA over 83 2/3 World Series innings. For the Yankees in the Fall Classic, Hoyt posted a 1.62 ERA over 77 innings.

"Waite was quite a guy. I remember catching him one day. I called for the changeup and Waite threw a fastball. And it went by my head. Well, it taught me something, I'll say that. I learned how to anticipate a cross-up. And I got where they couldn't throw a ball by me. I was kind of proud of that accomplishment, too. Because we had a pitcher on the club who would cross you up all the time [and] I could catch him just as well as if I knew what was coming. Hoyt was a good pitcher, and a fine fellow."

—Bill Dickey

Hoyt grew up in Brooklyn and was signed by Giants manager John McGraw after his sophomore year in high school, prompting the nickname "Schoolboy" that was often frequented upon cherubs. He wound up with the Red Sox for the 1919 season, getting a first-hand look at Ed Barrow's conversion of Ruth from pitcher to slugging outfielder. Ruth's first impression of Hoyt was one of surprise over such a young face, and Hoyt had responded by saying that is how Ruth must have looked when he broke in. It was typical of Hoyt's *braggadocio*, a self-confidence that usually served him well but sometimes got him into trouble.

When Ruth was sold to the Yankees for the 1920 season, it meant Hoyt had to pitch to him, but they were soon reunited. "Wake up, wake up!" Hoyt's father told him one day. "Your Christmas present is here! You've been traded to the Yankees!"

That eight-player deal happened after the 1920 season. The Red Sox got Del Pratt, Muddy Ruel, Hank Thormahlen and Sammy Vick, and Hoyt went to New York along with Harry Harper, Mike McNally and Wally Schang. Hoyt was part of an assembly line of talent that Harry Frazee was sending from Boston to New York, and for the right-hander it would be a homecoming.

"The secret," Hoyt once said, "was to get a job with the Yankees and joyride along on their home runs."

Hoyt won 19 games for the Yankees in 1921, his first year as a regular starter. The team had leaped to 95 wins in 1920 but failed to reach the World Series, and with Hoyt there was a major boost onto the big stage for the first time. It was the first year of a trend that would see the Yankees reach the Fall Classic regularly for the next 45 years. Remarkably, from 1923 – 64, the Yankees would never go more than three years without winning a World Series.

Despite falling short to the Giants in 1921, the series would garner plenty of attention throughout the baseball world. Not only was it played entirely in the media mecca of New York in the league's largest ballpark (Polo Grounds), but it was also the first to be broadcast over the radio, called by the legendary sportswriter Grantland Rice. Due to the backdrop, the 1921 Series may very well have put the Yankees on the map.

Hoyt was their star in the World Series, pitching three complete games without giving up an earned run—a description that would one day grace his Hall of Fame plaque. He won his first two starts and then lost the decisive Game Eight on a first-inning error when Yankees shortstop Roger Peckinpaugh allowed his positional counterpart Dave Bancroft to score an unearned run.

The New York Times wrote at the conclusion of that classic series: "To delve into the maze of excellent pitching that marked the series and bring out the names of the names of the hero pitcher is not difficult. It is Waite Hoyt, of course, to whom the laurels go."

The Yankees' AL-best offense fell flat in the series, hitting .207 with just 2.75 runs per game. But Hoyt had endeared himself to his local fan base. Hoyt nearly matched Christy Mathewson's iconic 1905 World Series performance, where the Hall of Famer had thrown complete game shutouts. Not coincidentally, Mathewson had served as a mentor to Hoyt years prior during the latter's time in the Giants' organization; they were crazy to let him go.

In 1922, Hoyt won another 19 games in the regular season and then allowed just one earned runs in eight innings over two World Series appearances. The Yankees lost to the Giants again, amid considerable clubhouse turmoil. But October was becoming the Yankees' domain. The following season was theirs, and the road to that first title went through the same Giants. Hoyt scuffled in the series but he had his first ring, and he became a fall fixture in the Roaring Twenties.

Hoyt always had baseball to keep him company, and a radio career would keep him in the public consciousness. But on October 11 – 12, 1981, he did one of the Hall of Fame's oral-history interviews for their collection and admitted how alcoholism had stripped him of everything during those Yankee glory years. He and Ruth clearly had much in common, and one day Hoyt would become the home run king's pallbearer at St. Patrick's Cathedral.

"In 1928, I had a great World Series," Hoyt said in the interview at his home. "We had beaten Pittsburgh in four straight in 1927, then we beat St. Louis in four straight in the 1928 World Series. In the 1928 World Series, I pitched and won two complete games of the four-game series, which was a record. The Yankees only used three pitchers to win the four games, me, [George] Pipgras and [Tom] Zachary. After the 1928 World Series, I was pretty much in demand [and] I went on the stage in Vaudeville, worked with [a] composer of some note. It was very successful and we did sixteen weeks. I was paid much more money from the stage than the Yankees paid me.

"Both Miller Huggins, our manager, and Ed Barrow, who was the general manager and had a vested interest in me, said, 'Waite, please don't go on the stage, you're making a mistake. You're going to lose your spirit or your dedication for baseball, which is after all the dog itself, and don't let the tail wag the dog.' I didn't pay any attention to them and I went on the stage, and it was a wonderful experience. We played the Palace Theater in New York, and in the process, I met Jimmy Durante, George M. Cohen, Mae West and a lot of other people [who] became close friends. I belonged to the Friars Club in New York. But it did just as those men said it would do, it took me away from my home and broke up my home, and I had a divorce and was stripped of everything. It had an effect on my pitching. I got to be rather loose in my operation and my personal life, so I really destroyed my own marriage in that sense."

Waite Hoyt warming up to pitch in 1922

Hoyt reported to 1929 camp about 17 pounds overweight and struggled so mightily that Huggins shut him down in mid-September. "You cannot do after thirty what you did before thirty," Huggins told him. "You do not recover as effectively as you do anything that tires you or wears you down, your recuperative powers are not as great." Rather than learn his lesson, Hoyt said, he "went back on the stage in 1929 and part of 1930, and that broke up my home, and in 1930 I was divorced, and it became a shock to me."

Huggins died and Bob Shawkey took over as manager, and he and Hoyt were oil and water. In May of 1930, a few weeks after dealing for Red Ruffing, the Yankees traded Hoyt and Mark Koenig to Detroit for Harry Rice, Ownie Carroll and Yats Wuestling. It was not a good trade for the Yankees, and Hoyt did not last long with the Tigers. Connie Mack was staying at a hotel near him in Detroit one day and invited him over to talk, and at that point informed him that he was pitching soon for Mack's mighty A's.

That led to one last World Series appearance for Hoyt, marking the 10th anniversary of his first one with the Bronx Bombers. Philadelphia lost to the Gashouse Gang of St. Louis, and Hoyt went on to work for the Pirates and Dodgers until throwing his last pitch in 1938.

Gradually his greatest Yankee teammates were lost, and Hoyt would entertain fans everywhere by regaling them with stories of Ruth and Gehrig, of Murderers' Row, of the big times. He hosted a Yankees postgame show called "According to Hoyt" and was the radio voice of the Reds from 1942 – 65. In that same 1981 interview with the Hall of Fame, Hoyt expressed his own idea about what made the Yankees' 3 – 4 combination of those years so special.

"I have a powerful belief in a power greater than ourselves, and that would be God or destiny or whatever you are to call it," Hoyt said. "I believe in predestination to begin with. It seems that Ruth and Gehrig were put upon this earth to fulfill a mission, or to fulfill a destiny of their own, which they did. Ruth fulfilled it despite a lot of transgressions, and Gehrig fulfilled it like Jack Armstrong, the All-American boy. Both were great stars, and both arrived at a pinnacle of success because of an innate talent with which they were blessed, given to them by God, because they did not create it. If we have talent, our abilities are only loaned to us. We use them until we pass on and they are given to somebody else. That is sort of my belief."

Lefty Gomez

Who threw the first pitch in All-Star history? Who drove in the first run in All-Star history?

The trivia answer for both is Lefty Gomez, who retired Pepper Martin to begin the first Midsummer Classic in 1933 at Comiskey Park in Chicago. In the bottom half of that first inning, Gomez singled to center off Wild Bill Hallahan to score Jimmy Dykes. AL manager Connie Mack had tabbed Gomez to start the inaugural event, over his own Philadelphia A's ace, Lefty Grove, and Gomez responded by pitching three scoreless innings and earning the win. It began the first All-Star trend: The Yankees' left-hander started an amazing five of the first six All-Star Games, so he was a fact of life in those days when MLB's best all gathered in July.

Gomez won 189 games between 1930 – 42, including four 20-win seasons, and he was 6 – 0 over seven World Series starts as the ace of a dynasty. "El Goofy" was known just as much for his jocular wit and self-effacing one-liners, for his sartorial splendor, for shielding longtime roommate Joe DiMaggio from the public through a record hitting streak, for counseling Lou Gehrig on the bench after the end of another streak, for marrying Broadway actress June O'Dea and hobnobbing with *hoi polloi*, for wearing an apropos 11 on his back to match his tall, wiry frame. Hall of Fame writer Bob Broeg called Gomez "the life of the party."

He filled notebooks and seats alike during a Depression and it took some pivotal help to get there.

Herb Pennock was similar to Gomez in many ways—same build and same high leg kick. He had been jettisoned by Connie Mack's A's due to their emphasis on more bulky pitchers, the same issue Gomez frequently had faced in coming up from California. Pennock had won more than 200 games en route to Cooperstown. The excellent 2012 book *Lefty: An American Odyssey*, written by Gomez's granddaughter Vernona (named after Vernon Gomez) and Lawrence Goldstone, recalls how the more refined and sophisticated Pennock helped Gomez with his mechanics and daily routine, not to mention how to dress and speak eloquently.

"Never throw a baseball without a purpose, even when you're shagging flies in the outfield to get in shape," Pennock told him. "When you toss the ball in, throw it slow or fast, see how close you can come to a marker, like second base or an individual player. Practice location with every pitch."

"In my book," Gomez said, "Pennock was one of the greatest left-handers in the history of the game. His curve didn't amaze anybody and he could scarcely break an egg with his fastball. But he had impeccable location and he could psych out the hitters. The ongoing battle in the center of the diamond. His pitches never arrived at the plate when or where the hitter expected them. Each pitch meant something. He taught me how to recognize the strength and weakness of every opposing hitter in the American League."

Another pivotal influence on Gomez was his fabled teammate, Babe Ruth. They got along famously. Gomez said in the book: "Babe taught me the basics of baseball. Win the game for your teammates and know that without the fans, you're nothing."

In 1932, Gomez emerged as the Yankees' top big-game pitcher. He was 24-7 with 21 complete games and 176 strikeouts in 265 innings, and his dominance in a Game Two victory that the Cubs thought they would win behind Lon Warneke was pivotal to that sweep. The series, best known for Ruth's "Called Shot," would put the Bombers back in the title business. Then Gomez was a fixture as the Yankees reeled off four straight championships from 1936 – 39.

"The greatest thrill of my career was my first World Series win," Gomez said. "A World Series game is not like any other game, and winning the World Series is the crowning event of a team's season. If you ask most ballplayers, they'll tell you the same thing. . . . it's peak performance under the maximum tension possible on a baseball diamond."

Joe McCarthy told *The Sporting News* how Gomez would demand the ball if he didn't offer it to him for those especially tough opponents.

"Lefty loved to pitch against the tough clubs," McCarthy said. "When he thought he should pitch, he would give me that look . . . just put the bead on me. Even if my back was turned, I could feel his eyes boring into me. I may have figured on pitching somebody else but when Gomez gives me that look I had to go with him. In 1932, we were on our way to winning the pennant, but the Yankees still had to knock off the A's. We were playing a doubleheader, and after Lefty beat them in the first game, he wanted to pitch the second game. In the clubhouse, between the games, he came to me and said, 'Joe, I can beat them again. Let me pitch the second game.'

"'No,' I said, 'I'm not doing that. But go down to the bullpen and if I need you, I'll call you.' Fortunately, I didn't need him, because we won easy. I knew if we got into trouble, he would have come running out of the bullpen without being called. I only sent him to the bullpen to keep him from driving me crazy on the bench."

Joe DiMaggio remembered his roommate as someone who kept the team loose off the field and kept them in games on the field.

"McCarthy wasn't one for gags or hilarity on the bench, but he loosened up for Lefty, feeling, I suppose, that even a business-like bunch like the Yankees could stand an occasional chuckle," DiMaggio said. "Of course Gomez was more than a comedian and master bench jockey, he was truly a great left-handed pitcher who averaged almost twenty wins a season for eight years."

Gomez also played a pivotal role behind the scenes during DiMaggio's record 56-game hitting streak in 1941. This is what number five wrote in "The Joe DiMaggio Story":

"It was a heavy strain, looking for that hit every game, but greater than that was the pressure of outside activities. During that period everybody I met wanted me to go some place and say something. I should have given half my salary to Lefty Gomez, my roommate, for protecting me during the siege. Without him, I wouldn't have had a minute's peace."

DiMaggio added: "During my hitting streak, we went to the ball park together for every game, and there was a long stretch when I hit a home run every time Lefty was pitching for us. It ran something like eight straight games. It got to be such a coincidence that I'd ask Gomez almost every day when he was going to pitch again."

There was a considerable backlash by some to Gomez's election in 1972 by the Veterans Committee. Some writers complained that he was elected more on personal charm than performance. *Daily News* columnist Dick Young deadpanned: "The next selection will be Joe Garagiola, because he's as funny as Gomez." True enough, Gomez is bottom-barrel at 177th all-time among starting pitchers in JAWS and 189th in WAR; no justification in modern analytics. However, Veterans Committee member Joe Cronin, a former Yankee opponent, expressed a cogent thought about that in Vernona's book: "If they'd had to stand at the plate with a bat in their hands when Gomez was pitching, they wouldn't have thought he was so damn funny."

He started all those All-Star Games for a reason, including the first one.

Elston Howard

In the 1958 World Series, the Milwaukee Braves had a 3 – 1 series lead and were looking for a repeat of their previous year's title won against the Yankees. Now it was the top of the sixth inning of Game Five at Yankee Stadium, and the home team was clinging to a 1 – 0 lead behind Bob Turley in hopes of staving off elimination.

Bill Bruton led off with a single to left for the Braves, and that brought up future Hall of Famer Red Schoendienst. With the hit-and-run on, Schoendienst looped one to shallow left-center, and left fielder Elston Howard swooped in and made a spectacular diving catch to rob him. Howard bounced up and doubled up Bruton at first. It was especially big because Eddie Mathews followed with a single that would have tied the game.

New York put up a six-spot in the bottom of that inning to win, and Gil McDougald's homer in the 10th inning of Game Six at Milwaukee sent the series to a deciding seventh. That's when the same Elston Howard singled in Yogi Berra with the eventual game-winning run that started a four-run rally in the eighth. Suddenly, the Yankees were champs again, having won the last three games and in large part because of Howard's pivotal performances.

Howard's production in that World Series was just one of many reasons his number 32 jersey was retired and a plaque dedicated in 1984 by the Yankees in Monument Park. "If indeed humility is a trademark of many great men—with that as a measure, Ellie was one of the truly great Yankees," reads the quote on Howard's plaque. The words from George Steinbrenner were uttered in December of 1980, when the Yankee family lost a legend due to heart disease.

Of course, the most pivotal role of all played by Howard was that of being the first black Yankee. He endured many of the same racial abuses as other black pioneers like Jackie Robinson and Larry Doby, but there was a stigma in the Yankees' case because their integration in 1955 happened so many years after Jackie broke the color barrier in 1947. "Branch Rickey wanted and supported Jackie Robinson," Arlene Howard, Elston's widow, wrote in her 2001 book *Elston and Me: Story of the First Black Yankee*. "Elston could never say the same thing about [then Yankees general manager] George Weiss."

Indeed, this is what Jackie once told Arlene: "You know, in a sense, Elston had it tougher than me. At least I knew Mr. Rickey wanted me, but Elston didn't know if the Yankees wanted him." The Yankees shifted Howard from outfield to catcher in his first Spring Training, knowing that Berra already commanded the position. Not until 1960 would Howard take over catcher from Yogi on a permanent basis, and in 1963 Howard would become the first black player to win an AL MVP trophy.

"There were lots of people who helped me develop as a catcher," Howard said after winning his MVP award, "but the big shove was given to me by Ralph Houk. One of the first things he did when he was made manager [for 1960] was to call me aside and tell me I was strictly a catcher from then on. No more outfield and no more first base. I started to become the kind of catcher I always dreamed I'd be some day."

The catcher who dominated the position through the 1950s was among those who made Howard feel most welcome around the team. Right from the beginning, Berra was happy to hear that his heir apparent at catcher was also from St. Louis.

"He was a helluva guy," said Berra, a pallbearer at Howard's funeral. "Any time you called him to do something, he was there. If he were alive, he'd be here."

If he were alive then, there would not have been a funeral, but that's another Yogi story.

Here's what Howard's longtime manager, Casey Stengel, had to say about the 12-time All-Star selection:

"He's the fella who came along at the right time. . . . Berra has been chasing all those men away for ten or twelve years, but Howard is the lucky fella who timed it right to do some catching."

Howard made key contributions to 10 Yankee pennants and another for Boston. "Ellie is the best handler of pitchers in the league," Ralph Terry once said. "You never shake him off when he calls for a pitch." Howard had good baseball instincts, coached for the Yankees, and hoped to be the first black manager—something Jackie always wanted to see. Frank Robinson got it done.

"He was a man who transcended any denomination," Reggie Jackson said at Howard's funeral. "He came up to me and said once that he cared about me. I needed that. He also reminded me once that Red Barber had said something about him: 'Judge a man as a man.'"

Lou Gehrig

It has been eight decades since the Hall of Fame affixed a bronze plaque in the Gallery for Lou Gehrig, and as I admire his smiling and slightly disheveled visage, with his Yankee cap riding up high on his head as if he'd just won another World Series with the "grand men," I am once again transfixed by the meaning found in the first of his plaque's two sentences. I stand here and stare at the wall art the way a Picasso connoisseur does at an art gallery. It reads:

HOLDER OF MORE THAN A SCORE OF MAJOR AND AMERICAN LEAGUE RECORDS, INCLUDING THAT OF PLAYING 2130 CONSECUTIVE GAMES

On September 6, 1995, I sat in the press box at Camden Yards in Baltimore and witnessed the impossible: someone breaking that "unbreakable" record. Cal Ripken Jr. played in his 2,131st consecutive game that night for the Orioles. Although the actual record moment simply involved the actuality of a game reaching the middle of the fifth inning, to make it official, the significance of that achievement, and Ripken's subsequent reluctant lap around the warning track to share it with fans, was one of the greatest things I have seen personally in sports.

It made all of us appreciate Gehrig even more.

Ripken was dubbed the "Iron Man," both in recognition of his durability and also as a nod to the "Iron Horse" label fixed

Lou Gehrig in 1930.

upon Gehrig in his time. Nearly a quarter-century after Ripken broke the record, it is still mind-boggling to think that someone actually surpassed Gehrig's mark. Looking at Gehrig's plaque now, it is ever as remarkable.

Gehrig gave his famous "Luckiest Man" speech on Independence Day of 1939, as his body was giving in to amyotrophic lateral sclerosis (ALS), known more commonly as "Lou Gehrig's disease." At the subsequent Winter Meetings, on December 7, the Baseball Writers' Association of America made an exception due to his illness and elected him immediately into the Hall of Fame. A plaque was arranged, and looking at it now, one can only imagine what it was like to compose that first sentence amidst the absolute certainty that 2,130 would stand forever.

MEL ALLEN

If you were a baseball fan in the 1980s and '90s, then you heard Mel Allen's trademark voice all the time. It was his narration of the TWIB ("This Week In Baseball") show that would typically be shown on a large screen during batting practice and pregame activities at any ballpark. *How about that?!* were the long-drawled words that famously rang out, and if you were a Yankee fan for a quarter-century in the 20th century, then you knew why he became a Hall of Famer.

"The Voice of the Yankees" was a key figure during the golden age of radio broadcasting, spanning the transition into television's popularity as well. Allen exemplified the early era of sports broadcasting. He grew up in Alabama and got his start in the booth for his alma mater, the University of Alabama, where he worked first as the public-address announcer and then as the play-by-play voice for Crimson Tide football games.

Allen became the Yankees' lead radio announcer in 1939 and would remain behind the microphone for the Yankees until 1964, having done both radio and TV broadcasts. During his long run with New York, Allen gave nicknames like "Joltin' Joe" to Joe DiMaggio and "Old Reliable" to Tommy Henrich. He was known for expressing his passion for his team on the air but believed he called the game fairly.

"Some guy once said to me, 'When I tune you in, I know you'll say something positive about the Yankees.' But there's a difference between partisanship and prejudice. I gave other players their due," he told the *Times*. The aforementioned catchphrase often followed an outstanding play.

Allen recounted a story from when Lou Gehrig was battling his illness. "Lou patted me on the thigh and said, 'Kid, I never listened to the broadcasts when I was playing, but now they're what keep me going.' I went down the steps and bawled like a baby."

When Allen was unexpectedly fired in 1964, no reason was given. His departure coincided with the downturn of the storied franchise. Whether that was a "pivotal" point in franchise history, only curse believers can surmise. For the next 10 years, New York finished at least 12 games out eight times and at least 20 games out six times.

Although they were often around .500, that was still far below the Yankees' lofty standards. They would go 12 years before the next Fall Classic appearance, the longest stretch since before Babe Ruth. The Yankees invited Allen back on many occasions after that. From 1978 – 85, he called 40 Yankee games a year on SportsChannel. He gained additional fame by hosting *TWIB*, the weekly TV program focusing on the biggest baseball highlights. The growth of ESPN and other around-the-clock sports outlets on cable soon rendered that show passé, but it made for good ballpark programming.

In 1978, Allen, along with his former broadcast partner Red Barber, was the recipient of the first Ford C. Frick Award given by the Hall of Fame for outstanding broadcasting. The Yankees dedicated a plaque to him in Monument Park in 1998.

"It's just a testament to Cal that he could play that many consecutive games, especially with expanded rosters and the bigger chance of getting hurt," said Hall of Fame president Jeff Idelson. "In a lot of ways, the streak is incredible, but in some ways, it also overshadows what Cal and Lou both did on the field. People remember them for their streaks, but both were players who did a lot more than show up for work every day."

Showing up for work every day began with what now has to be considered the second-most pivotal moment in Yankees history, after Babe Ruth's acquisition from the Red Sox.

The consecutive-game streak technically began on June 1, 1925, when Gehrig pinch-hit for Pee Wee Wanninger in the eighth inning and flied out to left against the great Walter Johnson (what a matchup!). But for all intents and purposes, the streak would have its true and legendary liftoff in the subsequent decision by manager Miller Huggins to start Gehrig at first base the following day against Washington and remove veteran Wally Pipp from the lineup.

Gehrig batted sixth and went single-double-single in his first three at-bats as a regular starter. The Yankees staged a come-from-behind victory with four runs in the eighth, and Gehrig finished 3-for-5. Huggins naturally kept it going. The Yankees came from behind to win again, this time in the 12th. Even though Gehrig was 0-for-3 in that one, Huggins kept it going. Gehrig hit his first homer two games later. The streak was on its way and Pipp's job was claimed.

For many years, the explanation for this pivotal lineup change was a tale that was fun to pass along to kin, like a good Jean Harlow story. Pipp, who may or may not have recently been beaned, supposedly asked outloud for aspirin in the clubhouse, and Huggins supposedly heard that and scratched out Pipp's name on the lineup card and wrote Gehrig's name in instead. This alleged reason has been sufficiently debunked by Snopes. com and other modern fact-checkers—even by Pipp himself before his passing in 1965—enough to disregard its authenticity.

Most Major Leaguers would have loved to put up the numbers Pipp did in his 15-year career. The Yankees had purchased him from Detroit in 1915, and he spent 11 years with the club. From 1920 to '24, Pipp hit .301 and averaged 29 doubles, 97 RBIs and 94 runs a season. The Yankees had beefed up with the addition of outfielder Bob Meusel, pitcher Waite Hoyt, third baseman Joe Dugan and, of course, Ruth, and Pipp played in those three straight World Series against the Giants from 1921 – 23, celebrating the team's first title in the last of those. He was a weak postseason hitter, but Pipp had been a decent player who was better around Ruth.

In 1925, Huggins's club was an aberration with only 69 wins, fated to go much of the way early without Ruth, and Pipp was among those slumping. Gehrig's defense was suspect, but Huggins saw it as an opportunity to give the rookie a chance. Headache or no headache, the reason for Gehrig instead of Pipp the next day and the day after that was very clear. To this day, being "Pipped" means failing to do "whatever it takes" to keep someone else from taking over your livelihood for keeps. And in the case of the New York Yankees, it meant an incredible turning point, the start of a legendary record and 1925 becoming a mere blip for club fortunes. With Ruth and Gehrig hitting back-to-back, the best was yet to come.

HOF ARTIFACT INVENTORY

Game-used equipment in the Baseball Hall of Fame:

LOU GEHRIG

B-24.48	According to ledger: Baseball glove taken from Lou Gehrig during Japanese barnstorming trip with Babe Ruth. Japanese Athletic Association replaced Gehrig's glove so that he might play. Upon his return to the Orient the glove was given to Herman Lang, who turned it over to his nephew. He in turn gave it to the Hall.
B-117.61	Baseball cap from his Barnstorming tour team, The Larrupin Lou's.
B-172.79	Yankee uniform cap.
B-232.39a	Yankees cap.
B-232.39b	Road uniform shirt worn in 1939 final season.
B-232.39c	Road uniform pants, part of complete uniform.
B-232.39d	Navy blue uniform belt, part of complete uniform donated to Hall.
B-262.79	Bat used in 1934 when he was AL batting champion.
B-295.57	Signed Louisville Slugger bat used with 1939 Yankees.
B-328.55	Yankees cap. Previously mis-labeled as the Larrapin Lou cap.
B-331.55	Spalding first baseman's mitt donated by Gehrig's mother upon her death in 1955. Listed in accession ledger as "First baseball glove of Lou Gehrig," and similar to a first baseman's mitt first shown in the Spalding Guide in 1924. However, the Hall found photos of Gehrig wearing a different-looking mitt while at Columbia, so it more likely dates from his days at Hartford in 1924 or early career with the Yankees.
B-332.55	His final mitt, according to ledger.
B-362.69	Locker used at Yankee Stadium.
B-393.55	Bat owned by Gehrig. Unsure if used by Tris Speaker or Gehrig.
B-394.55	Bat used by Gehrig.
B-395.55	Cane belonging to Gehrig.
B-396.55	Canvas bat bag.
B-397.55	Leather overnight bag.

B-398.55	Leather kit bag.
B-521.56	Baseman's mitt.
B-522.56	Single bronze shoe. Accession records state this was the "Last shoe" worn by Gehrig.
B-523.56a	No. 4 Yankees road uniform shirt.
B-524.56	Bat used in 1937 All-Star Game to hit homer off Dizzy Dean of the Cardinals.
B-549.56	Khaki duffle bag.
B-2758.63	Yankees uniform shirt worn in 1939.

After the 1925 season, the Yankees made it official by selling Pipp to Cincinnati for $7,500. No one then could have known how long Gehrig would be fixed at first base. In 1933, while the Yankees were in Washington, Dan Daniel of New York's *World-Telegram* asked him in a hotel lobby: "Do you know how many games you have played in a row?"

Gehrig shook his head. "No, I don't. Come to think of it, it must run up in the hundreds somewhere," he said. Told that it was up to 1,252, then just 55 away from the record set by former Red Sox and Yankees shortstop Everett Scott in 1925, Gehrig said: "Gosh! Why I never thought of that. I had no idea."

Daniel then asked Gehrig the obvious question: "What do you play ball every day for, anyhow? Why don't you take a day off once in a while?"

It was the only way Gehrig knew. He was a study in durability and determination from the start. On June 19, 1903, in New York, where the Highlanders baseball team was playing its inaugural season, a 14-pound boy was born in Manhattan's Yorkville district to German immigrants Heinrich and Christina

Gehrig. He was named Heinrich Ludwig Gehrig II, although his Hall of Fame plaque would read "Henry Louis Gehrig." This "Little Louie" was the only one of their four children to survive past infancy; one died before him and two after him. "He's the only big egg I have in my basket," Christina said. "So I want him to have the best."

One day while in grammar school, Gehrig woke up ill. He remembered that his mother left for her job that morning but first told him "I would have to stay in bed." Lou went to school after she left, and later that day his mother had to go to the school to pull him out and bring him back home. "I never had missed a day in school and I felt I just had to be there," Gehrig told biographer Frank Graham. "I guess it's . . . well . . . just like me. . . . The way I've always been and, I guess, the way I'll always be."

Christina saw to it that her son got into Columbia, and while there he was signed by the Yankees for a $1,500 bonus in 1923. Within two years he was the second name in what became arguably the most dynamic duo in global sports history. Gehrig's majestic career with those Yankees yielded 493 home runs, 13 consecutive 100-RBI seasons, a .340 career average, six World Series championships and, yes, 2,130 games in a row. He told the *Brooklyn Eagle* in 1936 that he had been hit in the head three times, broken "practically all ten fingers" plus his right big toe, among many other physical impairments; yet his goal, he said then, was to play in at least 2,500 straight games and break some of Ty Cobb's offensive records.

By 1939, however, Gehrig's on-field performance was mysteriously affected, and the Iron Horse was shockingly diagnosed with a degenerative muscle disease that the Mayo Clinic reported to the Yankees that summer as ALS. He left there thinking that in 10 or 15 years he would have to walk with a cane, as he assured his wife. But within two years, he was gone. Part of his legacy is the Lou Gehrig Sports Awards event each November in New York, where the ALS Association Greater New York City chapter raises large sums to help fund research to help with treatment and a possible cure. I covered about 10 of those in a row for MLB.com and the impact was so terrific that I would find myself bidding on auction items to raise money for ALS in Gehrig's name.

"When you think of Gehrig, you think of a guy who was a great humanitarian -- in the same vein of a Roberto Clemente, someone who cared as much about giving back as receiving," Idelson said. "It's hard to believe that someone of Gehrig's ability could actually be overshadowed by Ruth, which shows you how unbelievable Ruth was. Lou Gehrig, with any of the other fifteen teams, would have been by far the biggest name.

"Lou is a guy, from everything I have read, who didn't crave the spotlight, didn't need the spotlight, and was the perfect complement to Ruth. They balanced each other."

The Babe got the headlines; Larrupin' Lou just got it done and reveled in the relative tranquility. He was described by Marshall Hunt in the *New York Daily News* as "unspoiled, without the remotest vestige of ego, vanity or conceit."

As if to illustrate that point, the spotlight was all Gehrig's only in 1935—after the Babe and before DiMag. Gehrig hit 30 homers that year, between outputs of 49 in both 1934 and '36. His average dropped to .329. Yet it would be a stretch to say that Gehrig's own performance really declined per se. He led the league for the first time with 132 walks, indicative of seeing fewer pitches to hit, and he still led the league with 125 runs and a .466 on-base percentage.

That year, the Yankees finished 89 – 60, but they were three games out in the AL as Detroit went on to the title. It was the third year in a row that the Yankees finished second in the league. Remarkably, however, it would be 33 more years (1966) that they would go as many as three consecutive seasons without a world championship.

Gehrig played in seven World Series, and he might have been 7-for-7 in rings had Pete Alexander not struck out Tony Lazzeri in that 1926 seven-game classic. That was Gehrig's first year on the biggest stage, and in Game One of that series he had driven in both runs including the RBI single to score Ruth and win the opener. Whenever anyone talks about Ruth's "Called Shot" in the 1932 World Series at Wrigley Field, it is always worth remembering that Gehrig immediately followed it with a majestic homer of his own, one of two he hit out that day. Combined in those Fall Classics, Gehrig slashed .361/.483/.731 with 10 homers, 35 RBIs, 30 runs in 34 games—among the greatest postseason careers ever.

Gehrig's streak began on May 31, 1925, and ended at Detroit on May 2, 1939, when Babe Dahlgren played first in his place and a powerhouse Yankee club banged out 17 hits and scored 22 times. Americans had gone through Prohibition, the Great Depression, the New Deal and the invention of radio during Gehrig's run. Huggins had told him he was starting the streak, and Gehrig had told Joe McCarthy he was ending the streak. After watching that game on the bench, Gehrig told reporters: "This record for consecutive games always was meaningless to me. Some of you newspaper guys wouldn't believe it, but maybe you will now."

Eleanor recalled her husband's last words. She was at his bedside along with her mother and Lou's doctor. "He looked up at us and said, 'You are the best three pals of my lifetime,'" Eleanor said. "He never knew those were to be the very last words he ever said." Gehrig passed away on June 2, 1941—16 years to the day that he took over for Pipp as the Yankees' first baseman.

Gehrig's life as a ballplayer was the greatest paradox of them all. In the August 24, 1933, edition of *The Sporting News*, the magazine printed a letter thanking him for a trophy to commemorate passing Scott's record. Gehrig said "the continuous game record which I have broken required good luck and plenty of breaks, more than any outstanding ability of the player." Contrast that his famous speech on Independence Day of 1939: "I might have been given a bad break, but I've got an awful lot to live for." Good and bad breaks, but through it all he would always call himself fortunate, and ultimately "the luckiest man on the face of the Earth."

Alex Rodriguez

This book is about looking back, so in the case of Alexander Emmanuel Rodriguez one must consider the good with the bad. His name will appear for the first time on the Hall of Fame ballot that is mailed out in late 2021, and then we can settle in for up to 10 progressively vitriolic years of debate. Were his contributions so enormous that he absolutely must be in Cooperstown? Or will he be a cautionary tale about why aspiring ballplayers should never take performance enhancing drugs over and over and lie and apologize and lie and apologize? Do you remember his 2009 season for the awkward steroid confession that spring with teammates in attendance, or for the way he ended it with a huge double that led to the 27th world championship?

It always has been a roller coaster ride with A-Rod, so no one can really predict how that will all play out. On the one hand, my own Hall of Fame voting policy has been to exclude from consideration any player who is punished *subsequent* to the implementation of Major League Baseball's Joint Drug Prevention and Treatment Plan. I have consistently voted for such players as Barry Bonds and Roger Clemens, but planned to withhold votes from A-Rod and Manny Ramirez, to name a couple who were actually suspended by the Commissioner. On the other hand, though, any big leaps by Bonds and Clemens might open the door for Rodriguez, and then there is the matter of one of the greatest post-retirement breakouts we have seen.

Jim Bunning might be the ultimate example, the only former

player who went into both the Hall of Fame and the U.S. Senate. *That* was post-retirement impact. Derek Jeter, A-Rod's former teammate on the left side of the Yankees' infield, has been a leader on this front as well, first as a publisher and then in becoming an MLB owner. Most former players are happy to lead more secluded lives, or maybe to monetize their autographs, lend their names to products (Joe DiMaggio/Mr. Coffee or Jackie Robinson/Chock Full o'Nuts), or to coach. A-Rod has done the ultimate image makeover. He has helped Yankee prospects as a special advisor to the GM, developed into an Emmy-winning FOX broadcaster, become a guest panelist on Shark Tank, and emerged as a high-flying CEO. Oh, and he met Jennifer Lopez. "J-Rod" bought a $15 million apartment together at 432 Park Avenue, living high above the world.

Alex Rodriguez at bat in 2008.
Courtesy of Keith Allison

"Alex is back here because of his baseball content," Reggie Jackson, another Yankee special advisor, said after the position was created for Rodriguez during 2018 Spring Training. "No matter what you say, it's three thousand hits, two thousand runs scored, two thousand RBIs. Four homers from seven hundred. That's a lot of stuff."

Whether Reggie can help make a case for A-Rod with Hall of Fame voters will be quite another thing. The situation will resolve itself in due time, and maybe I will feel different about my own vote somewhere during his eligibility period. Who can say? His popularity with the public is soaring right now, and it was in that stratosphere that I found the 14-time All-Star and three-time American League MVP one recent day. He was on a red carpet at the Sports Emmys at the Jazz at Lincoln Center in New York when I interviewed him for an MLB.com article about his broadcasting prowess and also for my book *Diamonds from the Dugout*. As it turns out, his response to my question about what hit meant the most to him also covered the subject of what was his most pivotal moment throughout 12 seasons with the Yankees.

"The double in the World Series to score Johnny Damon in Game Four," Rodriguez said matter-of-factly. "That got us one game away from winning the world championship."

In 2009, A-Rod redeemed himself at last.

He batted .438 with five home runs against the Twins and Angels in the first two rounds of that postseason, but on the biggest stage once again, he was struggling under familiar scrutiny. In Game One of the World Series, he struck out three times and was 0-for-4 against Cliff Lee as the Phillies won at Yankee Stadium. In Game Two, the Yankees won despite Rodriguez, who again struck out three times and was 0-for-4.

Phillies left-hander Cole Hamels made the mistake of waking up A-Rod in Game Three by plunking him on the arm. "That at-bat kind of woke me up a little bit and just reminded me, 'Hey, this is the World Series. Let's get it going a little bit,'" Rodriguez said after that game. "So it worked out."

Then came the decisive double off Phillies closer Brad Lidge in the ninth inning that scored Damon to make it 5-4 and ultimately give New York a 3–1 World Series lead on the way to its 27th world championship. It was a solid shot to the left-field corner at Citizens Bank Park. Most people talked about the "Damon dash" that set it up, but that double was crucial to the Yankees and to Rodriguez's own legacy. He finally delivered in the clutch.

"There's no question—I have never had a bigger hit," Rodriguez said that night, and nearly a decade later, it had stayed firmly cemented as his own choice hit. Amid the various scandals and controversies that punctuated his long career, Rodriguez did just about everything a ballplayer could do. Ultimately, that included the ability to move on and be happy.

The Yankees had needed someone to help them get over the hump after losing to the Marlins in the 2003 World Series, especially after third baseman Aaron Boone tore a ligament in his knee playing basketball. The Red Sox had tried and failed in their own pursuit, offering Manny and Jon Lester in a trade nixed by the players union. "He was not only the best player in the game, but the best player by a huge, huge margin," said Jed Hoyer, then Boston's assistant GM. New York acquired Rodriguez with cash from Texas for Alfonso Soriano and a player to be named later (Joaquin Arias) after his first MVP season in 2003. Alas, those same Red Sox did the impossible in 2004 and came back to beat A-Rod and the Yankees and reverse the Curse of the Bambino, so Rodriguez was tied to that fiasco.

Rodriguez had been a regular season star but an October dud in ALDS eliminations from 2005-07, and the nadir had come when Joe Torre dropped him to the eighth spot in the order against Detroit in 2006. Torre was out after 2007, following 13 consecutive postseason berths for the Yankees, and in Joe Girardi's first year as his replacement the Yankees had watched idly. Then it was back to the postseason in 2009 for A-Rod, with then-girlfriend Kate Hudson in tow. She and Kurt Russell were there in the Yankees' celebratory clubhouse that night, and all was right.

Suddenly there was a parade up Broadway and Alex Rodriguez, once a boy in Washington Heights, was riding in it. In that 2009 postseason, Rodriguez finished with a .365 batting line, six homers and 18 RBIs. Three of those homers tied the game in the seventh inning or later.

When he was given the Babe Ruth Award by Ruth's family for being the postseason's most outstanding performer, Rodriguez said, "I've been to these dinners a couple of times to receive MVP awards and those, I'm very proud of those accomplishments. But none of those accomplishments will ever compare to the feeling you get from being part of a team that won a world championship."

Will I vote for him when that first ballot shows up with his name next to a box? There was a time when it seemed for certain, then a time when there seemed no way, and now we can let some time pass as he soars through an unconventional retirement. He ranks 16th all-time with a 117.8 WAR, but fought Baseball. He set a bad example for kids and might have influenced some to use steroids themselves, but he also has worked with so many kids including those at the Boys & Girls Club where he grew up in Miami. A-Rod is all over the place. Times change, and they are especially fluid in these decades of teeth-gnashing about steroids. Ask me in 2021.

Red Ruffing

On May 6, 1930, the Yankees acquired Red Ruffing from the Red Sox in exchange for outfielder Cedric Durst and $50,000. Ruffing proceeded to win 231 games as a Yankee, more than any other right-hander (a safe record), and he is the only pitcher in franchise history to put together four consecutive 20-win seasons, accomplished during New York's 1936 – 39 title run. He was a member of six world champions and seven pennant winners as a Yankee, was inducted into the Hall of Fame in 1967, and had a plaque dedicated in Monument Park in 2004.

Durst, meanwhile, became a Pacific Coast League fixture until he was nearly 50 and a trivia answer. It would not be a stretch to consider that deal one of the Yankees' 10 best trades.

It was a deal that almost never happened, though. Yankees manager Miller Huggins had tried for at least two years to acquire Ruffing. The Red Sox were reluctant after the Babe Ruth debacle a decade earlier, followed by a steady infusion of their talent to help create the Yankee machine. Ruffing had led the league in losses in the 1928 – 29 seasons, going 10 – 25 and then 9 – 22. At that point, he was a horrible 39 – 93 excuse of a Major Leaguer. He would be regarded as one of the best-hitting pitchers of all-time, though, and in that crucial time in his career he considered going the route of Ruth and becoming a full-time position player.

"It was a terrible club," Ruffing said. "I lost twelve games by one run and it was just one bad break after another. I decided that if I had to stay with the Red Sox I at least didn't have to pitch."

Huggins helped change his mind, especially after seeing Ruffing's weight blow up as the pitcher tried a beer-drinking diet to help add pounds. Huggins thought Ruffing was too slow for his six-foot, one-inch frame, and assured him he had a future as a pitcher. Unfortunately, Huggins died before Ruffing ever got to pitch with the Yankees.

From 1931 – 42, Ruffing failed to win 14 games only once and made six All-Star teams. That tradition began with the 1933 Midsummer Classic at Comiskey Park in Chicago. Ruffing won 273 career games, and he easily would have exceeded the 300 milestone if not for two stops: (1) the early years with Boston, and (2) World War II service that cost him 1943 – 44 seasons.

Then again, 300 is a passé number. It is doubtful another pitcher will reach that mark given the expanded emphasis on bullpens, pitch counts and overall decline of win opportunities. Today, 273 wins seems majestic, even if Ruffing's ERA of 3.80 is sky-high compared to other Hall pitchers. Ruffing also remains the Yankees' all-time leader in complete games with 261, and Lefty Gomez is a distant second with 173.

In 1938, deep into Ruffing's tenure with the Yankees, the *Milwaukee Journal* looked back at the trade and lauded Yankees owner Jacob Ruppert for his penchant of heisting talent. "Rufus the Red has proved one of his most profitable pieces of business," the newspaper wrote on May 27. "You'd have to go a long way to find a better right hand pitcher in baseball today."

Ruffing pitched his entire career without four toes on his left foot, a result of an accident while working for a mining company as a youth in central Illinois. Considering that and the early struggles, his path to Yankee greatness is even more impressive.

Ruffing had another advantage, as a pioneer of the slider. "The first game I ever worked behind the plate in the major leagues was against the guy who invented the slider and had the best slider ever seen—Red Ruffing," said former AL umpire Joe

Paparella. It is coincidental, then, that the same Whitey Ford whose pivotal moment in this book was the development of a slider would be the Yankee who passed Ruffing for most wins in the regular season and in the World Series.

Ruffing also was one of the best-hitting pitchers of all-time. Often sporting a bat that Babe Ruth had given him as a gift, Ruffing wound up with a career average of .269 along with 36 homers and 273 RBIs. Against Washington in 1932, he became the first player in history to win a 1 – 0 game, hit a home run, and strike out 10 or more batters. Early Wynn and Yovani Gallardo are the only others to do it. In 1935, Ruffing led the Yankees in wins (16) and batting average (.339)—not bad, considering that other hitters on the club included future Hall of Famers Lou Gehrig, Tony Lazzeri, Bill Dickey and Earle Combs.

The spring after that, Ruffing was introduced to a rookie outfielder from California and was quick to indoctrinate him into the clubhouse.

"So you're the great DiMaggio," Ruffing said. "Hit nearly .400 out on the Coast. Well you should hit .400 up here, hell, make that .450 because we throw away the scuffed balls. You get a nice clean, shiny one practically every pitch. You're a cinch to bat .450, DiMaggio!"

DiMaggio recalled later: "Red was a great needler and a great pitcher, too. He was our stopper in those days and could really relieve the tension during an important game or after a loss with some of his talk." DiMaggio added that Ruffing "could have been the most valuable Yankee of them all."

Aaron Judge

My first encounter with Aaron Judge was the day of the 2013 MLB Draft in New York. He was one of nine prospects who would be selected that night during the live show at the MLB Network studios in Secaucus, N.J. During the day, the group was given a grand tour of the Big Apple, and my job that day was to shadow them from morning to midnight for MLB.com.

They hopped on a red double-decker tour bus to take in Manhattan, then they spent time with Commissioner Bud Selig at the MLB Fan Cave social-media hub, and then we boarded a couple of buses and headed up to the Bronx for Yankee Stadium. They had a chance to sit in the Yankees' dugout, peep the home team's clubhouse, and walk through Monument Park.

That is what I remember most about Judge. He posed for a picture standing between the plaques of Miller Huggins and Babe Ruth, and it was like he somehow belonged. He had no way of knowing that the Yankees would select him later that night with the 32nd pick of the first round, but there was a dream that afternoon, as he walked amongst those legends. He could be a Yankee Legend himself, and based on what we have seen so far, I thought he should be included here.

Yes, it is early. Way early. The 2018 season was only Judge's second full MLB campaign. Still, you know when you know. He became the new face of the franchise during a 2017 season in which he led the Majors with 52 home runs, 128 runs, 127 walks and, yes, 208 strikeouts. He won the Home Run Derby in Miami. He led the Yankees to within one game of the World Series, easily won AL Rookie of the Year, and finished second to Houston's Jose Altuve in MVP voting only because of a mini-slump in the second half.

AT BATS PER HOME RUN

Here is the Yankees' all-time top twenty ranking for At Bats Per Home Run, including only players who have hit at least 100 homers with the franchise. We made an exception here for Aaron Judge and Gary Sanchez, both of whom are near 100.

Babe Ruth 10.95	Joe DiMaggio 18.89
Aaron Judge 12.52*	Tino Martinez 19.64
Gary Sanchez 14.04*	Charlie Keller 19.98
Jason Giambi 14.04	Nick Swisher 20.28
Roger Maris 14.81	Alfonso Soriano 20.29
Mickey Mantle 15.12	Yogi Berra 21.08
Alex Rodriguez 15.89	Mike Pagliarulo 21.66
Curtis Granderson 16.17	Dave Winfield 21.88
Lou Gehrig 16.23	Graig Nettles 22.08
Reggie Jackson 16.31	Jorge Posada 22.15
Mark Teixeira 17.10	

*Current through 2018

"I just try to have fun with everything," Judge said. "I'm getting paid to play a kid's game; it's pretty awesome what I get to do every day. So if I'm out in the outfield, if I'm on deck and I'm hitting, I just try to go out there and have some fun.

"I want to win, I want to compete. No matter what comes first, it's just about having fun for me. So that's talking to some fans, saying hello to some kids, tossing a kid a ball or something. Just trying to have fun out there."

I saw that confidence early one morning in December of 2016 on the floor of the New York Stock Exchange. We were there for the opening bell, and to promote a new partnership between MLB and Underarmour, which sponsors Judge. He was there with his parents, down-to-earth people who chatted with me about their water-weed problems back home in little Linden, Calif.

"I'm just working out every day, hitting every day," Judge said. "I'm kind of fine-tuning the craft a little bit, staying in shape and getting ready for the year. It's a long season, so you've got to be in shape. This is when you really work. The results that show up in October and November, that comes from what you do here in the fall and the winter."

He knew he had to earn the starting right field job on the Yankees the next Spring Training, and he did that and then some. All of that happened, and then we were in the AL clubhouse in the wee hours after the All-Star Game, and he and Robinson Cano were the last two players to leave. I asked him if all of this is what he had in mind when he had told me that at the NYSE. Judge didn't say a word; he just flashed that megawatt smile and beamed that same aura that I had first seen when he stood between two great monuments representing ultimate greatness.

Judge was part of a Baby Bomber movement that revitalized an aging club. While they had not been bad from 2013 – 16, the Yankees' only playoff appearance in those four seasons was a Wild Card Game loss to the Astros in 2015. However, that stretch saw the Yankees lose nearly all the star players that had been key to the dynastic run in the late 1990s and the 2000s. From 2013 – 16, the Yankees dealt with the retirements of Derek Jeter, Andy Pettitte, Mariano Rivera, Mark Teixeira and Alex Rodriguez, and the departures of Curtis Granderson and Cano.

In 2016, with the Yankees seemingly out of the playoff picture, Brian Cashman traded away key players like Carlos Beltran, Andrew Miller and Aroldis Chapman at the trade deadline, something the franchise had not done in decades. The following season was supposed to be a transition year, but Judge's rapid rise to stardom helped propel the club to a 91-win season and to the brink of a Fall Classic. There were plenty of other contributors, including young stars like Gary Sanchez and Luis Severino, but Judge stood out because of his incredible power and the appeal of a record for most homers by a rookie.

The 99 jersey became so omnipresent, Judge became the runaway number one in the annual Most Popular Jerseys story that I wrote for the last time before the 2018 season. That is pivotal power, and he seemed to have the confidence and drive to seek a higher place, like Monument Park. It is an unrealistic expectation at this stage, but Judge expects nothing less.

"I just think of myself as a little kid from Linden, California," he said. "I'm getting to live a dream right now."

Jacob Ruppert

All of those heady 100th anniversaries are now at hand for a new generation to learn, and Hall of Fame owner Colonel Jacob Ruppert will be a central figure in each of them. It will be a steady procession for ample social, print, broadcast and bookshelf banter among New York media and fans. There was his astute 1919 purchase of land directly across the Harlem River from the Polo Grounds for $600,000; his contract signing on December 26, 1919, allowing the transfer of "George H. Ruth" from the "Boston American League Baseball Club" to his "American League Base Ball Club of New York"; the first two pennants in 1921 – 22; the inaugural 1923 season of fabulous Yankee Stadium, complete with the first world championship; the first pinstripes and the first regular jersey numbers; Lou Gehrig and Joe DiMaggio; the best team ever in 1927; and a continuum of success unmatched in the United States.

"One of the most often-asked questions to me in 2013, when I would tell people that Jacob Ruppert had been elected to the Hall of Fame, the standard answer was: 'You mean he's not in yet?' Executives weren't really thought of for a long time," Hall president Jeff Idelson said. "You look at our executives, there are very few early execs in. You look at what Ruppert did: Ed Barrow, the pinstripes, Yankee Stadium, the numbers, that guy did everything."

"He brought baseball to the top," Babe Ruth said after Ruppert's passing in 1939, 20 years after the Colonel acquired the most famous athlete in American history to date. "Picked it up when it was a sort of hit-and-miss thing and made it a big business. He boosted salaries, built the greatest park in the business and was always a fine fellow to talk with and bargain with. I had my troubles when I was a young fellow on the Yanks. The Colonel always treated me with the greatest consideration. He was a great man."

Jacob Ruppert hosts a crowd at Yankee Stadium. From left to right: Harry New, the Postmaster General; Dr. Charles Sawyer, the President's physician; Albert Lasker; Jacob Ruppert; and President Warren G. Harding.

That man's rich life began on August 5, 1867, on the corner of Lexington Avenue and 93rd Street, and as a boy Ruppert used to play with local nines. His father, Jacob Sr., founded the Ruppert Brewery in 1867 and grew it successfully in a nation where alcohol consumption became so entrenched that a long era of temperance and Prohibition would help shape society and politics. The son graduated from Columbia Grammar School, and at the age of 19 entered both the family business and the crack Seventh Regiment of the New York National Guard.

Young Jake went from washing beer kegs to brewer superintendent four years later and took over as president upon his father's passing in 1915. At the age of 22, he was appointed colonel on the staff of Gov. David Hill. In 1898, Ruppert was elected as representative to Congress for New York's 15th District, and he served four terms between 1899 – 1907. He was one of the wealthiest men and most eligible bachelors in Gotham, and around the turn of the century, Ruppert foresaw the increasing popularity of the national pastime and started looking for a team.

"The very lucrative brewing business belonging to my family produced a great deal of profits, and I was always looking for ways to invest some of my money," Ruppert said on his 71st birthday, speaking as a guest on the "Out of the Past" radio show. "I have always enjoyed watching baseball and had been interested in purchasing a baseball team since the turn of the century but with truly no success."

He had initially sought to buy the New York Giants, but to no avail. Andrew Freedman, a real estate developer tied to the corrupt Tammany Hall political machine, was majority owner of that club and saw it finish a whopping 53 ½ games out of first place in 1902. Ban Johnson's American League was an upstart that was seen as a threat to NL bosses. During that season, in a bid to crush the fledgling AL, Freedman lured John McGraw to hop over from the Baltimore Orioles and bring key players with him. In addition, Freedman appointed his past nemesis, influential Reds owner John T. Brush, as managing director of the Giants. Freedman initially transferred day-to-day control to him and soon thereafter sold nearly all of his interests in the club to Brush. That dashed the hopes of the Colonel, who saw a great opportunity.

The Giants made a staggering turnaround, winning 84 games in 1903 and then 106 in 1904. They were so good, McGraw scoffed at the notion of playing the AL's best team in a winner-take-all series, as Pittsburgh had done when it lost the first of the "world's series" a year earlier. For Ruppert, it was the ultimate irony. He still wanted the Giants, but those Orioles had been so decimated that they were forced to relocate to New York after 1902 and become the Highlanders, fulfilling a Brush plot. Ruppert only wanted the best in life.

"I had wanted to buy the Giants for more than a decade, but I was never successful," Ruppert said. "The New York Giants [were] considered to be the finest baseball team in New York City at the turn of the century and into the second decade. John McGraw, manager of the Giants, was the friend, confidante and drinking companion of actors the length of Broadway. In 1914, he went with the Giants on a tremendously successful around-the-world publicity tour. Consequently, the Giants had an unmatched clientele that on almost any afternoon might include the cream of New York's sporting and social life. So you can understand why I would be interested in buying such a team. When I tried, the Giants had just lost their owner and patron, John T. Brush; but I was informed that there was no chance for me."

Ruppert turned down a chance to buy the Chicago Cubs in 1912, a New Yorker through and through. After that year's World Series, Brush was recuperating from an automobile accident injury and aboard a train headed West when he died suddenly in Missouri. His executor, Harry Hempstead, retained control of the Giants until selling to the Stoneham family at the end of the decade, dashing those hopes of Ruppert's for good.

YANKEES EXECUTIVES INDUCTED INTO HALL OF FAME

EXECUTIVE	INDUCTION YEAR
Ed Barrow	1953
George Weiss	1971
Larry MacPhail	1978
Lee MacPhail	1998
Jacob Ruppert	2013

"John McGraw, who was a friend of mine, said, 'If you really want to buy a ball club, I think I can get you one. How about the

Yankees?'" Ruppert recalled. McGraw introduced him to Col. T.L. Huston, who would become his baseball business partner.

"It had never really occurred to me to acquire the Yankees because they were such a, well, mediocre team at the time," Ruppert said. "Like all Giants fans, and like most businessmen, Col. Huston and myself weren't too interested. To us the Giants were still the only game in town and the Giants' hordes of public admirers formed the only swinging circle of fans in town. But McGraw convinced us and when a representative approached us with an offer to sell the Yankees, we eventually decided to purchase the team for a sum of $460,000.

"Many said that we were buying a 'pig in a poke' and that it was unwise to make such an investment with the Great War bearing down upon our country. At that time, they were certainly a poor team, but we believed that by acquiring a smart manager and good ball players, we could make the New York Yankees into a top-notch baseball club. We knew that it would be difficult, if not impossible, to draw the fans away from the Giants, but we hoped that we could offer New York an answer to the otherwise unanswerable Giants."

On January 30, 1915, in arguably the most pivotal and important moment in franchise history, Ruppert bought the New York Yankees for $430,000 from Frank Farrell and William Devery. They were reluctant sellers who were forced into an agreement by Johnson. The club formerly known as the Highlanders or "Hilltoppers" had been called "Yankees" since 1913, as editors needed a shorter nickname for headlines and the term made sense for an entity that had temporarily and aggressively moved into the home of another entity (Giants).

In 1918, while Huston was abroad as a lieutenant colonel in World War I, Ruppert hired Miller Huggins away from the Cardinals as his new manager. This infuriated Huston, who was not able to weigh in and never warmed up to the skipper. One of the two would have to go, and after the Yankees won their second consecutive pennant in 1922, Ruppert assured Huston that it would not be his manager. Ruppert bought out the interests of Huston for $1.175 million, and in announcing the news in a rare visit to the Yankee clubhouse, he killed two birds with one stone by completely removing any internal strife. "Gentlemen, I am now the sole owner of this ball club. I want you to know that Miller Huggins is manager."

Ruppert's most famous—and shrewd—transaction was the purchase of The Bambino. Ruth had been an electric two-way player, dominating on the mound for the Red Sox and setting himself apart with a revolutionary big-bang style at the plate. Ruth had shattered the single-season home run record with 29 in 1919, 17 more than the next-highest total. "It was an amount the club could not afford to refuse," said Red Sox owner Harry Frazee, who received $100,000 ($25,000 up front) plus a loan against his Fenway Park mortgage. On January 5, 1920—10 days after the actual contract was signed—the Yankees announced Ruth's acquisition.

"It was quite by chance, actually," Ruppert said of the Ruth deal, speaking on the radio show in the last months of his life. "I was instrumental in helping out the Red Sox financially; I realized that Ruth was an invaluable player [and] the Yankees could use him . . . so as part of the agreement, I asked for him and got him! Yes—Babe Ruth's home runs so captured the imagination of the fans that his reputation helped brand the Yankees as a team of sluggers—'The Bronx Bombers.'"

Ruth hit 54 homers in 1920 and 59 the next year. On Opening Day, he hit the first longball at brand-new Yankee Stadium, an edifice that the Two Colonels had delivered on a grand scale for $2.5 million. After losing to the Giants in consecutive World Series, the two teams met a third time and the first year of a new ballpark was completed by the Bronx Bombers' first title. At long last, Ruppert was finished with chasing the "Jints," and his team was just warming up.

Another profound part of Ruppert's legacy can be seen simply by strolling through the Gallery at the Hall of Fame. So many of the plaques are a direct result of his impact, such as the hiring of executives Ed Barrow and George Weiss, managers

Huggins and Joe McCarthy, and powerhouse players including Gehrig, Waite Hoyt, Tony Lazzeri, Earle Combs, Red Ruffing, Herb Pennock and Joltin' Joe. Ruppert said he most remembered "all the pennants and the World Series" and also the "amazing, astounding feat" of Ruth's 60 homers in 1927.

Ed Hughes wrote in the Brooklyn *Eagle* on January 13, 1939: "As a baseball magnate he was extraordinary—and the tops. . . . He thought his competitors should spend as much money as he did, if that was the only way they could get star ball players. Colonel Ruppert wanted the best in baseball, and he got it." Jimmy Powers eulogized with all caps in the *Daily News*: "He bought us the BEST BASEBALL CLUB IN THE WORLD!" Frank Graham wrote in the *Sun:* "The part that he played never can be minimized and never will be forgotten." On April 19, 1940, a plaque was dedicated for the Colonel, joining that of Hug.

In his last will and testament, Ruppert provided for the perpetuation of the New York Yankees for as long as possible. He was proud of his possessions, and especially his ball club. In January 1945, six years after his death, Ruppert's heirs and assigns were pressed for cash and sold the Yankees for nearly $3 million. In 1955, the brewery would sponsor Giants broadcasts, and in 1965 it would go out of business and sell its flagship Knickerbocker brand "The Beer That Satisfies" to Rheingold. But the Colonel's greatest legacy would carry on strong, his winning philosophy still at the core. His Yankees won six titles and he hated defeat with a passion.

"He never took a backward step the whole time he was owner of the Yankees," said Ruth, his final visitor. "We'll never see another owner like him."

Bill Dickey

Removing the Yankees from the equation, catcher is easily the least-retired jersey by position in the history of baseball. Consider this list of active MLB clubs:

RED SOX:	Carlton Fisk
WHITE SOX:	Carlton Fisk
REDS:	Johnny Bench
DODGERS:	Roy Campanella
METS:	Mike Piazza
RANGERS:	Ivan Rodriguez
NATIONALS/EXPOS:	Gary Carter

That's it, until Buster Posey, Yadier Molina, Joe Mauer and maybe Salvador Perez are duly honored. One catcher's jersey was retired by two teams, so only six catchers. I am not counting Craig Biggio, who caught for his first four seasons for Houston but spent his last 16 as a second baseman or outfielder. There are clubs who *should* retire catcher jerseys: no-brainers Gabby Hartnett (Cubs) and Mickey Cochrane (by either the Athletics or Tigers). Also: Ted Simmons (St. Louis), Roger Bresnahan (New York Giants, before jersey numbers), Ernie Lombardi (Reds), Manny Sanguillen (Pittsburgh), Gene Tenace (Oakland), Bill Freehan (Detroit) and maybe Carlos Ruiz (Philadelphia) and

Jason Varitek (Boston, hey they finally won) among them. There is so little thought given to this subject and catchers direct the game. Then there are the New York Yankees, home of the catcher. Bill Dickey started this proud tradition, and the Yankees almost match that total of MLB retired catchers all by themselves. He was followed by protégés Yogi Berra and Elston Howard, then Thurman Munson, then Jorge Posada. All world champions as well. Gary Sanchez has the early makings of a sixth, and he is motivated by this rich tradition. (Hey, even Joe Torre, whose number six was retired as a manager, was a catcher for part of his career.) The Yankees are so far ahead of any other Major League franchise in this department, they even retired the same number (eight) for two catchers, and that goes back to Dickey's numeric spot in the great lineups.

The pride of the Ozarks attended Little Rock College, and by 1927 he was playing in 101 games for the Jackson Senators with a .297 average, three homers, .989 fielding percentage, 84 assists and only nine errors. "That's when I really learned to catch," Dickey said. He was seeing the field better and working with pitchers better. "I just decided I was a pretty good catcher," he said of that year. "Which I never was before. I was a lousy catcher."

He was hitting about .315 late in the season, and veteran Yankee scout Johnny Nee told him with a week left in the season, "If you wind up hitting over .300, I'm gonna buy you for the Yankees."

Dickey didn't get another hit and wound up at .297, although they won the playoffs.

"I said, 'uh-oh,' there goes my chance with the Yankees," he said.

Jackson waived its rights to Dickey, adding to his concern. But veteran scout Johnny Nee was hell-bent on getting him into pinstripes. "I will quit scouting if this boy doesn't make good," Nee pleaded with Yankees general manager Ed Barrow, who was hesitant. Nee's job was safe. The Yanks purchased Dickey's contract for the $12,000 waiver fee.

"I was on my way home, on the train, and I saw a little piece of paper, *The Sporting News*, on the floor," he recalled in a 1987 interview for the Hall of Fame, just before his 80th birthday. "I picked it up and it read: 'Yankees buy catcher Dickey.' I said, 'Heck, that's me.' And that's how I found out."

He debuted with the Yankees on August 15, 1928, playing 10 games in that regular season.

THE TEAM, THE TALENT, THE TITLES

From Babe and Lou, to Joe and Bill, to Yogi and Mickey, to Reggie and Lightning, to Jete and Mo, to the current cast, the Yankees have been constantly in title-hunting mode. Entering 2019 as contenders, the Yankees had won 27 World Series, leading MLB and North American pro sports in general for sustained success. Here are numbers to consider as the count goes on.

Fun Facts

- Six players have eight or more World Series rings: Yogi Berra (10), Joe DiMaggio (9), Bill Dickey (9), Phil Rizzuto (9), Frankie Crosetti (9), Lou Gehrig (8)
- 26 players have won six or more World Series rings: Eddie Collins is the only one to have never played for the Yankees
- There are only five MLB teams the Yankees have never faced in the postseason: Rays, Blue Jays, White Sox, Rockies, and Nationals (entering 2019)
- Only franchise in modern era to have three seasons of at least a .700 winning percentage (1927, 1939, and 1998)
- The Yankees have not had a losing season since 1992
- 21 losing seasons in 118 years
- Only 12 losing seasons in last 100 years (since 1918)
- Between 1921 (their first appearance) and 1964, the Yankees never went more than three consecutive years without reaching the World Series

"You have an idea how a kid would feel going to a ball club that had just won the World Series in four straight ballgames and had the greatest ball players at that time that there was in the country," he said. "Babe Ruth and Lou Gehrig, they were both my idols. I never saw two guys who could hit in as many runs and hit the ball out of the park in any direction that they could, or as far."

He saw Ruth and Gehrig slam baseballs into Crescent Lake beyond the old Huggins Field in St. Petersburg, and that is where the field's namesake (now it's Huggins-Stengel Field) took exception to Dickey trying to copy their splashes.

"Little Miller Huggins called me over one day and said I think you're trying to hit the ball as far as Babe and Lou," Dickey recalled. "I said, 'Yes sir.' He says, 'You'll never hit the ball as far as them as long as you play baseball.' He says, 'I'll tell you what I want you to do . . . I want you to get one of Earle Combs's bats and I want you to choke up and hit the ball all around.' So that's what I did."

From 1929 – 38, Dickey batted at least .310 in nine of 10 seasons, including a remarkable 1936 campaign in which he hit .362 with an OPS of 1.045. The left-handed hitter's .313 average leads all catchers with at least 7,000 plate appearances. For perspective, it should be noted that the league average was .280 over Posada's career, a full 33 points less than during Dickey's; a great batter could hit .400 back in Dickey's day.

He was not generally fast, but he got out of the box and down the line quickly. Applying Huggins's guidance, Dickey found that homers came with just driving baseballs all around. He hit 202 home runs and drove in 1,209 runs, winding up with a 35-ounce bat. Once the All-Star Game was instituted in 1933, he became a regular choice with 11 selections.

Of course, those stats only tell part of the story. Dickey was synonymous with winning. He played in eight World Series from 1932 – 43 and won seven rings to go with the one he received as a regular-season member of the 1928 champs. His best WAR seasons came in the 1936 – 39 run when Joe McCarthy's club won every year. The Yankees had been through 47 serviceable catchers until Dickey arrived, so without question the pivotal moment was his creation of an important tradition.

Suddenly Murderers' Row had filled its only real weakness, catcher. It would rarely ever be a weakness for the club again. Besides his offensive prowess, Dickey emerged as a defensive standout and an authoritative handler of pitchers. From 1932 – 1943, all years when Dickey was the team's primary catcher, the Yankees gave up the fewest runs in the AL 10 out of 12 seasons.

"Bill Dickey is the best [catcher] I ever saw," Indians Hall of Fame ace Bob Feller said. "He was as good as anyone behind the plate, and better with the bat. There are others I'd include right behind Dickey, but he was the best all-around catcher of them all. I believe I could have won thirty-five games if Bill Dickey was my catcher."

"I was lucky to work with Hall of Fame catcher Bill Dickey, who was always one pitch ahead of the batters," Yankees pitcher Charlie Devens said. "He not only called a great game, but had the best arm I'd ever seen."

Hall of Famer Red Ruffing, a 20-game winner for four of the seasons he served as Dickey's batterymate, said: "Dickey never has bothered me, never has shaken me off. He just lets me pitch my game."

Dickey caught more games than any Yankee catcher before or after, and that includes catching 100 or more games in 13 consecutive years. He was a model of consistency, a trait he shared with his roommate, Lou Gehrig. Dickey said he thought *he* was strong, but soon found that Gehrig was the "strongest" person he'd ever known. Dickey was the only Yankee invited to Gehrig's wedding, the first Yankee to know of Gehrig's ALS, the only teammate to represent the club at Gehrig's funeral, and a speaker at Gehrig's memorial at the Stadium. They shared the same approach, to the game and to life—quiet leaders by example.

Dickey was a fierce competitor on the field, though. In 1932, he drew a 30-day suspension and $1,000 fine for breaking the jaw of Washington's Carl Reynolds in two places with one punch after a collision at home plate. Dickey expressed remorse for that later.

"He was a great catcher, great hitter and a great man to have on the ball club," McCarthy said. "The records prove Dickey was the greatest catcher of all time." Maybe even greater acclaim came from Connie Mack, the all-time managerial win leader who even had Cochrane on his roster back then. Mack said Dickey was "the game's greatest catcher."

Dickey hit the World Series-clinching home run in 1943, and in doing so he kind of went out of in style. He missed the 1944 and '45 seasons while serving in the Navy, and attempted to return to his usual role in 1946 but wound up managing the Yankees when McCarthy abruptly resigned that May due to health issues. It was a short-lived assignment, and Dickey submitted his resignation before the year was out, returning home to Arkansas.

He was ecstatic to get an invite back into the Yankee organization as a member of Casey Stengel's coaching staff in 1949 and began mentoring young Yogi Berra—another Navy vet—in the transition from outfielder to catcher.

"Bill is learnin' me his experience," Berra would say. Eventually Dickey would do the same thing for Howard, inspiring him to say: "Without Bill, I'm nobody. Nobody at all. He made me a catcher." It was an indication of how long Dickey continued to have influence on the club and especially on the tradition of high catching standards.

In 1954, Dickey was enshrined in Cooperstown. He returned to Yankee Stadium for the retirement of his number eight jersey in 1972, and then for a ceremony to dedicate his plaque in Monument Park in 1988. Johnny Bench would be inducted a year after that plaque ceremony, so there might have been a little extra bravado in these words on the plaque:

BILL IS CONSIDERED THE GREATEST CATCHER OF ALL-TIME.

Even Dickey himself would have told you at the time of that unveiling that Yogi deserved such lofty inscription. In 1988, suffice to say it would have been accurate to describe Dickey as "one of the best catchers of all-time." To this day, he is generally considered in the top 10.

More important is what he started and what he nurtured into the future. Too many clubs have paid too little attention to the legacy of their backstops. The Yankees have no such qualm. They own the position outright, proof in all those retired numbers. It is an interesting prospect when considering that it was the last position they finally addressed back in the late 1920s.

"That's the high-rent district because of the history behind those positions and the people that manned them for a decade," Yankees general manager Brian Cashman said recently, when asked about Sanchez. "It's almost like a Supreme Court justice. Those types of players that man that position for a very long time."

Catfish Hunter

"**Ever since I was** a little boy I wanted to be a Yankee," Catfish Hunter once said. "I think it's a goal of every ballplayer to be a Yankee. It's a real thrill."

By the time it happened to him, Hunter already had pitched 10 years in the Majors, all with Oakland. He already had won 161 games and three rings, with a Cy Young Award and six All-Star selections along the way. After pitching Oakland to a threepeat in the 1974 World Series, Hunter became notable for what happened off the field. His agent successfully claimed that the A's had failed to make an insurance-annuity payment for Hunter in time, and the pitcher's contract was then voided and arbitrator Peter Seitz declared him a free agent.

That paved the way for a five-year, $3.75 million contract from the Yankees, who had the help of former MLB catcher Clyde Kluttz, a fellow North Carolinian who had been a father figure to Hunter. The deal revolutionized the process of free-agent shopping, popularizing the concept of a multiyear deal and bringing arbitration to the forefront. For the Yankees in particular, it began the Steinbrenner family tradition of going after the best free agents on the market. Just two years later, the Yankees would sign another A's star, Reggie Jackson to a record-setting contract. Nowadays, the Yankees are expected to make a play for many of the biggest names in baseball, so Hunter's signing was one of the most pivotal moments in franchise history.

After four consecutive 20-win seasons, Hunter not only picked up where he left off, but he also proved that he could excel anywhere by giving the Yankees his best season: an 8.1 WAR, compared to 6.9 in his Cy Young season of 1974. He finished second to Jim Palmer in Cy voting in 1975, after leading the Majors with 23 wins, 30 complete games, 328 innings and a 1.009 WHIP. And in the process, he brought a brand of success back to pinstripes.

Hunter's new team missed the postseason in 1975, but soon became the elite team in the American League, replacing the A's, who would not return to the World Series until 1988. The Yankees won the pennant in 1976, followed by world championships in 1977 and '78. That gave Hunter an incredible stretch of five world championships in seven years—something like Michael Jordan's later run with the Chicago Bulls.

"Catfish was the cornerstone," Steinbrenner said. "He taught us how to win."

Although Hunter had left the A's for big money, he never allowed the money to change him. Teammates like Jackson, who played with him in both New York and Oakland, observed the same down-to-earth personality that he had always featured.

"When you have a [deciding] game," Reggie Jackson told the *New York Times* in 1973, "he's the one you want pitching for you."

To friends he made outside of baseball, the pitcher remained Jimmy Hunter of Hertford, North Carolina. Prior to his MLB career, he had to have one of his toes removed due to a hunting accident. This caused some reluctance by teams to sign him, but he debuted with the A's just past his 19th birthday. Hunter never pitched in the Minors, aside from a winter ball stint in 1964. On May 8 of 1968, the Year of the Pitcher, Hunter threw the first AL perfect game since Don Larsen did it for the Yankees in the 1956 World Series.

Hunter was soon to emerge as an elite right-hander, and he came with a "catchy" nickname, if you will. It was given by the same Charles O. Finley who would later sue to try to prevent him from becoming a free agent and thus a Yankee. The flamboyant A's owner wanted every player have a moustache and a good nickname.

"He told me, 'A player's got to have a nickname,' and he asked me what I liked to do," Hunter explained in 1991. "'Hunting and fishing,' I said, and he said, 'Let's call you Catfish. . . . The story is, when you were six years old you ran away from home to fish and by the time your parents got to you you'd caught two catfish and were just about to bring in a third. Got that? Now you repeat it to me.'"

Hunter joined Cy Young, Christy Mathewson and Walter Johnson as the only pitchers in Major League history to win 200 games by the age of 31. He retired after the last year of his Yankees contract in 1979 at the age of 33 because diabetes and arm trouble hurt his effectiveness. His final record was 224 – 166 with a 3.26 ERA and 1.13 WHIP. Hunter was 9 – 6 with a 3.26 ERA in 132 1/3 postseason innings.

In 1987, Hunter was inducted into the Hall of Fame, and unlike Reggie, his plaque would be without a logo in recognition of two franchises with magnificent contributions. "THE BIGGER THE GAME, THE BETTER HE PITCHED,"begins the text on his plaque. Twelve years after that enshrinement, back home in Hertford, Hunter died at the age of 53 due to the same ALS disease that had taken the life of another Yankee champion, Lou Gehrig.

Graig Nettles

If we may start here with some housekeeping, Yankee fans would be wise to mount a Hall of Fame campaign for Graig Nettles. His qualifications look better today than they did in the immediate decades after he left the game.

Nettles ranks 12th all-time among third basemen with a 55.2 JAWS and a 68.0 WAR. Everyone above him on that list already has been enshrined except for number three Adrian Beltre (possible first-ballot when he is eligible), Number 10 Scott Rolen (I voted for him in his first year, but he barely reached double digits in voting percentage his first year) and Number 11 Edgar Martinez (expected to either be elected or come close for 2019). Nettles is more deserving than some other Yankees in Cooperstown, and definitely more deserving than some other third basemen with Hall plaques such as George Kell and Freddie Lindstrom.

As a defensive-minded player—albeit one who was also one of the better power hitters of his era—Nettles often was overshadowed by bigger stars, such as Thurman Munson, Catfish Hunter, Reggie Jackson and Ron Guidry. Yet, Nettles was with the team for 11 years, even becoming the captain in 1982. His highlight-reel defensive performance in the 1978 World Series earned him wider national appeal and marketability, much like his rival Brooks Robinson had enjoyed in the 1970 World Series. Additionally, Nettles won the ALCS MVP in 1981 and went on to hit .400 in the Fall Classic that year as well, although in a losing effort.

It solidified his standing in Yankee history as a key part on multiple pennant-winning teams. A strong argument could be made that he was the best third baseman in Yankee history for the first 100 years of the franchise, before Alex Rodriguez came along, and also that his acquisition was one of the most pivotal by the Yankees in the years following the 1964 World Series and fade from contention.

Nettles was selected in the first MLB Draft, a fourth-round choice by Minnesota out of San Diego State. When the Twins traded former ace Dean Chance to Cleveland after the 1969 season, they threw in Nettles as part of the six-player deal. The Indians made him their everyday third baseman and he responded by belting 54 homers combined over his first two years. That would become standard production for him over the next decade, along with about 85-90 RBIs a season. Nettles was durable and above-average, and the Yankees eyeballed him.

On November 27, 1972, Cleveland sent Nettles and Jerry Moses to New York in exchange for John Ellis, Jerry Kenney, Charlie Spikes and Rusty Torres. Although Indians general manager Gabe Paul boasted that 11 teams wanted Nettles and that they had waited out the Yankees for just the right time, it was about as lopsided as deals come. The players they got amounted to nothing. Cleveland would never finish above fourth place in the AL East again and would become a laughingstock serving as the basis for the movie "Major League."

"If I could have picked the spot I wanted to go, it would have been the Yankees," Nettles said. "I always wanted to play for New York and for Ralph Houk. I hope I'll satisfy the team and be here for ten years or so."

Lee MacPhail said of the Yankees: "Now we feel we have as good a club as anybody in baseball. Our fans have been waiting long enough." Ralph Houk, who was about to manage his last season with the Yankees, said at the time: "I'm not worrying about youth. It's time to go out and win it. Our offensive line up now should be the best since our winning teams of ten years ago."

Nettles was given number nine, the same number Roger Maris had worn through his glory years. Marty Appel, who served as the Yankees PR Director at the time, wrote in *Pinstripe Empire* that he told Yankees equipment manager Pete Sheehy, "Pete, you gotta give Nettles number nine! He's Maris." Interestingly enough, in 1976, Nettles became the first Yankee to lead the AL in home runs since Maris's famous 61-in-'61 season.

The acquisition of Nettles proved pivotal to the franchise. It helped to reignite an organization that had not made the playoffs since 1964. By Yankee standards, that was a massive drought, the longest since before Babe Ruth was purchased. The Yankees had slowly crept back to respectability, and Nettles became a key missing piece for a contender.

Nettles had set the single-season record for most assists at third base with 412 in 1971, and in 1973 he tied for second with Brooks Robinson (410). Nettles was now a key figure as the Yankees finally returned to the Fall Classic in 1976. Although he batted only .190 (4-for-21) and .160 (4-for-25), the Yankees won it all in 1977 – 78.

In the 1978 World Series, it was Nettles's glove that is remembered by many. You want a pivotal moment? Try the top of the third inning of Game Three. The Dodgers had won the first two games in Los Angeles. Now New York was clinging to a 2 – 1 lead for Ron Guidry at home. With Bill Russell on first base and two out, Reggie Smith smashed one down the third base line. Nettles dived to his right, snagged the shot, and threw out Smith to end the inning. In the fifth inning, Smith again was batting with two out when he again smashed one to Nettles, this time with runners on first and second. Nettles knocked it down, holding Smith to a single that loaded the bases. Steve Garvey batted next and drilled yet another ball to third. Nettles made the play from his knees, spun and threw to second for the force.

And as if that were all not enough, then came the number one play of Game Three, according to the Baseball Reference box score. Davey Lopes batted with the bases loaded in the sixth, hit one to Nettles, and the result was another inning-ending force at second to end the inning. It was shades of 1970 Brooksie. "It's Dodgers Two, Nettles One," Reggie Smith said after the game. Dodgers third base coach Preston Gomez went one further: "I said to Nettles, 'You're the best' . . . I say he's as good as Brooks Robinson."

In 1981, Nettles was ALCS MVP (6-for-12, nine RBIs) as the Bronx Bombers made it back to the big stage. He played in 53 postseason games over seven seasons, a large number in those days. Overall in his career, Nettles played from1967 – 88 with six teams, earning two Gold Gloves (a category owned by Robinson) and six All-Star selections. He finished his career with 390 homers, and of those, the 372 as a third baseman ranks sixth all-time behind Mike Schmidt, Eddie Mathews, Chipper Jones, Beltre and Aramis Ramirez.

Nettles was the Yankees' captain from 1982-84. Despite not leaving New York on the best of terms in 1984, he has returned to Yankee Stadium for Old-Timers' Days and he served as a coach for the club in 1991. He was traded to his hometown Padres in part because he co-wrote a book, *Balls,* that heavily criticized The Boss. The Yankees retired Maris's number nine the year before trading Nettles, and the latter suggested that the timing was no coincidence. There was plenty of rancor in those days to go around for everyone in the clubhouse, and Steinbrenner was not one to settle for another extended run without a ring.

"I mean, Roger had a couple of great years there, but look over the career, and I had a longer and better career than Roger did," Nettles said. "So they could've mentioned both of us wore that number, especially with me being the most recent. But George chose not to, and that's his prerogative."

In 2017, I covered Nettles's appearance at the 37th annual Thurman Munson Awards Dinner, where he was named a recipient of an honor bearing the name of his beloved former teammate. Nettles was presented with his award by Roy White, his teammate on those Yankee clubs that won it all in 1977 – 78.

"We had some good teams," Nettles said in his acceptance

speech. "We had come from a time when the Yankees were not so good, in the late sixties and early seventies, and we slowly put the puzzle together and ended up being a very good team at the end of the seventies."

Nettles was very good, and maybe even good enough that he warrants another look for Cooperstown.

Reggie Jackson

As I interviewed Hall of Fame president Jeff Idelson in his office, we got to the subject of Mr. October. Jeff, who oversees the best collection of baseball memorabilia anywhere, reached into a bookcase beside him and pulled out one of his own personal favorites.

"The first book I ever read was *Reggie Jackson: Superstar.* Here it is," he said as he proudly showed it to me. It is a 1975 paperback by Dick O'Connor and published by Scholastic Book Services, with 91 pages on the inside and a bearded Reggie resplendent in green and gold while in full power stride, left knee touching the dirt, launching a home run for the Swingin' A's and launching a legend. I took the accompanying photo of Jeff holding the book.

"This one and the one right after, it, *Slick Watts.* Slick had the headband and he's bald, and I'm like, 'What does this dude need a headband for?' Maybe Reggie's wasn't the *first* book, but the first chapter book, let's put it that way. I probably read *Harold and the Purple Crayon* and stuff like that. You could buy books, and they had *Reggie Jackson: Superstar.*"

For me as a boy, it was Matt Christopher books, like *Catcher with a Glass Arm.* So I can appreciate why that Reggie book stays right there in Jeff's office, a little wear and tear but the memory in mint condition. It takes you back to your own discovery of magic. That is how Idelson remembers the flamboyant slugger on an Oakland team that dominated baseball with a 1972 – 74 threepeat, and a nearby bronze plaque in the museum is even better.

"Reggie always has had a flair for the dramatic," Idelson said. "I found him annoying when I worked for the Red Sox, and then when I went to the Yankees, I got to know him and understand him a little better. So I developed a little different opinion.

"When you think of Reggie, you think of a guy who lived for the big moment, and when the big moment arrived, he didn't fail. He loved putting a team on his back and being the guy who could get them to the next level."

Jackson hit 563 home runs over 21 Major League seasons, at the time of his retirement the most homers by any left-handed hitter other than Babe Ruth. Jackson slashed .262/.356/.490 with 139 OPS+ (leading the league in OPS+ four times), finishing with 1,551 runs and 1,702 RBIs. Of course, when you think of Jackson, though, you think of a time when leaves changed colors and a three-homer clincher for the Yankees symbolized his command of a calendar month.

Hall of Fame President Jeff Idelson proudly shows off his first chapter book which was about Reggie Jackson. *Courtesy of the author*

He played in 11 postseasons and was a member of five world champions—three straight with Oakland (1972 – 74) and two straight with New York (1977 – 78). He hit 10 home runs and drove in 24 runs over 27 World Series games, and his batting average on that stage was nearly a full 100 points higher than in regular seasons. "MR. OCTOBER" is the text right under the name on Jackson's Hall of Fame plaque, one of the best nicknames in history, even if it was originally meant in a sarcastic way when Yankee captain Thurman Munson first said it.

"I can't say I relished those moments under pressure—at least, not at the moment—but I succeeded in them. I rose to the occasion," Jackson said. "I knew what to do, how to control it. . . . It is nerve-racking. But you have to adjust to the clutch, do what you have to do—that's what they're paying you for."

Jackson has been imparting wisdom like that to generations of Yankees now, in his role as a special advisor. It has been a quarter-century since he became a first-ballot Hall of Famer (receiving 96.3 percent of the vote) and had his number 44 retired by the Bombers. After all those years of loud actions on the field and in the press, the reality is that Jackson, whose ego was among the most famous in baseball history, has continued to have a quietly profound and sustained impact on the team whose logo adorns the cap of his Hall plaque.

"My dad talked about him all the time, 'Mr. October,'" said Aaron Judge, one of the latest in a long line of aspiring Yankees with whom Jackson has worked at Spring Training and during regular seasons. "Just getting a chance to meet him and talk about hitting, defense and even stuff off the field has been huge."

Judge is from Oakland Athletics country, and that is where his father saw the rise of a legend, the true superstar gracing those yellowing pages of Idelson's book.

The A's were in their brief iteration as a Kansas City club when they drafted Jackson out of Arizona State with the second overall pick in 1966, a year after they made Rick Monday the first overall selection in draft history. The Mets had the number one pick in that 1966 draft, and they could have had Jackson but went instead with California high school catcher Steve Chilcott. Reggie became a first-ballot Hall of Famer and Chilcott never made it out of the Minors.

Jackson hit a combined 23 homers in 68 games for two Class A teams right after being drafted, and the A's wasted no time bringing him up. He appeared in 35 games for Kansas City in 1967, and then he led the club's move to Oakland for the next season. Jackson quickly became a face of Charlie Finley's franchise, belting 29 homers with 74 RBIs, 82 runs and 14 steals while playing all 154 games in 1968. One harbinger of note: Jackson led the league with 171 strikeouts, building toward a Major League record of 2,597 strikeouts that still stands.

The next summer was a quantum leap. Pitching mounds were lowered for 1969 to counter the domination of overall pitching, and it also was a year of two new expansion clubs per league. Offense busted out, and Jackson led the way. He topped the Majors with a 189 OPS+ and 123 runs, hitting 47 homers and driving in 118 runs. Jackson had 34 homers by July 5 and was drawing national attention for what looked like a potential bid at Roger Maris's record that had happened at the start of the decade. The 1969 season also brought Jackson's first of 14 All-Star nods.

The Swingin' A's won titles from 1972 – 74, earning their first one despite Jackson missing that series against Cincinnati due to an ALCS hamstring injury. He won his first of two World Series MVP awards after the 1973 Fall Classic against the Mets, and he continued to produce when it counted as Oakland eliminated the Dodgers for the threepeat.

It was the dawn of free agency, and after an arbitrator declared Andy Messersmith and Dave McNally free agents, Finley got more serious about moving Jackson to avoid a big payday. Jackson was going to be a free agent at the end of 1976, so Finley traded him to Baltimore just before that Opening Day, an odd mix. Jackson was still determined to test the free agent market after that season, and George Steinbrenner, a few years into his quest to end the Yankees' long title drought, signed him for five years and 2.96 million.

BOB SHEPPARD

Good evening, ladies and gentlemen, welcome to Yankee Stadium

He was the Vin Scully of public address announcers, or perhaps Vin Scully was the Bob Sheppard of broadcasters. In both cases, it was a welcoming voice that you could not ever imagine being without. "You're not in the big leagues until Bob Sheppard announces your name," Carl Yastrzemski once said.

Sheppard introduced Yankee lineups and batters for some 4,500 games, mixing in the occasional need to implore fans to stop throwing items onto the field (see: Chris Chambliss). He was 12 when he came to Yankee Stadium for the first time, and it was only fitting when the Yankees talked him into working day games for 15 bucks instead of teaching.

The pivotal moment came on April 17, 1951 for Opening Day against the rival Red Sox. It was Mickey Mantle's big-league debut and Joe DiMaggio's last opener. Here is the lineup Sheppard read:

Jackie Jensen	LF
Phil Rizzuto	SS
Mickey Mantle	RF
Joe DiMaggio	CF
Yogi Berra	C
Johnny Mize	1B
Billy Johnson	3B
Jerry Coleman	2B
Vic Raschi	P

Amazingly, six of those nine are in the Hall of Fame—Rizzuto, Mantle, DiMaggio, Berra, and Mize as players, and Coleman as a broadcaster. Make it nine if you want to include Ted Williams, Bobby Doerr, and Lou Boudreau from the Red Sox lineup that day. And so began the middle season of a five-year run of Yankee titles, and it was the beginning of a beautiful relationship between a guy in the booth and his audience, lasting through 2007. He was the PA announcer from the Yankees' 14th championship through their 26th: the sound of success.

Mantle told Sheppard in the 1990s that he had gotten "goose bumps" every time Sheppard announced his name, and Sheppard told Harvey Frommer that "I felt the same way about announcing him." After Sheppard passed away in 2010 at the age of 99, Derek Jeter requested that a recording of this iconic intro be played each time the Captain stepped to the plate in the Bronx for the remainder of his career: "Now batting for the Yankees, number two, Derek Jeter. Number two." It lives on in the hearts of pretty much every fan who ever saw a Jeter at bat at home, slowly and regally delivered from a faceless voice that was like an old friend to generations.

It was the largest free agent contract to date, and resistance within the Yankees' clubhouse would begin right away and reach historic levels as a Bronx Zoo era began. The team had finally returned to the Fall Classic in 1976, thanks to Chris Chambliss's big walk-off homer. Some, notably manager Billy Martin, failed to understand why they needed Jackson and his exorbitant ego. In an interview with *Sport* magazine at his first Spring Training, Jackson said, "I'm the straw that stirs the drink; Munson can only stir it bad." Munson was sure there was no misquote. Here is what Reggie said about it in the *Times* 16 years later, a week before his Hall induction:

"I felt I was misunderstood about that straw stirring the drink remark. I mean, I came to the Yankees after they'd just lost the Series in four straight to Cincinnati. And I said they had great players like Munson and [Ron] Guidry and [Lou] Piniella and Chambliss, but I said I was the last ingredient that could win the championship. The straw that stirs the drink. When it was printed, everyone went nuts."

They heard him say: "I didn't come to New York to be a star, I brought my star with me." Then they saw the Reggie! Bar, a candy bar promotion by Reggie's people for the home opener. Then they saw him clearly loaf on Jim Rice's lazy fly ball while playing right at Fenway Park on a nationally televised game, followed by his replacement by Paul Blair in right that same inning and the subsequent skirmish between Reggie and Billy in the dugout. Then they saw him benched for the decisive Game Five of the 1977 ALCS before coming through as a pinch-hitter. It was a daily watch for media in the zoo.

"I only ask one thing as a manager—that my players hustle," Martin said after the Fenway episode. "I told them this spring that if you show the club up, I'll show you up."

Here is the pivotal thing about Reggie Jackson as a Yankee: That all happened right in the middle of his career, in his prime, the stuff of so many stories and books, and yet you wouldn't think twice about it if you only look at his career stats. Nothing got to him, ever. That 1977 season, when most of the clubhouse was against him (and justifiably so), Jackson hit .286/.375/.550 with 32 homers, 110 RBIs, 93 runs, 39 doubles and 17 stolen bases. His 150 OPS+ was easily the best on the team.

Then came his ultimate moment: Game Five of the World Series against the Dodgers. The Yankees had a 3 – 2 Series lead entering that night of Tuesday, October 18. Reggie was coming out of his slump with home runs in each of the previous two games. After walking in the first inning, he homered on the first pitch he saw from starter Burt Hooton in the fourth inning, chasing Hooton. With two out in the fifth and Willie Randolph on first base, Jackson hit a laser over the right field fence on the first pitch he saw from Elias Sosa, chasing Sosa. Then in the eighth, Jackson led off with a towering drive beyond the right-center wall off Charlie Hough, making it three homers on three pitches from three different hurlers.

"*Reg-gie! Reg-gie! Reg-gie!*" the crowd chanted. Babe Ruth had been the only player to homer three times in a World Series game, doing so twice. Albert Pujols subsequently did it. But three homers on three pitches in a game, and four homers on four pitches if you include the previous game . . . nothing could compare or probably ever will.

"It was probably the greatest [single-game] performance by a player I've ever seen," said third baseman Graig Nettles, one of those who had bridled upon Jackson's arrival. "It gave me chills when he hit that third one . . . And it didn't matter in the slightest whether you liked him or detested him. You put away whatever you felt for the guy and just bathed in the magnitude of the achievement. He was my teammate and I was pulling for him and so was each and every guy in the Yankee dugout."

Nettles and Jackson led the Yankees to a repeat title in 1978, so Reggie was in pinstripes for club championships number 21 and 22. Jackson finally tasted World Series defeat when the Dodgers beat the Yankees in 1981, and he was a collective 10-for-32 with three homers that postseason. He spent the next five years with the California Angels, leading them to 1982 and '86 ALCS appearances but never making it back to his personal showcase event.

Steinbrenner always said that his biggest mistake was not re-signing Jackson after the 1981 World Series, even though Jackson had emphasized that was not going to happen. There had been enough drama, and Jackson had nothing left to prove on that scene. He had become an expert on the matter, about how to thrive in New York, and he has helped shape the perspective of bright Yankee prospects for all these years now.

ONE OF THE MOST COLORFUL AND EXCITING PLAYERS OF HIS ERA
A PROLIFIC POWER HITTER WHO THRIVED IN PRESSURE SITUATIONS

So begins the description on his plaque in Monument Park, unveiled on July 6, 2002. He did it his way and was a major reason that winning ways returned to the Bronx. The 1977 title ended a 15-year drought that had been the club's longest since before Ruth's arrival.

"It's part of the deal, part of New York and part of the Yankees," Jackson said of playing amid pressure. "It's what makes the Yankees the Yankees, the demand for excellence after all the Hall of Famers and twenty-seven world championships. You have to have it inside like Jeter, Pettitte, Whitey, Mickey and the Babe."

Reggie Jackson: Superstar. It was a chapter no one will ever forget.

Tino Martinez

There have been plenty of pivotal moments at first base in Yankees history, none more important than the day Miller Huggins wrote Lou Gehrig's name onto a lineup card instead of Wally Pipp. Another one was Game Five of the classic 1995 American League Division Series in Seattle, where Don Mattingly played the last game of a brilliant career while Tino Martinez was winding down his Mariners days before taking over for Mattingly the following spring.

"That was not an easy set of footsteps to try to fill," Yankees manager Joe Torre said of the transition to Martinez, while speaking at Cipriani across from the Wall Street bull about his guest of honor at a 2017 Safe at Home Gala fundraiser in Manhattan. "Tino Martinez never wanted any notoriety, which I think really set our ballclubs apart. The guys never stopped to admire what they did. They never said, 'Look what I just did.' It was always 'we.'"

Constantino Martinez began his Major League career with Seattle in 1990. He emerged as the team's regular first baseman in 1992 and by 1994 looked as though he were primed for stardom, blasting 20 home runs in only 329 at bats before the labor stoppage ended the season. The raw power Martinez showed in '94 was on display again when play resumed the following year, as he made his first All-Star team and hit 31 homers with 111 RBIs on the abbreviated 144-game schedule. He and the Mariners finished in a tie for the AL West title with the Angels and advanced in the one-game playoff. Then Martinez batted .409 with five RBIs in those five games that eliminated the Yankees and ended Donnie Baseball's career.

New York acquired Martinez that December, and he proceeded to help the Yankees to four World Series championships, in 1996 and 1998 – 2000.

"Tino obviously is a perfect guy for the Yankees, I thought coming in," Mattingly recalled. "He was a guy who loved to play, not afraid to fail at all. A lot of people probably didn't know him when he got here, but [he was] a guy that I think a lot of people knew was going to be a really, really good player."

Martinez filled those shoes immediately, hitting 175 homers and driving in 690 runs over his first six years in pinstripes. He would return for a final stint in 2005. His best season was actually the only one that did *not* result in the title in those first five seasons. In 1997, Martinez slashed .296/.371/.571, produced 44 homers and 141 RBIs, topped out with a 143 OPS+ and 5.1 WAR, earned his second All-Star selection, and was runner-up to Ken Griffey Jr. in AL MVP voting.

"Tino gets such a lot of credit on the teams that we were able to build and win championships with, because of his leadership, his toughness . . . He played every day," teammate Jorge Posada said. "He played great baseball at both ends of the game, a great defender and a clutch hitter. At times you needed that big home run, and he was the one who provided that for us."

As a member of the Yankees, Martinez had the opportunity to play in 77 postseason games in his first six years with the club between 1996 – 2001. His numbers were ordinary at best in the postseason with the Yankees, but there was one moment in the 2001 World Series that rose above all others in his career.

A month and a half earlier, the Twin Towers had fallen in the 9/11 terrorist attacks. A grieving city—and nation—came together with a World Series played just a borough away. The Yankees had rallied from a 2 – 0 series deficit to win Game Three on Scott Brosius's RBI single, and now it was Martinez's turn for heroics as a tense crowd watched in Game Four at Yankee Stadium.

With Arizona up by two and Paul O'Neill on first, the Yankees were down to their final out. Martinez launched the first pitch from Arizona's submarine closer, Byung-Hyun Kim, into the right-center field seats to send the game to extra innings. *"Oh, the Bamtino delivers big-time!"* John Sterling exalted on the radio. Derek Jeter said it was "as loud as I've ever heard Yankee Stadium," and he would personally take over from there the next inning with a walk-off homer to even the series at 2 – 2.

"It gave the fans a brief break from thinking about the tragedy," Martinez said of his own homer. "To tie the game with two outs in the bottom of the ninth was another big hit I'll never forget.

"I was looking first pitch fastball. My goal was to get a good pitch, hit it hard somewhere, and keep the rally going. Fortunately, I hit it perfect, and it went out of the park."

On June 21, 2014, the Yankees unveiled a plaque for Martinez in Monument Park. He said he was "speechless" to receive the honor, and humbly attributed it to being part of dominant teams.

"Tino was a perfect addition to our team," Torre added. "He felt he was letting you down if he didn't get hits, but he helped you in so many different ways—not the least of which was his passion for the game."

Thurman Munson

The annual Thurman Munson Awards Dinner in Manhattan is nearly four decades old, and Diane Munson has been there for each one of them to carry on the legacy of her late husband. It has been my honor to cover them on multiple occasions for MLB.com and Yankees.com, not only to interview and write about the award recipients, but also to see the joy on the faces of fundraising beneficiaries: jubilant attendees with intellectual and developmental disabilities who are recognized at their designated table in a packed ballroom each offseason.

There is another reason, and that is simply to see the virtues of Thurman extolled by Diana.

"I know I say this every year, but I'm still blown away that Thurman is still so loved and well-thought-of by everyone, and New York in particular," Diana said at the 2017 event. "They took him to heart and they have honored him and have been loyal to his memory and legacy. . . . He didn't realize how loved he was."

It is always as if it happened just yesterday, when in fact it was on August 2, 1979. The Yankees had just left Chicago after a six-game road trip that ended at Comiskey Park. They were 58 – 48, and 14 games behind Baltimore and in fourth place. Any hopes of a possible threepeat were gone as they settled in for a long summer. There was an off-day that Thursday, and Munson had gone home to Canton, Ohio, before returning to Yankee Stadium that next night. He had just received his pilot's license, and the small plane he was flying crashed nearby in Summit County.

Munson died on his way to a Hall of Fame induction. He was taken at the age of 32, already a seven-time All-Star, a two-time world champion, a Rookie of the Year and an MVP.

"He was a tremendous teammate, a tremendous leader," said Bucky Dent, the shortstop on those Yankee teams. "He was tough as nails, kind of a crusty old guy who would sometimes say things to you, to get you motivated. Like if you weren't playing very well, he'd walk up to you by the batting cage and say, 'Hey, you ever thought about retiring?' It was something to kind of get your attention. That's the kind of guy he was. He was a fun guy. Even playing against him, when I was with the White Sox, you would walk up to the plate and he was always chirpin', throwing dirt on your shoes, trying to distract you. I just loved him to death."

"There is very little that I can say to adequately express my feeling at this moment'" Yankees owner George Steinbrenner said in those dark days. "I've lost a dear friend, a pal and one of the greatest competitors ever known. We spent many hours together talking baseball and business. He loved his family. He was our leader."

Steinbrenner made sure that Munson's empty locker would remain a fact of life in the Yankees' clubhouse, even through the opening of a new Yankee Stadium. That has helped keep Munson's memory alive, and a reminder of a proud Yankee tradition at catcher that has gone from Bill Dickey to Yogi Berra to Elston Howard to Munson to Jorge Posada and Gary Sanchez. Steinbrenner also was responsible for what may have been the most pivotal aspect of Munson's Yankee heritage, and that was the naming of him as team captain.

The title had been commonplace in the early days of the franchise, going back to the Highlanders. In January of 1976, after his suspension was lifted, Steinbrenner suggested to Billy Martin that he might want to consider appointing a captain to impose leadership. Marty Appel, who was PR director at the time, tells the story in *Pinstripe Empire* of what happened next. He spoke up and reminded all parties that Joe McCarthy had retired the position after Lou Gehrig played his last game in 1939—never to allow its use again.

"Well," Steinbrenner said, "if Joe McCarthy knew Thurman Munson, he'd know this was the right time, and this is the right guy."

The Captain Hiatus was over. "George likes people to assume leadership roles," Munson said after the title was conferred upon him. "I guess that's what being Captain is all about." Berra had insisted that the Yankees teams in the glory days of the 1940s and '50s did not lack leadership. "We were all captains," he said. But in this case, the designation for Munson did seem to pay off.

He led the Yankees to their first World Series in 12 years and was named 1976 AL MVP after hitting .202/337/.432 with 17 homers, 105 RBIs, 14 steals and a 126 OPS+. That Fall Classic was dominated by Cincinnati, but the Yankees would go on to win it all in 1977 and 1978. Just as importantly, Munson was a rock as the team endured frequent clubhouse turmoil.

Over his 11-year career, Munson hit .292/.346/.410 with 113 homers, 1,558 hits, a 116 OPS+ and three 100-RBI seasons.

Nettles said Munson "was my best friend, he was a great teammate. Everybody thought he was a gruff, mean guy, but I think he was a shy person. I just think he didn't want people to know what was going on in his life. But in the clubhouse, he was the best. I am so happy to have been a teammate of his, and to have been a Yankee for eleven years. I wouldn't have traded it for anything."

Nettles was eventually named Captain after Munson's passing, from 1982 – 84. Then came co-captains Willie Randolph and Ron Guidry from 1986 – 88, followed by Don Mattingly from 1991 – 95 and then Derek Jeter for the longest haul of any Yankee Captain: 2003 – 14.

After Munson, the parade of legendary Yankee catchers subsided for a number of years, as the team cycled through options at the position for roughly the next two decades until Posada became the regular catcher in 1998. The team's eras of greatness have been marked by the presence of an elite backstop. Sanchez emerged as the likely successor to the tradition, and as a rookie he was one of those honored at the Thurman Munson Awards Dinner.

"It means a lot to me to receive an award in Thurman Munson's name," he told the crowd. "Diana, the best way I can show my appreciation for this award is playing hard and trying to be a great man like your husband was, and I promise you that I will do my best."

Joe Torre

Miller Huggins. Joe McCarthy. Casey Stengel. They combined to manage through the first 20 of 27 Yankee world championships. They are almost pharaoh-like now when you look back at their times in history as legendary leaders of men and success.

So I was slightly surprised when Marty Appel, author of so many definitive books about the Yankee franchise and its immortals, told me with utter certainty: "I'd like to tell you the reason why I think Joe Torre is the best manager the Yankees ever had."

"To begin with, you've got to compare him to the big three," Appel said. "Unlike those three, Torre had to win three rounds of the playoffs for a world championship. He had to beat twelve or thirteen league opponents just to get into the postseason."

Marty was just warming up.

"He had to manage a multicultural team of players of all races from all countries. The other three guys had pretty much an all-white team the whole stretch. Torre's players had multiyear multimillion dollar contracts. They didn't really have to put out as much on a daily basis as those other guys. Torre had to deal with sports-talk radio and more second-guessing than those other guys ever did. Torre had to do live interviews questioning his every move with reporters after the game."

All true. Huggins, McCarthy and Stengel all managed at a time when sports was the toy department of life, when sportswriters were buddies, when taboos were honored by media. None of those three was on a hot seat after a few bad losses, at least not in the press.

"Torre had to deal with a boss with a short lease, where they didn't," Appel said.

This might be his best point of all. Torre managed for George Steinbrenner, and somehow, they achieved mostly tranquility—in such stark contrast to the Billy Martin years. Torre was the longest-tenured manager in the Steinbrenner Era and second-most in Yankees history, behind McCarthy. No other skipper in Steninbrenner's tenure (1973 – 2010) lasted more than four full seasons. Either the Boss was mellowed, or Joe was a master employee, or they just made a great match. Probably all of those were true. That is why, after giving his own Hall of Fame induction speech in 2014, Torre sought to immediately apologize to everyone that he had forgotten to thank George and the whole Steinbrenner family.

"You just have to give it to Torre," Appel continued. "Casey gets all the accolades for winning five straight in his first five years, and Torre won four in his first five years with all those things I just mentioned. When you look at all those facts, my god, I don't think people give Torre as much credit as he should have."

It is hard not to be completely convinced after that conversation. Torre managed the Yankees from 1996 – 2007, reaching the postseason *every* year. The Yankees posted a .605 winning percentage and earned six pennants and four world championships.

Previously as a manager with the Mets (1977 – 81), Braves (1982 – 84) and Cardinals (1990 – 95), Torre's teams had combined for just five winning seasons and zero postseason victories. His managerial record was a losing one in those three combined stints, and even though he had been a catcher and infielder for all three clubs back in the day, each of those clubs unceremoniously jettisoned him. Working for Gussie Busch in the first half of the '90s, Torre had the dubious distinction of following a decade of success in which the Cardinals had been to the Fall Classic in 1982, '85 and '87. They fell from grace in the Torre years, as Ozzie Smith and others aged. Torre left St. Louis as a person with a reputation as an outstanding former player—the 1971 NL MVP and a nine-time All-Star—but a very ordinary manager.

After the Yankees were bounced by Seattle in the dramatic first AL Division Series, the Yankees announced one of the most pivotal moves in their modern era. They let Buck Showalter go and replaced him with a Brooklyn native. It was hardly popular at the time, in fact quite similar to the greeting Stengel had received after being hired despite prior futility as a manager. *Oh, and by the way, Joe, you won't have Don Mattingly on your roster, either; he retired.*

The *Daily News* headline on the day of the Torre hiring read: "Clueless Joe." Wow. Did he know what he was getting himself into as manager for Steinbrenner, they wondered? Torre, though, was characteristically calm and composed at his introductory news conference before media who were ready to pounce. He showed candor and humor, and he talked about his lifetime ambition of winning the World Series. The Yankees had gone 17 years without winning it all, their longest drought since their first in 1921, and he knew it.

"When you get married, do you think you're always going to be smiling?" Torre said then. "I try to think of the potential for good things happening. That's the World Series. I know here we'll have the ability to improve the team . . . To have that opportunity is worth all the negative sides."

Torre was undaunted about his rude welcome. "It didn't matter to me," he said in his autobiography *The Yankee Years*, written with Tom Verducci. "I was so tickled to have the opportunity that none of it mattered. I was a little nervous starting out with it. Every time you get fired there is always something you think you can do better. I started thinking, maybe I have to do this different or that different. And then one day before spring training began, I was thumbing through a book by Bill Parcells, the football coach. He said something like, 'If you believe in something, stay with it.' And that was enough for me."

POWER OF THE PINSTRIPES

The Yankees topped Forbes' annual list of most valuable franchises in 2018 for the twenty-first consecutive year, listing the value at $2 billion. That's quite a return on the $8.8 million George Steinbrenner spent to purchase the club from CBS in 1973. Tradition means everything and here are some other numbers that help explain such financial dominance:

	YANKEES	NEXT-BEST TEAM
World Series championships	27	11 (Cardinals)
North American titles	27	24 (Montreal/NHL)
World Series appearances	40	20 (Giants)
World Series title streaks	5 (1949-53); 4 (1936-39); 3 (1998-2000)	3 (Athletics, 1972-74)
Postseason appearances	54	32 (Dodgers)
LCS appearances	16	13 (Cardinals)
LCS victories	11	7 (Cardinals)
MVP Award winners	20	AL: 11 (Tigers); NL: 17 (Cardinals)

Like Stengel nearly a half-century before him, Torre removed any doubters with wins. The Yankees won and they won often. The 1996 Yankees racked up 92 wins and rallied from an 0 – 2 start to beat Atlanta in the World Series. That long stretch of white space in the "Playoffs" column on the Yankees' Baseball Reference page was enough. Torre earned AL Manager of the Year honors in his first season at the helm, and followed with titles in 1998 – 2000. Entering 2019, that was the last time any Major League team ever repeated, and they came one pitch from a possible four-peat in 2001, the year Torre managed a club in a city coping with 9/11.

"The 1996 team brought back that atmosphere of 'these are the Yankees—this is the team that's supposed to be on top,'" Bernie Williams said. "It set the precedence for the rest of the teams that came after that."

Torre was blessed with talent: Derek Jeter, Mariano Rivera, Andy Pettitte, Jorge Posada and Williams among others. Their nucleus grew up within the Torre years, and they won together. Back to Appel's argument, one might note that Huggins and McCarthy had to manage an outsized personality like Babe Ruth, whereas Torre had utter princes. The fact is, future Hall of Famers like Rivera and Jeter thrived and defined themselves in a workplace where Torre's cool demeanor fostered consistent work habits and professionalism.

That tremendous character was the hallmark of the Torre years, and in many ways he led by example off the field. Most notable was his work to help kids who grew up amongst domestic violence. Torre and wife Ali started his "Safe at Home" foundation in 2002 and then grew it into a formidable institution that has reached more than 25,000 children. More than a dozen Margaret's Place sites—named for Joe's mother—have been opened in the New York, Los Angeles and Cincinnati areas.

Through all that time as a writer for MLB.com, I typically would cover Torre's summertime Safe at Home golf event and then the annual gala dinner each November. While we were always there to talk to the many Yankee legends who would walk his red carpet, unfailingly Joe would go before every camera and tape recorder at all of these and share the same story about how domestic violence had been a constant presence in his boyhood home.

"It's a subject that's uncomfortable for people," Torre said. "I can just speak from what my feelings were as a kid growing up in a house where my dad abused my mom. As the youngest of five, my older siblings were trying to protect me from it, and they were doing a lot of whispering. When you hear whispering, you say, 'Oh, I must have done something wrong.' You were embarrassed by what was going on in the house. Even though I never saw my dad hit my mom, you did hear him throw dishes against the wall if he didn't like what she put on the table for lunch or dinner.

"He was a New York City policeman and I did witness when he went for his revolver in the drawer to threaten my mom and my older sister. He created a lot of fear in the house, and I never really connected the dots until later in my life that it is what was causing these feelings of nervousness and low self-esteem, which I thought I was born with. I realized through the counseling that we went through that the fear he created was what was causing that. I wanted to shout it from the rooftops, I wanted to share it, because there are so many other kids out there who feel they are doing something wrong and that they are why their parents aren't getting along."

This commitment from Torre always rubbed off on those who played for him. That included Jeter, who said Torre has been "like a father to me."

"There are so many athletes and managers who do great things in the community and give back," Jeter said. "He and his wife deserve a lot of credit for what they have done. People always want to talk about legacy, and I think a lot of times your legacy off the field, or away from the field, is much more important than what you were able to accomplish while you were in uniform. This is a legacy with him having an impact on so many kids in the community."

Torre finished out his managerial career with the Dodgers, and then went on to work for the Commissioner as MLB's Chief Baseball Officer to keep a steady hand in the game. His legacy is a profound one, both on and off the field, and going back to Appel's case, it is easy to argue that he was even the best manager in Yankee history. It was Huggins who managed the 1927 team that most people generally regard as the best in baseball history, but experts also have made a strong case for Torre's 1998 squad that breezed to a 114 – 98 record and a World Series sweep of San Diego. It was yet another reason to induct him in 2014 into a place where he already had been a borderline candidate as an 18-year player.

"You play the game, and then you manage the teams you played for—and now they all fired you," Torre said. "And you wonder what's next and wonder, 'Where can I go because I have no connections?' And then I get a Yankee opportunity and the best part of my life starts after I'm fifty-five years old."

Dave Winfield

On December 15, 1980, the Yankees gave Dave Winfield the richest contract in sports history at the time. He could attack the ball like no other and, at six feet, six inches, was the biggest five-tool star ever. It was a 10-year deal worth $23 million, although owner George Steinbrenner reportedly had understood that it would be worth $16 million, a confusion over cost-of-living increases. Either way, the new outfielder would be the Player of the Eighties in New York.

Indeed, Winfield was an All-Star in every full season he gave the team. But that did not quite capture the reality of how that decade turned out. So far, it has been the only decade since Babe Ruth was signed that the Yankees failed to win at least one World Series. It was even more frustrating when considering that the Yankees' combined record of 854 – 708 (.547) was *easily* the best of any Major League team over the entire decade.

For the Yankees, titles matter more. New York even became a *Mets* town during the eighties, with Dwight Gooden, Darryl Strawberry, Gary Carter and the rest. Steinbrenner and Winfield dominated the tabloids at times, the finest hour for neither, and the pivotal moment in the whole thing was Game Five of the 1981 World Series against the Dodgers.

It was the turning point in the Winfield-Yankees relationship, looking back. If things had happened differently, maybe Winfield does not go to Toronto and embrace his 1992 World Series clutch double for all of Canada as the most memorable hit in his life. Maybe he does not pick up his 3,000th hit with his hometown

Twins in 1993. When he is inducted in 2001, he likely goes in with a Yankee cap instead of the San Diego franchise that drafted him. And number 31 surely would be in Monument Park. That's baseball. What-ifs don't matter. Winfield is content today, and said in his Hall of Fame speech that he and Steinbrenner had long since cleared the air between them. He said there were no regrets. But go back to that night of October 25, 1981. The labor strife had caused the season to be split into halves, and these two familiar postseason rivals had survived. The Yankees had won the first two games at home, the ultimate recipe for a championship.

After batting .350 in the first-ever Division Series round to help eliminate Milwaukee, Winfield turned cold. He was just 2-for-13 in the ALCS sweep of Oakland, going hitless in his final six at-bats of that series. That meant his slump was now up to 0-for-22 at the worst possible time for the Yankees, when he came up to bat against Jerry Reuss in the fifth inning of Game Five.

Winfield finally got a hit. It was a single to left on an 0-1 pitch, and he jokingly asked for the game ball. Steinbrenner was in no mood for that brand of humor. The Yankees were clinging to a 1 – 0 lead at that point in the game, and everyone knew that Fernandomania's next event was going to be Game Six back at Yankee Stadium. The Yankees needed to win this to avoid losing all three at Dodger Stadium, but Ron Guidry gave up back-to-back homers to Pedro Guerrero and Steve Yeager in the seventh inning, and Los Angeles won. Sure enough, Fernando Valenzuela was too much for the Yankees in Game Six, and the Dodgers were champions.

It would be the Yankees' last trip to the World Series until 1996, a 15-year drought that remains the team's longest since before Babe. Steinbrenner and Winfield went 'round and 'round. In 1982, Steinbrenner said Winfield "isn't a winner, the way Reggie Jackson was. Winfield can't carry a team." In 1984, when Winfield was leading the league in batting average, Steinbrenner told the *New York Times*: "I think it's a great individual accomplishment . . . But more important than Dave Winfield hitting .368 is winning the American League pennant. . . . individual numbers don't mean a thing if the team doesn't win." In 1985, The Boss asked reporters, "Does anyone know where I can find Reggie Jackson? I let Mr. October get away, and I got Mr. May, Dave Winfield. He gets his numbers when it doesn't count." Steinbrenner would go out of his way to run Winfield out of town, and he would pay the price for it. After paying gambler Howard Spira $40,000 to try and dig up dirt on Winfield in an attempt to get his large contract voided, Steinbrenner was banned for life by the Commissioner's Office. That banishment would be lifted, but the long suspension still happened. In May of 1990, the last year of the 10-year contract, Winfield was traded to the Angels for pitcher Mike Witt, and a turbulent decade without a ring was over.

"Dave's a great human being who hasn't been treated in his career as well as he should have been," Hall of Fame executive Pat Gillick said after the 1992 World Series, following Winfield's heroics. "It was probably a little bit of redemption that his hit won this championship for us."

During his time in New York, Winfield hit .290/.356/.495 (134 OPS+) with 205 home runs, 818 RBIs, a 26.9 WAR, five Gold Gloves and five Silver Sluggers. He did that despite missing the entire 1989 season with a back injury. In his eight full seasons, Winfield was either first or second on the Yankees in RBIs every year and only once did he finish out of the team's top three in homers. He had four seasons where he was top 10 in the American League in OPS+ and received MVP votes six different times as a Yankee. But he once said: "Only I know how much better I could have been without the distractions."

For the record, Winfield said in 2008 that he believes Steinbrenner to be worthy of the Hall of Fame "for what he's done to resurrect the Yankees and their image, that team and that Stadium as a baseball institution."

OTHER HALL OF FAMERS WHO PLAYED FOR YANKEES

PLAYER	POSITION	INDUCTION YEAR	YEARS WITH NYY	PRIMARY INDUCTION TEAM
Willie Keeler	RF	1939	1903-09	Brooklyn Suberbas
Frank Chance	1B	1946	1913-14	Chicago Cubs
Paul Waner	RF	1952	1944-45	Pittsburgh Pirates
Frank "Home Run" Baker	3B	1955	1916-19; 1921-22	Philadelphia Athletics
Dazzy Vance	SP	1955	1915-18	Brooklyn Dodgers
Burleigh Grimes	SP	1964	1934	Brooklyn Robins
Stan Coveleski	SP	1969	1928	Cleveland Indians
Joe Sewell	SS	1977	1931-33	Cleveland Indians
Johnny Mize	1B	1981	1949-53	St. Louis Cardinals
Enos Slaughter	RF	1985	1954-55; 1956-59	St. Louis Cardinals
Gaylord Perry	SP	1991	1980	San Francisco Giants
Phil Niekro	SP	1997	1984-85	Atlanta Braves
Dave Winfield	RF	2001	1981-90	San Diego Padres
Wade Boggs	3B	2005	1993-97	Boston Red Sox
Rickey Henderson	LF	2009	1985-89	Oakland Athletics
Randy Johnson	SP	2015	2005-06	Arizona Diamondbacks
Tim Raines	LF	2017	1996-98	Montreal Expos
Ivan Rodriguez	C	2017	2008	Texas Rangers

Joe McCarthy

One afternoon while pondering all the Yankee plaques in the Hall
of Fame, I noticed some interesting juxtapositions of the bronze
faces. My favorite example features Lou Gehrig and Commissioner Kenesaw Mountain Landis. Each looks off to one side,
and because they are on perpendicular walls of their alcove, it
means they stare for eternity exactly at each other, as if to say,
"We did the right thing for Baseball, and we did all we could."
(See for yourself next time!) In another alcove is a symbol of
the Yankees' winning tradition. Miller Huggins, the team's first
championship manager, looks off to his right, or to the center of
the Gallery. Directly across from him on the opposite wall of the
same alcove, Joe McCarthy looks admiringly right at him, as if
to say he carried on what Hug had started . . . *and how about
that Babe Ruth!*

Huggins's plaque was mounted in that very spot in the
summer of 1964, while the Yankees were making another
World Series run. On that day that Huggins was posthumously
inducted—after eight previous appearances on the ballot—
McCarthy paid tribute to him.

"This is the man who cut the Yankees' pennant pattern,"
McCarthy said.

McCarthy followed the pattern and added his own imprint.
He won nine pennants (including one with the Cubs) and seven
world championships with the Yankees. He managed 24 years
in the Majors (1926 – 50) and *not once* did his team finish with

a losing record or out of the first division. Eight of his clubs finished second, three third and four were fourth.

His .615 winning percentage (2,125 – 1,333) is still the best in MLB history, and it is worth noting that no one else has even topped .600; Huggins ranks 14th and Billy Martin 15th. With the Yankees only, McCarthy's percentage rises to .627 (1,460 – 867). That is nearly two wins out of every three games of a regular season—over an era.

Joseph V. McCarthy. As one reporter put it during the 1941 season, "The middle initial stands for victory, fifth pennant and Vincent."

Joe McCarthy and Bill Terry shake hands before taking the field for the 1937 All-Star Game.

By various measures, and with an obvious nod to Connie Mack and John McGraw, one could argue that the long-sleeved McCarthy was the greatest manager in baseball history. The late Hall of Fame scribe Bob Broeg made a case for that claim in *The Sporting News*, and that was on February 25, 1978. If he was in correct in that assessment, then certainly no one in 40 years hence has superseded that case—not Sparky Anderson, not Tony La Russa, not Joe Torre or Bobby Cox. Broeg noted that even with the empirical evidence for such lofty status, what set McCarthy apart was his leadership ability, how he handled his roster and commanded their respect.

"Joe McCarthy made and developed the Yankee players to his own pattern, and they made him as a pennant-winner," said Tommy Henrich, who played for him from 1937 – 46. "Those who didn't fit into his ball club didn't stay around."

"A ball game lasts approximately two hours," McCarthy said. "All I ask is that my men go out there and hustle every minute for two hours every day. If I have any one on the team who does not want to do that I get rid of him."

McCarthy demonstrated that in his first year as a Cubs manager by asking for waivers on veteran Grover Cleveland Alexander. As sportswriter Joseph Durso tells the story in a McCarthy obituary, Old Pete undermined the manager during a clubhouse strategy discussion, and a month later found himself pitching for the Cardinals. Cubs owner William Wrigley told McCarthy after that: "Congratulations. I've been looking for a manager who had the nerve to do that."

Wrigley had the nerve to let McCarthy go later, and he would have to regret losing someone whose arrival proved so pivotal to the succession of Yankee glory.

After managing the Cubs to 98 wins and the NL pennant in 1929, McCarthy seemed plenty stable. His teams had improved their victory totals in each one of his first four seasons with Chicago. But the wheels came off in the World Series against the Philadelphia A's. Connie Mack surprised most people by starting 36-year-old righty Howard Ehmke, who would have only a few more appearances left in a 15-year career. Ehmke responded in the opener by mowing down the Cubs, with a then-record 13 strikeouts. Worse yet, the Cubs blew an eight-run lead, and people second-guessed McCarthy's decision to bring Art Nehf out of the bullpen. The percentages were in McCarthy's favor, because two left-handed batters were coming up and Nehf was a southpaw. Mule Haas promptly ripped a fly to left and Hack Wilson lost it in the sun—a key blow in Philly's 10-run seventh inning. The A's won that game, 10 – 8, and then clinched the series in five. Blame was widespread in Chicago, and McCarthy got much of it.

The Cubs were still competitive as a second-place team the following season, but the sting of that World Series loss never went away. Wrigley said he was not sure that McCarthy was the person to give him his first world championship. During the 1930 season, McCarthy was interviewed by Warren Brown, then sports editor of the Chicago *Herald-Examiner*. Brown asked him: "Would you like to manage the Yankees?" McCarthy replied, "Who wouldn't?"

Done.

Colonel Ruppert and Ed Barrow were on the case, and that same season, Ruppert received Wrigley's blessing to work out the change. Barrow and Ruppert discussed terms with McCarthy, and the Cubs announced that September that McCarthy had resigned and was being replaced by second baseman Rogers Hornsby. The Red Sox were in the hunt, but they were no match for the Bronx Bombers in this fight. The news for Yankee fans came a bit later, in a Philadelphia hotel room during Game Three of the World Series between the A's and Cards.

McCarthy called Landis during that Series to discuss the opening, noting that he had two of three other clubs interested in him. "I want you to get the best job in baseball," Landis told him. McCarthy replied that Landis already had that title, and Landis laughed. "Then get the next best," he told the manager, and by that he meant managing the Yankees.

Sailor Bob Shawkey had managed them in 1930, the season after Huggins passed away, his Yankees finishing with a respectable 86 – 68. Of course, "respectable" was not in the Colonel's lexicon. He demanded only the best, whether it involved his racehorses or St. Bernard show dogs or real estate or his baseball team. Ruppert and Barrow wanted someone they could give talent to and know it would result in titles, the way they had been comfortable with Huggins. Shawkey was out, and probably was right in later saying that he felt he had not been given enough time. McCarthy was introduced to the New York press as the new manager.

After managing Louisville to a minor league championship in 1921, Joe McCarthy wrote a top-10 list that goes on today as a metaphor for life. Right-hander Bill Zuber pitched on Marse Joe's Yankee staff during the World War II years and later printed the list on the back of a black-and-white baseball card given to customers at Zuber's restaurant in Homestead, Iowa. A copy of this list, with the restaurant's stamp, is on file at the Hall of Fame.

The Ten Commandments

By Joe McCarthy

- Nobody ever became a ballplayer by walking after a ball.
- You will never become a .300 hitter unless you take the bat off your shoulder.
- An outfielder who throws back of a runner is locking the barn after the horse is stolen.
- Keep your head up and you may not have to keep it down.
- When you start to slide, S-L-I-D-E. He who changes his mind may have to change a good leg for a bad one.
- Do not alibi on bad hops. Anybody can field the good ones.
- Always run them out. You can never tell.
- Do not quit.
- Do not find too much fault with the umpires. You cannot expect them to be as perfect as you are.
- A pitcher who hasn't control hasn't anything.

Printed in the interest of Baseball by
BILL ZUBER'S DUGOUT RESTAURANT
Homestead, Iowa

"I think we need a man of more experience," Ruppert said at the presser. "Someday I may regret this move. For [Shawkey's] sake I hope so. But at the moment I think I am right in replacing him with a man of McCarthy's proven managerial ability."

The contract-signing event for media, including "talking-picture" press, did not go without a hitch, though.

"McCarthy," Ruppert said, "if you will sign this contract it will make you manager of the Yankees for two years."

The Colonel handed Joe a pen and McCarthy said:

"Colonel Huston" –

"Ruppert, Ruppert," his new boss interrupted. The degree of gaffe was obvious to media who had covered the drama about eight years earlier with the departure of Ruppert's partner, Colonel Huston. The cameras were re-started, and McCarthy re-did his part of the show.

Ruppert laughed with others and said, "Maybe McCarthy will be around here long enough so he will get to know me better."

More importantly, Ruppert left McCarthy with this message: "McCarthy, I finished third last year. I realize that you are confronted with problems that it will take you a little while to solve, so I'll be satisfied if you finish second this year. But I warn you, McCarthy, I don't like to finish second!"

"Neither do I, Colonel," McCarthy countered.

Then McCarthy assumed management of about $8 million worth of baseball property. It was a two-year contract, and he told Ruppert he hoped the next one would be for five. Along the way, McCarthy would ride in parades up Broadway, sadly fill out a lineup card that did not include the name of his favorite player (Lou Gehrig), watch from the bench as Joe DiMaggio hit safely in 56 consecutive games, and manage an iconic club that provided relief as life went on during a war.

McCarthy's Hall plaque blurb actually begins with the sentence:

**OUTSTANDING MANAGER WHO NEVER
PLAYED IN MAJOR LEAGUES.**

That dated disclaimer not only reflects how rare it was for a Major League manager back then to be devoid of such big-league experience, but also what external forces he would have been up against. Ruth was just one of many players who scoffed at McCarthy's qualifications to manage the Yankees, feeling McCarthy could not possibly know more than them about the game's intricacies.

McCarthy brought discipline and new rules to the Yankees, including the end of card games on trains, but he generally let Ruth be Ruth, citing the numbers he produced. He knew how to manage stars—hardly a "push-button manager," in the words of Jimmy Dykes, who conversely posted the second-worst all-time winning percentage among longtime managers.

DiMaggio remembered him as a "taskmaster" who "made every game an important one and demanded a serious, businesslike attitude." He refused to allow "horseplay" and made them wear suits off the field and "wear the uniform with dignity." But DiMaggio also remembered him for "a gentleness and understanding that brought about mutual appreciation. McCarthy always wanted his men to be successful as humans and not merely as athletes.

"McCarthy would let a guy ride out a slump" DiMaggio said during his retirement. "He'd come around and cheer you up, saying, 'Hang in there, fellow, things are going to get better. We all have slumps.' Believe me, it always helped. A guy feels low enough when he has the hitting miseries. Other managers, however, will bench a player as soon as his average tails off a little. This only makes it tougher for the guy to get going again. I know, I've heard them cry."

There was another cry that became an inevitable issue in the McCarthy years. The 1934 season was Ruth's last with the Yankees and his interest in managing the club was well-known by then. He had told Joe Williams of the *World-Telegram* that he would not return to the club the next year "unless I'm manager. Don't you think I'm entitled to the chance?" McCarthy reportedly offered to resign, but the Yankees were not about to let that happen.

Barrow said Ruth's condition "made things easier for the

Colonel and myself . . . I don't know what we would have done if the Babe hadn't solved the situation himself." Ruppert and Boston Braves owner Emil Fuchs agreed that Ruth could sign with Boston, and on February 26, 1935, all parties gathered at Ruppert's brewery office to announce that The Bambino was released and was joining the Braves. McCarthy was staying put. They had it good.

"I never saw him miss a trick," Barrow said. "And you wouldn't think it, but he handles men better than anybody I ever knew."

McCarthy had free rein of his club while Ruppert and Barrow were heading the front office, as Huggins had enjoyed. But Larry MacPhail arrived in 1945 as Yankee president and the two personalities clashed. McCarthy resigned on May 24, 1946, and was replaced by his catcher, Bill Dickey. McCarthy managed the rival Red Sox from 1948 – 50, winning 96 games in each of those first two seasons, and then resigned because of poor health and physical exhaustion on June 23 of that final year. He died in 1978 at the age of 90 at home in Buffalo, N.Y.

The year before his passing, McCarthy told the story about taking a taxi over to the Colonel's Fifth Avenue apartment right after the 1937 World Series clincher. Ruppert was sick in bed and had not been able to attend. Ruppert was smiling because he had heard it on the radio.

"Colonel, you're the champion again," McCarthy told him.

"Fine, fine, 'McCarddy.' Do it again next year."

Phil Rizzuto

About nine minutes into his rambling, fly-swatting, half-hour Hall of Fame speech in 1994, Phil Rizzuto told the crowd: "Anytime you want to leave, just leave. This is going to nowhere." The crowd and his fellow Hall of Famers were in stitches. It was maybe the best speech in Cooperstown history.

Then Rizzuto touched on one of his many pivotal moments in a great baseball life, and probably the most pivotal to his enduring success as a Yankee shortstop.

"I was happy to just be at the right spot at the right time," he said. "Frank Crosetti was just about ready to hang up his spikes, and I got in there, and all I had to do was make a few double plays, beat out a bunt. Crosetti taught me how to get hit with a pitch so I wouldn't get hurt. All these things. And I'd just collect that World Series check and it was so great."

Crosetti had been the Yankees' shortstop since 1932, and a catalyst during the 1936 – 39 dynasty run. However, he had averaged just .194 in 1940, and that one-year hiatus was something the club took seriously. They would have to fix something, and the main addition was a five-foot, six-inch "Scooter" from Brooklyn, signed by superscout Paul Krichell after the Giants and Dodgers passed on a tryout. Crosetti was still kept around, and Dan Daniel speculated in the November 27, 1940, issue of the *New York World-Telegram* that it might be an insurance move just in case Uncle Sam entered the war and called upon any young, unmarried talents like Rizzuto.

HOF ARTIFACT INVENTORY

Game-used equipment in the Baseball Hall of Fame:

PHIL RIZZUTO

B-2856.63	Baseball shoes from 1956, Phil Rizzuto's final season.
B-130.93	Batting helmet, 1955. Among first players to wear helmets.
B-75.94	Glove from 1946-56.
B-2721.63	Signed glove from 1953.
B-293.76	1950 Hickok Professional Athlete of the Year award, mounted.
B-202.2004	1950 Hickok Professional Athlete of the Year belt.

Rizzuto started Opening Day in 1941 and then every game after that for a solid month, from April 14 to May 15 (team game Number 29). He had nine multi-hit games in April; so far, so good.

During that impressive early stretch, Rizzuto made his first visit to St. Louis as a Yankee for a series against the Browns, and he was invited to the old offices of The Sporting News downtown. When I got there a half-century later to work for the publication over most of the 1990s, its office was moved several miles west on Lindbergh Boulevard. J.G. Taylor Spink, the legendary editor of the old Bible of Baseball, did an exhaustive Q&A in the office to introduce Rizzuto to national readers. Spink asked him: "Did you have a model whom you imitated?" The rookie lit up.

"Now you have something, Mr. Spink," came the reply. "I think this is one of the most interesting stories I ever ran into. Before I signed with the Yankee chain, I used to come to the Stadium whenever I could lay my hands on half a buck. I was interested in Gehrig. I liked Dickey. I was a DiMaggio rooter in 1936—still am, for that matter. But my idol was Frankie Crosetti. I watched him closely, tried to imitate every mannerism and movement. Even to hitching the belt. I said, 'Here is the champ.

Poise, class, big league all over.' Imagine me playing short for the Yankees and Crosetti on the bench. Why, that's incredible. I think he is the greatest shortstop that ever played ball." That was insightful for the lesson that was about to come. Rizzuto soon began to struggle against big-league pitching and was in a 3-for-25 slump. After May 15 games, Cleveland was 21 – 9 and threatening to run away with the AL, the Yanks were 14 – 15 and 6 ½ games out in fourth place, and manager Joe McCarthy returned Crosetti to shortstop.

For the next month, McCarthy platooned the pair at the position, making sure Rizzuto's head was in the game for every pitch while on the bench. It was a lesson that would stick with the young shortstop, and Crosetti mentored Rizzuto. Then on June 16, Crosetti was spiked in the throwing hand by Hal Trosky in the second inning, and Rizzuto ran out to shortstop to replace him. Rizzuto went 2-for-3 that game and sparked a three-run rally in the eighth for a come-from-behind victory that put the Yankees just a game behind Cleveland.

Fiero Francis Rizzuto was Yankee shortstop for good. He went on to play in 10 World Series, winning eight rings, including one in that 1941 campaign. He was named 1950 AL MVP, the only year he reached a WAR of 4.0 or better.

"Players have come and gone, but the Yankees have kept right on winning world's championships," Rizzuto said in a first-person article for *The Saturday Evening Post* in 1953. "A lot of the credit has to go to the Yankee organization, under Ed Barrow at first, and now under George Weiss. They've kept the good replacements coming along. . . . They get the kids with the right temperament, and they know how to develop them."

Rizzuto missed the 1943 – 45 seasons while serving in the Navy, and he was released in 1956 after the long run. Then came the second part of his Yankee career, and even he concedes that all those years broadcasting Yankee games kept him part of the conversation and enhanced his Hall outlook. With Rizzuto, you can't separate the ballplayer and the broadcaster. They were like two buns on a great burger. And in his classic Hall of Fame speech, Rizzuto pointed out the most pivotal moment that set him on his way in the booth:

"Howard Cosell told me the first week, he says, 'You'll never last. You look like George Burns and you sound like Groucho Marx.' So thirty-eight years later, I'm doing it my way and still here in broadcasting."

Rizzuto died in 2007 at the age of 89. Hall of Fame president and former Yankee publicist Jeff Idelson said his memories of Rizzuto were as a broadcaster because of their time together.

"You got a sense for how beloved he was by the number of times you had to go to the back of the press box and open the door for someone who had yet another cannoli," Idelson recalled. "Once in a while you'd get cannolis that were like the size of your forearm.

"It was constant the number of times people would bring gifts for Phil. He was a man of the people. The attendance [at Cooperstown] when he was inducted in 1994 was strong, even though it had been years and years since he had played. He certainly was popular. It was like Richie Ashburn; two different careers, one playing and one broadcasting."

Visitors to Cooperstown are greeted immediately upon entrance by the large "Holy Cow" fixture, attired in pinstripes. It was part of the 2000 New York City Cow Parade, and Hall of Fame Chairperson Jane Forbes Clark purchased it at the conclusion. It is on loan to the museum.

"I know she had Phil in mind when she bought it," Idelson said. "It quickly became one of the big photo opps. Here you have the plaques of the all-time greats of the game, and everybody's clustered around a cow. I guess you could say they find the sculpture moo-ving."

Ed Barrow

Discovering Honus Wagner would have been enough for a lifetime of stories, but Ed Barrow was just warming up. The baseball executive had a monumental impact on the national pastime over a half-century, with 14 pennants and one championships under his guidance, and his signature success was as the builder of an unmatched pro sports empire. "Cousin Ed" did most of his work at his desk on 42nd Street, staying away from the clubhouse except for emergency or World Series celebration. Here were 10 of his most pivotal moves:

1. **Created a Home Run King:** While they were together in Boston, Barrow persuaded Babe Ruth to play the outfield and bat on days when he was not pitching. That was in 1918, and two years later the Bambino would be swatting 54 homers for the Yankees.

2. **Signed Lou Gehrig:** The streak of 2,130 consecutive games played does not happen if Barrow and his top scout Paul Krichell don't pay close attention to what the future Iron Horse does on the field for Columbia University. John McGraw of the Giants and Clark Griffith of the Senators had opportunities to snag a legend, but Barrow was the winner.

3. **Bought Joe DiMaggio:** A bum knee scared off every other club, but the Yankees were confident that the San Francisco Seals hitting star had a future. Barrow had

him sent to a specialist down the coast, the knee was deemed playable, and the Yankees beat the Red Sox to the punch. Earle Combs, Tony Lazzeri, Mark Koenig and others were snapped up off minor league rosters as well under Barrow's oversight.

4. **Freed Miller Huggins:** In his early days as Yankee manager, Hug had a thorn in his side in the form of co-owner Col. Tillinghast Huston, who wanted him out. Col. Jacob Ruppert was on Hug's side. Both owners freely stepped into the clubhouse to criticize, and the dissension was getting out of hand. Barrow made peace between the warring owners. Ruppert bought out Huston's interest, and from then on there was no executive interference to undermine Hug's authority. "After that, I let Miller Huggins, a great little manager, run things on the field," Barrow said in 1953. "I just got him players who I thought could win. That's the way baseball should be."

5. **Made the Red Sox miserable:** After watching his boss Harry Frazee decimate his own Boston club once too often, Barrow turned it around. The Bombers won their first pennant in his first year with them, and he gave hug what he needed by acquiring Waite Hoyt, Wally Schang, Harry Harper and Mike McNally from Boston. It was a long litany of key moves after that.

6. **Hired Joe McCarthy as manager:** "The greatest manager who ever lived," Barrow called him. Barrow actually forced out Ruth, who had wanted to manage the team. "I knew Babe didn't have the qualities for the job," Barrow explained. "Babe was a great player, but managing is different."

7. **Constructed a farm system:** To do this, Barrow hired George Weiss. Barrow didn't care for the man personally, but he knew Weiss was the right person to grow a far-flung farm system, as Branch Rickey had done for the Cardinals. Barrow's influence was

everywhere. Lefty Gomez, Frankie Crosetti and many others came up and into Yankee fame.

8. **Innovations at the old ball game:** When asked what he recalled most out of that special 1936 – 39 quad title run, Barrow said: "The thing that made me proudest was the manner in which we cleaned the gamblers out of Yankee Stadium. They were becoming a menace. We had to train a special group of private police to get rid of them, but we did the job." Speaking of the crowd, Marty Appel noted in *Pinstripe Empire* that everyone began hearing "The Star-Spangled Banner" played on a daily basis instead of just on holidays, thanks to Barrow's new PA system that allowed recordings. He also put numbers on players' backs (the first team to do so regularly), and marked the distance from home to the outfield fence.

9. **Bill Dickey and the catching tradition:** Barrow's Yankees developed Dickey behind the plate, and that led to Yogi Berra to Elston Howard to Thurman Munson to Jorge Posada to Gary Sanchez.

10. **Wilcy Moore:** Who? He wasn't around long and few fans today will recognize his name, but Barrow was especially proud of this acquisition. Barrow regularly pored over the minor league data in *The Sporting News*, looking for a knockabout who might be a diamond in the rough. He plucked this Texas righty out of the Class B Sally League, where he had 30 wins, ignoring advice that Moore was not big-league material and could not even throw a curve. Moore went 19 – 7 for the 1927 Yankees and went the distance in the World Series Game Four clincher. "We paid four thousand dollars . . . sight unseen," Barrow said. "Only Ruth's record of sixty home runs rivaled Moore's pitching as a baseball performance in 1927."

Yogi Berra

Recently I went through boxes and boxes in my New York basement to prepare for a move, and I came upon a batch of worn-out steno notebooks filled with scribblings from interviews for MLB.com over the years. I had been wishing I could have talked to Yogi Berra for this book and was wishing, as usual, that he were still around. Then, almost like he was granting a bonus interview from above, I stumbled upon a notebook that began on the first page with the scribbled word, "Yogi." Here were the first words I scrawled:

"If you work at it. You can't just go out there and play a new position."

Wait, was I getting a Yogi-ism from an angel? What does this mean?

On the pages were answers but no questions, so I flipped through them to get some context about the subject and setting of this interview. Following Yogi's quotes were fan responses galore, first from Yankee fans and then from Red Sox fans. It gradually hit me that this notebook was from the 2004 Spring Training and specifically the Yankees' first game against the Red Sox in Fort Myers with newly acquired Alex Rodriguez now moved over to third next to shortstop Derek Jeter. And with Nomar Garciaparra starting that day for Boston, you had three superstar shortstops all at once. The Rivalry was on absolute fire and the hype and price of a ticket that day was sky-high. Everyone was talking about A-Rod being part of this rivalry now and that included Yogi, who was there around the field in batting practice as a special instructor.

HOF ARTIFACT INVENTORY

Game-used equipment in the Baseball Hall of Fame:

YOGI BERRA

B-125.68	Glove used by Yogi Berra to catch Don Larsen's perfect game in 1956 World Series.
B-240.70	1951 MVP Award, his first of three.
B-185.82	Windbreaker as 1981 Yankees coach.
B-1163.67	Harmonica and box signed by Berra, from a scuffle between players' band and Berra.
B-517.64	Ball used in first game managed by Berra at Yankee Stadium on April 16, 1964.

You can't just go out there and play a new position.

That's what A-Rod was doing that day, because Joe Torre wrote him into the lineup at third base. But looking back, you know what Yogi meant. This Hall of Famer that Billy Crystal once called "a wonderful piece of American folk art" always had a way of saying things that made sense, even if they didn't make sense.

So to solve the mystery of "The Notebook," it was apparent that I had gone up to Yogi and asked if he thought Rodriguez would make a successful transition from short to third. Here is the rest of what Yogi had to say to me:

"I didn't care, as long as I got to hit. I had fun doing it. I was horseshit, my first two years. [Laughs]."

Now we had turned it on himself, going back in time to the golden age of baseball.

In 1946, Bill Dickey caught his last game for the Yankees and Yogi caught his first. The former was finishing a 17-year Hall of Fame career, and the latter debuted that September and homered in each of his first two starts behind the plate. The Yankees finished third in the AL that fall. At the next Spring

Training, manager Bucky Harris stuck the five-foot, seven-inch kid from St. Louis out in right field. In 1947 – 48, Berra split time between outfield and catcher, and even though he had made his first All-Star Game and batted .305 with 14 homers and 98 RBIs, the Bombers started looking to acquire a catcher with strong defensive skills.

LARRY MACPHAIL ON YOGI BERRA

Larry MacPhail was inducted into the Hall of Fame in 1978 as an executive, with a resume that included pioneering night baseball, the development of broadcaster Red Barber, air travel by teams between cities, and televising regular games. As a Yankees president, two of his most important moves were ones that he did not make. In neither case was he particularly astute, but these were nevertheless change-the-world pivots had either of them gone down.

One was the famous meeting MacPhail had with Red Sox owner Tom Yawkey at Toots Shor's. Well into the bottle at around two a.m., the hard-drinking MacPhail proposed a straight-up swap of Joe DiMaggio and Ted Williams. It was the equivalent of today's radio sports-talk chatter—Vinnie in Queens calling in to propose an outlandish trade. MacPhail reasoned that each player's ballpark dimensions would mean more home runs for the other, and the two magnates verbally agreed. "Helluvan idea," Yawkey told him. But the next morning, a woozy Yawkey backed away, citing the Babe Ruth deal's legacy and what Sox fans would do to him if he dealt the Splendid Splinter.

The other important no-deal made it possible for Yogi Berra to become a Yankee legend. Berra had served in the Navy and saw action on D-Day as a machine gunner on a rocket boat off the Normandy coast. The fact that he came home from the war at all has to be perhaps his most pivotal fact of life here. Berra was shipped to a submarine base at Groton, CT., just before he was discharged. It was there that he played for the base's baseball team and when he went 3-for-4 in a contest between the sailors and the New York Giants. Berra made an impression on Giants manager Mel Ott, who promptly offered the Yankees $50,000 to part with him. MacPhail turned Ott down and Berra went on to the Hall of Fame as a Yankee, and MacPhail would confess years later that he never had even heard of the young player. All MacPhail knew was that $50,000 was big money, and if Ott wanted him that much, then Berra must be of use to the Yankees.

They liked Yogi's bat but longed for the heyday of Dickey. Enter Casey Stengel. Hired to manage in 1949, he saw Berra as "my assistant manager" behind the plate and tasked Dickey with teaching Berra how to catch. Dickey worked for hours with his protégé, focusing on mechanics and teaching him how to think ahead while behind the plate.

"Bill Dickey, he taught me everything," Yogi told me as I kept reading The Notebook. "I owe a lot to Bill Dickey."

Berra caught 108 games in that 1949 season, and won his second of a record 10 World Series rings despite a 1-for-16 performance in that Fall Classic. *Professor Dickey Gives Yogi Berra Gold Star*, read *The Sporting News* headline on May 25, 1949. Here is what Dickey told reporters at that time:

"Berra now is moving ahead on all fronts and will get increasingly tough at the plate, and increasingly effective behind the bat. In two years, Berra will be far and away the greatest catcher in the American League. It all depends on him. And I don't believe there's any danger of his losing interest.

"He has the natural ability, and aptitudes except in one detail. Berra has improved vastly in every feature of receiving except getting the bad pitch that bounces in front of the plate. I have been trying to teach him to fall over on the ball, but he just won't do it. He is at his best getting the ball that is tucked into his glove.

"I have regarded my job with Berra as a challenge to me. You writers told me, when I came back to this club, that you never again wanted to see Berra go behind the bat. I think you have changed your minds."

In 1950, everything clicked. Berra was a true catcher and a force for a generation of Yankee fans. He hit .322 with 28 homers and 124 RBIs and won his third ring. Dickey told Grantland Rice after the 1950 season: "Yogi Berra is the best catcher in baseball. You can also add that he will be the best catcher in baseball for a long time."

In 1951, Berra was given the first of three AL MVP trophies in his career and was now being paid more than Roy Campanella of the Dodgers, thanks to Stengel. Over a seven-year stretch from 1950 – 56, Berra was always in the top four in MVP voting—similar to Mike Trout's extended run in his first decade at this level.

In 1952, Berra caught 15 different pitchers who threw at least 15 innings apiece. He was a good listener and he was sort of a psychologist and wordsmith with his pitchers, which is funny given the way he often manipulated the English language. Sam Walker wrote in a 2017 leadership book called *The Captain Class*: "Truth be told, he was one of the most talented communicators baseball has ever seen."

In Ford's first full season of 1953, Berra already had such a strong reputation for reading hitters, Ford would throw whatever pitches the catcher called for. "I rarely had to shake him off, and usually when I did, it turned out Berra was right, after all," said Whitey Ford, who would partner with him to form one of the greatest batteries in MLB history.

Berra could put the young lefty at ease in any rough patch. One time, the catcher went out to the mound and said a movie was starting at six and he wanted to be at the theater on time.

Berra developed a reputation as a "pitcher whisperer." He talked to them for hours about their approach to hitters and he studied their temperaments and learned to adjust to their moods.

Berra finished his playing career with the Yankees in 1963 after compiling 15 All-Star selections and many Major League records for a catcher. He managed the '64 Yankees to the AL pennant, and appeared in four games in 1965 for the Mets, going on to manage them to a '73 pennant. The retirement of two number eight jerseys, one for teacher and one for student, representing a great transition in Yankees history, is one of the most beautiful things in baseball.

In 1972, Berra was inducted into the Hall of Fame. You can find one of his MVP trophies there today and his boundless presence in many other exhibits.

"Yogi was delightful. He loved Cooperstown," said Jeff Idelson, the Hall of Fame president and former Yankee publicist. "When the Hall of Fame invitations went out in the mail, invariably he was the first guy who would call. He would call me and say, 'I'm comin' in July. Carmen and I are comin' on Thursday.'

"He was a super-early riser, which I am as well. With the Yankees, you never slept. So I'm at The Otesaga, about 2006, and I go out on the back porch. It's about six-thirty in the morning and Yogi's sitting out there. There's nobody anywhere else out there except for Yogi. So I'm sitting next to him on the rocker, we're rocking, and it's misting a little bit. He says, 'How come it always rains Hall of Fame weekend?' I said, 'Look, we're between two mountain ranges, the Catskills and the Adirondacks, we're at the base of a nine-mile-long lake, and at this time of year you invariably get showers that come through. That's why it mists and rains a little bit.'

"We sit there and we rock and he's silent, and then he goes, 'Well, why don't you move it to another weekend when it doesn't rain?' I said, 'How do you do this?' And he says, 'I don't know, you're the smart one.'"

I knew there was a reason I kept those old notebooks.

You can't just go out there and play a new position.

"What is great about Yogi is that everybody loved him," said Idelson. "He was a man of few words. Everybody thought he was this profound sort of a yogi, I guess, a Buddha, someone with great thought process. He basically did have great thought process, but it was always very simple and made sense. He just had a habit of it coming out funny. But beloved. He got huge ovations when he was here. To see the other players crowd around him and want to hear his stories as a three-time MVP. Yogi and Carmen, too—his wife was absolutely part of the package. Seriously, she was really beloved as well. He is beloved, absolutely beloved. He never had a bad word to say about anybody. I think players found it hard to believe that this little guy had three MVPs and ten rings with the New York Yankees. He was very respected by other players."

New Yankee Stadium

After the Yankees lost to the Dodgers in the 1981 World Series, two especially pivotal turns happened in the franchise's history. One of them was bad: the advent of a 15-year drought before the next sighting of a Yankees World Series. The other was good: the dream of a new pantheon that would be as majestic in its time as his predecessors had dreamed before opening the first Yankee Stadium in 1923.

Roughly a quarter-century of vision, proposals, discussions, controversies, emotion, politics and progress went by and George Steinbrenner's dream finally became a reality in 2009. The new ballpark not only was the most expensive baseball stadium ever built, but it also matched the 1923 inauguration by producing a world champion immediately. The 1923 title was the first in team history, and this one would be the 27th and still most recent entering 2019.

Even as his teams were building a dynasty around the turn of the millennium, The Boss had been after a modern venue that would have more luxury boxes and club seating to vastly increase the value of the franchise. He wanted wider concourses and restaurants. The big issue always was the proportion of public vs. private financing, and whether the Bronx could keep their Bombers. At one point, Mayor Rudy Giuliani pushed for a West Side Yard location that would cost $1 billion and be funded primarily by taxpayers. His successor, Michael Bloomberg, reversed that logic, unveiling blueprints for new ballparks for both the Yankees and Mets that eventually would cost a combined $3.1 billion-plus, with taxpayer subsidies of $1.8 billion.

Derek Jeter, who had given the memorable speech after the final game at the old Stadium in 2008, made the symbolic transition by saying right after his first batting practice in the new digs: "It looks like the old Stadium unless you look into the stands—the stands are a lot bigger." He said it probably will be "second to none."

In hindsight, there could not have been a much worse time to open a new Major League stadium—and in New York's case, it was opening two. It was the bottom of a big recession. The average person now had less disposable income and there was worry about spending. Suddenly there were exorbitant costs at a Yankee game, including Legends seats that often remained empty-blue. "I think if anybody in business had known where the economy was going to go, they would have done things differently," Hal Steinbrenner, George's son, told the *New York Times* on the first day of April, 2009. Indeed, few foresaw such a crash while the Yankees' construction and pricing strategies were in their initial stages, and they would require a quick correction.

The Yankees lost that home opener to Cleveland, 10 – 2. Joe Girardi, the team's former catcher who was in his second year as manager, said: "It's not how you want to start out a new Stadium, but one game is not going to make the history of this Yankee Stadium or this year."

The Yankees went on to finish with the best record in baseball at 103 – 59, and then they marched through the postseason with a three-game sweep of the Twins, a pennant clincher in six against the Angels, and finally the Game Six triumph over the Phillies that led to a parade. The last time an AL team had opened a ballpark with a World Series title had been Fenway Park, and the only other time it happened in the meantime had been new Busch Stadium in St. Louis, in 2006.

Jorge Posada became the first player to homer in new Yankee Stadium, and home runs drew plenty of attention in that first campaign. Jim Kaat, the pitching legend and longtime broad-caster, opined at the time: "The playing field is a disaster. It's like making a Little League park out of Yankee Stadium. Balls go over the fence in right-center field so easily it's a joke." When asked about the homer-happy ballpark, Girardi said, "It's fun to watch, that's for sure." It has been a prime launching pad ever since.

New Yankee Stadium was inspired by the grandeur that Col. Jacob Ruppert, Babe Ruth and everyone introduced in 1923. The Great Hall inspires wonderment with immortals on the giant banners overhead. Even the famous frieze was carried over. Menu choices and social access around the concourses gradually have been upgraded. Amenities are so much better for fans, and players now had spacious clubhouses and the best practice capabilities. What I remember most about the new Yankee Stadium clubhouse when it opened was the computer that had been built into each locker for players to take care of digital business.

Ultimately the new ballpark will be measured by the number of Octobers (and Novembers) it hosts. That is a high expectation, considering how many World Series were conducted in the one that once stood across the street.

The former Yankee Stadium in 1923

Sparky Lyle

Among all the pivotal moments of the 1970s for the Yankees, one of the most important was Sparky Lyle vs. George Brett in Game Four of the 1977 AL Championship Series at Kansas City. It paved the way for the first of two straight Yankee titles and still stands today as a symbolic reminder of the most successfully versatile season ever by a Yankee pitcher.

Lyle pitched 16 years in the Majors, all in relief and seven of those seasons with the Yankees. Capping a Cy Young Award season in which he was 13 – 5 with 26 saves, Lyle was called upon in a key situation against the Royals. Yankee starter Ed Figueroa had been staked to an early 4 – 0 lead in Game Four, but Dick Tidrow had to replace him in the fourth and surrendered an RBI double to Frank White that cut New York's lead to 5 – 4 with the top of the order due up.

Tom Poquette grounded out and Hal McRae walked, making it men on first and second with two out. The Yankees were hoping to get over the hump after losing to Cincinnati in the 1976 World Series, and hoping to end a World Series title drought that was now up to 15 years, the longest since before Babe Ruth. Yet here they were, facing elimination, and facing the 1976 AL batting champion who was into his prime as one of the game's top superstars.

Brett had tripled in a run in his previous at-bat, and manager Billy Martin wanted his best weapon in this matchup with the player who would one day become the alpha to his omega in a future Pine Tar episode. Martin brought Lyle out of the bullpen, despite backup catcher Fred Stanley telling pitching coach Art Fowler after bullpen warmups: "Sparky ain't got nothin', Art." Martin was adamant, so it was lefty vs. lefty. On a 2-and-1 pitch, Brett smashed a liner to left that was caught by Lou Piniella. The Yankees were out of the jam, and Lyle would go the distance in relief as Kansas City never threatened. Lyle pitched 5 1/3 innings of scoreless relief, relying on his slider and allowing just two hits, facing 16 batters and inducing 15 outs. He was at his best pitching in a tight situation.

"Sparky saved us all season," Yankees third baseman Graig Nettles said. "He had an amazing year, but to do that in the playoffs and to pitch almost six innings was unbelievable."

After the game, Lyle said he would be available for Game Five. "I get better as I go along. My slider is better when my arm is tired."

It was one of three consecutive postseason wins in relief by Lyle, a rare feat in MLB history.

He came in to pitch the Game Five clincher, against at Kansas City. In the bottom of the eighth, the Royals had a 3 – 2 lead and were threatening to extend it with two out and runners on second and third. Rather than intentionally walk Cookie Rojas, Martin summoned Lyle and Rojas struck out swinging. The Yankees broke through for three runs in the top of the ninth, and then Lyle retired the side in order to secure the pennant.

In the World Series opener against the Dodgers at Yankee Stadium, Don Gullet was outstanding for New York but ran into trouble in the ninth. He left with two on and one out, clinging to a 3 – 2 lead. Lyle came in and blew the save, as Lee Lacy tied the score with a single that scored Dusty Baker. But Lyle proceeded to pitch three straight one-two-three innings, and he recorded his third straight win as Paul Blair gave New York Game One with a walk-off single against Rick Rhoden.

The Yankees were counting World Series championships again, winning the first of two in a row from 1977 – 78. In that stretch, they also became the first American League team to

have two different pitchers win the Cy Young Award consecu-
tively. Sandy Koufax and Don Drysdale had pulled it off for the
Dodgers in 1962 – 63, respectively, when there was just one Cy
across MLB. Lyle and Ron Guidry not only matched that but
also became the first pair to do it within back-to-back world
championship seasons.

For style points, this one was much different as well.

Koufax and Drysdale were traditional dominant starting
pitchers. Guidry was as well, but in Lyle's case, it was from the
other end of the pitching staff. Lyle became the first reliever in the
AL and the only one other than Mike Marshall of the Dodgers
(15 – 12 with 21 saves in 1974) to win the Cy Young. Lyle
led the Majors with 72 appearances, usually handling whatever
assignment Martin gave him. It was perhaps a harbinger when
Lyle began the regular season with a two-inning save followed
by five yeoman innings.

Although he did not have his best ERA or WHIP that year,
Lyle did pitch a career-high 137 innings. His unique combination of wins and saves were certainly a driving force in taking
home the Cy Young. Of those 72 appearances, Lyle recorded
more than three outs in 50 of them, and six or more outs in 34
of them. On seven different occasions in the regular season, he
completed at least four innings.

It was quite an achievement for someone who was told after
trying out for his hometown youth team at the age of 13 that "You
can't throw hard enough to be a pitcher." Lyle was so dejected
that for the next few years, he only played pickup baseball. "I
wonder what Ben Shingledecker thinks of my winning the Cy
Young," Lyle later said of that team's presumed manager.

Lyle began his career with the "Impossible Dream" Red Sox
in 1967 and quickly established himself as a valuable member of
the bullpen. Before the 1972 season, Boston traded Lyle to the
Yankees for Danny Cater and a player to be named later (Mario
Guerrero). Keeping within tradition, neither Cater nor Guerrero
ever helped Boston much. "Lyle's my lock-up man," Yankees
manager Ralph Houk said of that trade.

As a Yankee, Lyle compiled a pristine 2.41 ERA and saved 141 games. He still ranks fourth in Yankees history in saves and fifth in MLB history among left-handers. With the Yankees, his adjusted ERA+ was 148. During that seven-year span (1972 – 1978), only two pitchers who threw at least 500 innings were better. One was Guidry and the other was another dominant reliever, John Hiller of the Tigers. Using regular ERA, only Guidry was better during that period.

Here's another pivotal note about Lyle: He was among the first pitchers who made reliever entry music popular—long before Mariano Rivera's "Enter Sandman" or Trevor Hoffman's "Hell's Bells" or even Charlie Sheen's "Wild Thing" in the movie *Major League*. Lyle would be driven in from the bullpen in a pinstriped Datsun, and then he would get out and toss away his warmup jacket and walk to the mound. Former Yankees publicist Marty Appel thought Lyle's entrances from the bullpen were theatrical, so he wanted a song to go with it.

Appel and Lyle first tried to think of rock songs, but none seemed to work. They settled on "Pomp and Circumstance", the graduation song, for no apparent reason. Yankee fans liked it, but Joe Posnanski wrote that Lyle hated it. That was the end of graduation music at Yankee games, but just the start in the pontification of future closer tunes.

Alas, Lyle was rewarded for his Cy Young season by being benched, and one of his other great contributions to Yankee posterity would be a different kind of title. He wrote the best-selling book *The Bronx Zoo* with Peter Golenbeck, "a hilarious but scathing baseball tell-all." The Yankees acquired free agent future Hall of Famer Goose Gossage after the 1977 world championship, relegating Lyle to an observer who told it like he saw it in 1978.

"Never in a million years did I even secretly believe that the writers would give me the award," Lyle wrote about his Cy Young, "because it's so rare for a relief pitcher to get it. Mike Marshall won it once with the Dodgers, but he had been the only one. I thought for sure Jim Palmer would win it. He won twenty games, he's a great pitcher, and, besides, every year he campaigns for the thing. No one can blow his own horn the way Jim Palmer can. . . .

"On this one day, at least, I can be excited and proud and fart in public if I want. I was on a team that won the pennant and the World Series, despite enough crap to last an entire career, and now that I've won the Cy Young Award everyone can say that Sparky Lyle was an important part of that team."

In 1978, the Yankees beat the Royals and the Dodgers again for a repeat, but Lyle's status showed just how much some things had changed. He made one ineffective appearance against Kansas City and did not appear against Los Angeles. The Yankees ended their Sparky Lyle era a month later, trading him to Texas in a 10-player swap. There would be another versatile left-hander in that trade who would make his mark in pinstripes: Dave Righetti.

Jorge Posada

"I am simply a man who was born passionate about baseball and the New York Yankees."

Jorge Posada did most of his talking behind the plate and in the batter's box over 17 years with the Yankees, so when he spoke on the day of his induction into Monument Park, those words from a man of action were loud and everlasting. It happened on August 22, 2015, and one day after his number 20 jersey was retired, Andy Pettitte's number 46 followed suit.

It was a time of transition for the Yankees and the imminent rollout of tributes for key figures who had built the team's latest dynasty. Mo, Joe, Bernie, Jorge, Andy and Derek: Their six jersey numbers were retired within a span of about 3 ½ years, easily the most-bunched stretch of such formalities in club history, even more than the five jersey retirements in a five-year stretch from 1969 – 74 (Mickey Mantle, Casey Stengel, Yogi Berra, Bill Dickey and Whitey Ford).

At the time of Posada's emotional speech that day—as well as his choked-up retirement announcement that had preceded it—the natural order of life was being felt. They could not stay young forever. How many millions of Yankee fans across generations had felt the same pangs? The more important these heroes become in your life, the harder it is to say goodbye. In that instance, it was easy to look at Posada and think about how it all began.

"I got to play the same position as my idols and Yankee greats, Yogi Berra, Bill Dickey, Elston Howard, and number fifteen, Thurman Munson," Posada said to the crowd.

It took a while before one could envision Posada's name mentioned on that legendary list. He came up through the Yankee farm system with his Core Four friends and made his Major League debut by taking over behind the plate for Jim Leyritz in the ninth inning of a blowout victory over the Mariners on September 4, 1995. Unlike Jeter, Pettitte and Rivera, though, Posada would have to fight for a regular role in a budding dynasty.

Although Posada debuted in 1995, it would take him until 1998 to have more starts at catcher than Joe Girardi. Posada was growing impatient along the way. That Puerto Rican "passion" was burning, a stubborn persistence that he inherited.

"They keep saying I'm the catcher of the future. For me, the future is now," Posada said to Jack Curry in January 1998. "I've been working hard all these years to win the job. My time is now. I don't want to be too late. I'm going to be 27 in August. They keep saying I'm the future. By the time I get there, it's going to be too late."

That 1998 team was one of the two or three best in Yankees history, and perhaps in hindsight, having a two-headed catcher was a valuable commodity at the time. Girardi was a right-handed batter, and Posada was a switch-hitter, so Torre had the lineup advantage depending on opposing starting pitchers. Girardi, technically considered Posada's backup catcher, started 76 games that season while Posada started the bulk. Posada had his first true center-stage moment that season, catching David Wells's perfect game.

Posada's first postseason start came in Game One of the 1998 ALCS against Cleveland, and he drove in a run with a single in his first-at bat, followed by a solo homer later in the game as New York won, 7 – 2. It would be his first of 11 postseason homers.

In the 1998 and 1999 World Series sweeps by the Yankees,

Posada and Girardi split two starts apiece both times. Posada started Games One and Two against the Padres in 1998, and Girardi started the last two (with Posada playing the second half of Game Three). Posada started Games One and Four against the Braves in 1999, and Girardi started the middle two. Torre still valued Girardi's leadership and defensive contributions, yet even Girardi knew that Posada was the catcher of the future. Girardi's starts dropped from 76 to 64 in 1999, and Posada's continued to rise slightly. Girardi stuck around through 1999, and then signed with the Cubs as a free agent. So the pivotal moment in Posada's tenure can be traced back to that clincher against the Braves and Girardi's subsequent move to Chicago.

A new millennium arrived with Posada in the new position of full-time catcher for the Yankees. Finally, at age 28, he exceeded 112 games played in a season. He played in 151 games in 2000, and that would remain his career-high. He was an All-Star from 2000 – 03 (should have been in 2004 as well), and then added a fifth All-Star selection during his brilliant 2007 season when he batted .338/.426/.543 with 20 homers, 42 doubles, 90 RBIs and a 153 OPS+. Posada finished with 275 homers—passing Berra's club record for a catcher—as well as 1,065 RBIs and six Silver Sluggers. He was a member of five World Series champions, and memories such as his 2001 postseason, the first homer at new Yankee Stadium, his revenge double off Pedro Martinez in the 2003 ALCS clincher and his gallant effort to hold on to his job at the end are among the priceless memories of this absolute warrior.

"I just remember how fiery he was," said former NBA great Karl Malone, who I interviewed at an October 2015 awards dinner to benefit The Buoniconti Fund to Cure Paralysis, which honored Posada. "I can't remember when he missed a game. Just old school in the way he played the game. He never took days off. He took days off when the coach wanted him to take days off."

Posada was born on August 17, 1971 in Santurce, Puerto Rico, and he would especially embrace his connection to that island, even though his heritage is a mix of Dominican, Cuban and Puerto Rican. He was always fascinated with the history of the Puerto Rican people, and one reason he loved playing in New York was its large Puerto Rican population.

"No one is more important to my identification as Puerto Rican than Roberto Clemente," Posada wrote in his 2015 autobiography. He was not one to get caught up in personal honors, but the Robert Clemente Award (won by Jeter in 2009) is one that would have meant a great deal to him. Posada and his wife Laura have done extensive work to help research craniosynostosis, a disease that affects their son, Jorge Luis, and along the way the Jorge Posada Foundation has had widespread impact. Posada's trips back and forth to Puerto Rico on relief missions after the 2017 hurricane destruction there were the latest example of his love for that homeland and his respect for Clemente's legacy.

Posada's father Jorge was a scout for the Blue Jays in the 1980s, allowing his son to join him on Spring Training trips at a young age. In 1983, Posada took his first trip to Yankee Stadium with his family. "Someday I'm going to be out there," he said at the time.

Growing up in Puerto Rico gave Posada the opportunity to play baseball year-round, and he enrolled in 1989 at Calhoun Community College in Decatur, Georgia. The Yankees chose him in the 43rd round of that June's draft (1,116th overall), but he chose to attend college instead. Posada would be drafted again by the Yankees the next year, this time in the 24th round.

Posada was drafted as a middle infielder, but it became apparent that his lack of speed would be a hindrance to his development. Mark Newman, then the Yankees' coordinator of Minor League instruction, approached Posada about moving behind the plate for the 1991 season.

"You have a great arm," Newman told him. "You're going to be very strong because your legs are very strong. You haven't been catching, so you're going to be very durable. Your knees are not [worn out]. They haven't caught." He added: "It's the fastest way to get to the big leagues."

Looking back on those words when he was in New York for his jersey retirement ceremony, Posada reflected: "When he said that, that was it. That was it for me. I wanted to get to the big leagues. That's all I wanted." He said that if he had not switched, "I'd probably be working some job in Puerto Rico right now. I'd have been one of those guys who was out of baseball after two or three years."

That same stubborn persistence to become the Yankees' full-time catcher would be his driving force in the final years, as he battled to maintain his position and his impact.

Girardi was back on the scene in 2008, this time taking over for Torre as manager, and things were never quite the same from Posada's perspective, per his subsequent autobiography. He followed his banner season by playing in just 51 games due to a labrum injury, DHing in 15 of those games. But in a new Yankee Stadium, Posada came back strong. In fact, he hit the first home run there.

Few catchers have ever been so good at such an old age. As the Society for American Baseball Research noted in 2011, his OPS through age 30 was an impressive .835, but from age 31 to 38 it was .872, an outstanding rate for a catcher. He was a stalwart in the Yankees' 27th world championship, producing five hits and five RBIs in the series against Philadelphia. But the inevitable final chapter was unfolding.

Posada played in 120 games in 2010, including 83 at catcher and 30 at DH. On June 12 – 13 of that season, he hit a grand slam in each game against Houston at home. There was no doubt that Posada was going to go out proudly. He was 5-for-19 in the ALCS loss to Texas, and then came his swan song season of 2011. Girardi benched Posada in the middle of the season, and after five days without appearing in the lineup, he returned and hit a grand slam—his 10th and final one. In 2011, Posada caught in one game, and appeared in 90 games at DH and 14 at first base. He was the lone bright spot for the Yankees in their ALDS exit against Detroit, hitting .429.

The next month, he attended Joe Torre's Safe At Home Foundation Gala, and Don Mattingly was there. Mattingly hugged him and asked if he could have a word with him privately. "You don't have anything to prove," Mattingly told him. "If you really have to play, then go play, but if you're not sure, retire as a Yankee."

"I thought about what he said, and I realized that there weren't too many players who could say they played their entire careers as Yankees," Posada recalled. "That conversation made me understand how important my legacy as a Yankee is, and after that, I didn't want to wear another uniform. That's when I decided to retire. That's when I decided to be a Yankee forever."

Posada's career was finished. Five years later, his name appeared on the Hall of Fame ballot for the first time, and I felt embarrassed on behalf of the entire BBWAA voting body that he failed to receive the minimum five percent of votes needed to remain on the ballot. There is really no way to make a legitimate case for him in the Hall, but in this day and age, there is no way a Jorge Posada should get one crack at the ballot. There should have at least been a social discourse.

Either way, Posada wrote his name on the list of great Yankee catchers. It is a tradition no other baseball team can match.

"I never saw myself as part of that group," Posada said. "Just a lot of respect for the guys. It's just being there with them now is such a great honor."

He said that on the memorable day when his jersey was retired, and one of the most telling reminders about his impact came in the form of a message from Yogi Berra on the giant scoreboard during the plaque unveiling. It read:

> *Dear Jorge,*
> *I am very sad that I cannot be with you today, but my knees hurt too much—just wait, one day your knees are gonna hurt too!*
> *You were a real good ballplayer for a long time—I'm proud of you kid.*

Herb Pennock

On January 30, 1923, the Red Sox completed their most recent disastrous trade of the time to the Yankees. They sent yet another future Hall of Famer, Herb Pennock, to the Yankees for Norm McMillan, George Murray, Camp Skinner and $50,000. It was the missing piece for a franchise that would promptly win its first world championship and 26 more after that.

Pennock is the answer to many trivia questions, and not the least of them is: *Who was the winning pitcher of the first title clincher in Yankees history?* He had made one scoreless appearance in relief in a previous World Series, for Connie Mack's 1914 Philadephia A's. This one would be the first of five World Series starts and a 5 – 0 record in all of them.

October 11, 1923, Game Two vs. Giants

The Yankees had been swept by the Giants in 1921 and '22 while sharing the Polo Grounds with them, and this series would mark their first chance to play the NL powerhouse with home games in their own new ballpark. But Waite Hoyt had been knocked out in the third inning after starting Game One at Yankee Stadium and blew a 3 – 0 lead on the way to an opening loss. Pennock calmly took the ball in Game Two at the Polo Grounds and emerged as a stopper. Backed by two Babe Ruth homers, he went the distance in a 4 – 2 Yankees victory.

"The experts were predicting another rout of the American Leaguers, then along came Pennock," said umpire Billy Evans.

"Unquestionably, it was the turning point of the series." Despite the Yankees having a better record, they did not yet have the winning pedigree of the Giants, and therefore, were considered underdogs.

Herb Pennock gets loose in 1913.

October 15, 1923, Game Six vs. Giants

Pennock had closed out a Game Four victory for the Yankees at the Polo Grounds, and in Game Five, a home team finally won as Bullet Joe Bush pitched a three-hitter. Protecting a 3 – 2 lead in the best-of-five series, Pennock was not as commanding, scattering four runs and nine hits across seven innings. The Giants were ahead, 4 – 1, but the Yankees erupted for five runs in the top of the eighth, Sad Sam Jones threw two scoreless innings in relief (retiring a mighty pinch-hitter named Casey Stengel for the last out of the eighth), and they held on for the clincher as Pennock was credited with the W. Finally the Yankees had bragging rights . . . and their first ring.

"Lack of proper rest seemed to have robbed him [Pennock] of much of his stuff," Evans said of the Game Seven outing. "A less courageous pitcher would have grown careless and the Giants would have probably made a dozen runs. Not Pennock. . . . Then came the break, five runs in the eighth and victory. Pennock's work richly deserved it."

October 2, 1926, Game One vs. Cardinals

By this point, Pennock was the clear choice by Miller Huggins to start a World Series opener. The left-hander won a career high 23 games during the regular season and led the Majors a second straight year with a 1.265 WHIP. Pennock did not disappoint. After allowing one run in the first on a Jim Bottomley single, he shut down St. Louis for the rest of the game and won a pitcher's duel behind Lou Gehrig's RBI single.

October 7, 2006, Game Five vs. Cardinals

Ruth had tied the series at 2 – 2 with his historic three home runs in Game Four, and now Pennock was on the hill to finish the third of the three middle games in St. Louis. He and Bill Sherdel each pitched all 10 innings, and Pennock improved to 4 – 0 in World Series play thanks to a clutch sac fly from Tony Lazzeri in the top of the 10th. It is worth noting that game-winning RBI here, because it has sort of been lost in history. Lazzeri would hear many years later about the time he struck out against Pete Alexander in the decisive at-bat in this series' seventh game. Pennock pitched three scoreless innings in relief of Hoyt in that Game Seven, by the way, and would have improved to 5 – 0 there had Lazzeri in fact delivered a game-winner in that ninth inning.

October 7, 1927, Game Three vs. Pirates

As noted on his Hall of Fame plaque, Pennock worked on a no-hitter until Pie Traynor singled with one out in the eighth. Pennock finished with a three-hitter, and Gehrig's two-run triple in the first inning was all he needed. That gave New York a 3 – 0 Series lead and they swept their way into American lore the following day as the best team in baseball history was crowned. It was Pennock's second ring, and now he was 5 – 0 in the Fall Classic.

"Herbie's work Friday was perfect," Ruth said. "He never pitched a wrong ball, never once lost control and never lost his stuff."

For Pennock, those five World Series starts were complemented by brilliance in relief. He also closed out Games Three and Four of the 1932 World Series against the Cubs, throwing the last pitch of the series to Riggs Stephenson for a final fly out to right.

Pennock was said to have been "used up" at the age of 29 when New York acquired him, but he won 79 games in four seasons with the Yankees, including 23 in 1926. The three players Boston received for Pennock all amounted to busts, playing a total of four years with the Red Sox between them. Pennock had an array of curveballs with varying sweep, the sidearm style that perplexed lefty batters, and he meticulously studied opposing hitters.

"Always pitch to the catcher and not the hitter," Pennock said in his *10 Commandments of Pitching* that became widely circulated. "Keep your eye on that catcher and make him your target before letting the ball go."

Huggins once described him as the greatest left-handed pitcher of all-time, and credited Red Sox owner Harry Frazee for the last piece of the puzzle that started the Yankees on a title tradition.

Allie Reynolds

The Yankees acquired Allie Reynolds from Cleveland in exchange for future Hall of Fame second baseman Joe Gordon on October 11, 1946. Reynolds was a hard-throwing right-hander from Bethany, Oklahoma, known as "Superchief" due to his Creek Indiana heritage. The Indians wanted Gordon so badly, they reportedly offered the Yankees any pitcher other than Bob Feller.

"Take Reynolds," Joe DiMaggio said after then-GM Larry MacPhail asked his opinion on acquiring a pitcher. "I'm a fastball hitter, but he can buzz his hard one by me any time he has a mind to."

Gordon would pay quick dividends for the Indians, helping them to their only World Series championship in 1948 by hitting 32 homers and driving in 124 runs that year. Reynolds, meanwhile, would last longer in the Majors and become the picture of success. As his Monument Park plaque attests, he became one of the most reliable right-handers in Yankees history, writing his name into the record books with two no-hitters in 1951 and pitching on world champions in an astounding six of his first seven years with the team.

Reynolds's no-hitters that season came on July 12 at Cleveland (Gordon was out of baseball by then) and September 28 against Boston. It was the first time an AL pitcher had thrown two in one season, and the only pitcher other than Johnny Vander Meer, who threw no-hitters in consecutive starts for the Reds in 1938.

NO-HITTERS

DON LARSEN

He was a symbolic example of the phrase "be patient and good things will happen." The journeyman right-hander came to the Yankees in the massive 17-player trade with Baltimore after the 1954 season, was rocked in his Game Four start in the 1955 World Series loss to the Dodgers, and had early troubles in Game Two of the 1956 Fall Classic. But manager Casey Stengel brought him back to start Game Six and the rest is history. Larsen pitched the only World Series perfect game, throwing 97 pitches against a Dodger lineup loaded with four future Hall of Famers. He struck out Dale Mitchell for the electric final out, with a borderline call from outgoing ump Babe Pinelli. Yogi Berra leaped into Larsen's arms, a moment frozen in time.

"It was just a great day. I think about it every day," Larsen said in 2010 after watching Roy Halladay throw only the second postseason no-hitter, for Philadelphia. "No one has to remind me what happened. I was just happy to be a part of it with the New York Yankees and against Brooklyn in the World Series, everybody was watching."

Fittingly, perhaps, Larsen was traded after the 1959 season in the deal that would bring Roger Maris to New York. It was a connection between two of the most iconic individual feats in Yankee history. Larsen pitched for eight teams in all and finished with a career 81 – 91 record (4 – 2 in the World Series) and a 3.78 ERA.

JIM ABBOTT

In the media reception before the 2016 Thurman Munson Awards Dinner in Manhattan, we asked Jim Abbott about receiving such an important honor and about how he had thrown a no-hitter for the Yankees in 1993 despite being born without a right hand.

"Baseball has always had a message of ability, rather than disability—of ability versus perception," he replied. "They didn't care if I threw a baseball and caught the baseball with the same hand. If I could go get Rickey Henderson out, or if I could get Ken Griffey Jr. out, then there was a place for me in the game. I think it would be a wonderful message for a lot of workplaces, to think the same way: What can you do, instead of what can't you do?"

Abbott would throw with his left hand while positioning his right-handed thrower's glove on the end of his right arm, and then he would quickly slide his left hand into the glove to be ready for a comebacker. He lasted a remarkable 10 Major League seasons and compiled a 4.25 ERA over 1,674 innings—not too shabby considering he pitched almost his entire career against the vaunted lineups of the 1990s. The highlight, of course, was the 4 – 0 shutout against a stacked Cleveland club, finishing the 119-pitch masterpiece with a Carlos Baerga groundout to short. Abbott would go on to be a successful motivational speaker.

"The specialness of it, I didn't know how lasting it would be when it happened," Abbott said of his gem. "Everywhere I go, people talk about that game, how exciting it was. That makes me very proud."

Yankees No-Hitters

DATE	PITCHER	OPPONENT	SCORE
4/24/1917	George Mogridge	Red Sox	2 – 1
9/4/1923	Sad Sam Jones	Athletics	2 – 0
8/27/1938	Monte Pearson	Indians	13 – 0
7/12/1951	Allie Reynolds	Indians	1 – 0
9/28/1951	Allie Reynolds	Red Sox	8 – 0
10/8/1956 (W.S.)	Don Larsen	Dodgers	2 – 0
7/4/1983	Dave Righetti	Red Sox	4 – 0
9/4/1993	Jim Abbott	Indians	4 – 0
5/14/1996	Dwight Gooden	Mariners	2 – 0
5/17/1998	David Wells	Twins	4 – 0
7/18/1999	David Cone	Expos	6 – 0

Going into the second of Reynolds's gems, he had been dealing with bone chips in his elbow and was feeling under the weather. It was the first game of a doubleheader, and Reynolds was almost certain he had lost the no-hitter on a deep fly off the bat of Aaron Robinson in the eighth inning that was caught by Hank Bauer. "I didn't even look back at it," Reynolds said after the game. "I was sure it was out of the park."

Years later, Reynolds would make a case for looking beyond those two outings, though. "A no-hitter is not the best standard by which to judge a pitcher," he said. "That's just luck. I've pitched four games better than the no-hitters and lost three of them."

Reynolds led the Majors in ERA the following season, reached 20 wins for the only time in his career, and finished second to Bobby Shantz in regular season MVP voting. Reynolds certainly would have made a case for 1952 World Series MVP if one had existed at the time. He pitched in four of those seven games against Brooklyn, going 2 – 1 with a save.

One key pitch came in the bottom of the sixth inning of Game Seven, when he got Gil Hodges to ground into a 6-4-3 double play following a leadoff single by Roy Campanella. That preserved the Yankees' 3 – 2 lead on the way to a 4 – 2 clincher at Ebbets Field.

After his banner 1952 season, Reynolds worked more frequently out of the bullpen. He won 13 games and saved more in 1953, and then won 13 and saved seven in his swan song of 1954.

"That really was a career-shortener," Reynolds said of the dual role. "But to me, that was important. Teamwork was more important than some kind of honor."

Casey Stengel had taken over as Yankee manager in 1949 and became known for his platooning and unconventional lineup moves—including his usage of Reynolds.

"Reynolds was two ways great, which is starting and relieving, which no one can do like him," Stengel said. "He has guts and his courage is simply tremendous."

Reynolds retired after the 1954 season with a 182 – 107 record and a .630 winning percentage. That percentage soars to .686 when roping off those eight Yankee seasons.

His career stats are virtually identical between Cleveland and New York:

5 years with Cleveland: 792.1 IP, 51 – 47, 3.31 ERA, 1.43 WHIP, 7.9 H/9, 5.0 BB/9, 5.2 K/9

8 years with New York: 1,700 IP, 131 – 60, 3.30 ERA, 1.36 WHIP, 7.9 H/9, 4.3 BB/9, 5.1 K/9

Reynolds's 7 – 2 record with a 2.79 ERA in the Fall Classic made him an October standout. Despite these accomplishments, his 13-year career, which included five seasons in Cleveland, was not long enough to build a strong Hall of Fame resume. He topped out at 33.6 percent of the BBWAA vote in 15 years on the ballot and fell one vote shy of election by the Veterans Committee in 2009. He is unlikely to garner much more than the same tepid support he received from the writers more than 30 years ago, but Reynolds, who died in 1994 at age 77, had said he was "indifferent" about the whole matter, anyway.

"He was a dominating pitcher," said Dr. Bobby Brown, who played third base behind him for the Yankees and delivered his eulogy. "He was as good as any pitcher that pitched during his time. He was extremely instrumental in the success of the Yankees."

Miller Huggins

William Howard Taft made two notable contributions to baseball, one renowned and one relatively unknown. He was the first U.S. president to throw out a ceremonial first pitch, starting a proud tradition at Major League ballparks. He also taught a local student named Miller Huggins at the University of Cincinnati Law School.

Toward the end of the nineteenth century, Taft delivered two hour-long lectures per week as Professor of Property and introduced the case system to the school's curriculum. Huggins absorbed the facts, arguments and summary judgments, and he learned to apply an analytical method of fairness and reason. He obtained his law degree there, fulfilling the wishes of his immigrant father, and ultimately passed the Ohio bar but chose to play professional baseball.

Taft not only became president after their paths crossed, but he also served from 1921 – 30 as Supreme Court Chief Justice. During that term, his former law student would manage the Yankees to six World Series and three championships. They obviously followed each other's progress. What he had learned from Taft and his other law professors eventually became a prerequisite strength for him as a Hall of Fame manager in the Babe Ruth era.

"I studied the characters of my players," Huggins said. "One system will not rule. It is impossible, because you will find temperamental players, you will find players who do not need any rules, and you will find players who insist they know more than the manager."

MANAGERS INDUCTED INTO HALL OF FAME AS YANKEES

MANAGER	INDUCTION YEAR	YEARS WITH YANKEES
Joe McCarthy	1957	1931-46
Miller Huggins	1964	1918-29
Casey Stengel	1966	1949-60
Joe Torre	2014	1996-07

Huggins grew up in Cincinnati's hardscrabble Fourth Ward, a diminutive (five feet, four inches) figure who would have to overcome constant and cruel size labels throughout life. He was a tough, above-average second basemen over a 13-year NL career (1904 – 16) with his hometown Reds and then the Cardinals, rounding out the top 50 all-time WAR list (35.6) at his position. Considered one of the game's best leadoff hitters of his times, with a good eye and a good glove, Huggins scored 90 or more runs four times in his career and led the NL in walks four times. "He sputtered like a little gamecock as he raised himself on tip-toes to thrust his chin against that of a two-hundred-twenty-pound rival player or a husky umpire," Fred Lieb wrote in *The Sporting News*.

With the Cardinals, Huggins served as player-manager from 1913 – 16 and then managed the Cardinals to an 82 – 70 record in 1917. He was a contender to buy the Cardinals from Helen Britton in 1916, but a St. Louis syndicate headed by James C. Jones stepped in and coaxed St. Louis Browns player-manager Branch Rickey to become the Redbirds' president. Browns owner Phil Ball tried through court action to block Rickey's departure, and although that effort failed, AL chief Ban Johnson did his best to settle the score. Johnson encouraged Yankees owner Jacob Ruppert to bring the Cardinals' manager over to the AL. Col. T.L. Huston, Ruppert's co-owner who had fancied the Dodgers' Wilbert Robinson as the Yankees' next manager, was in France with the U.S. war effort when Ruppert unilaterally hired Huggins for the 1918 season.

For Huggins, it meant a great opportunity . . . and five years of grief to go along with it. His ability to adroitly handle it with that same fairness and analytical perspective, as well as Ruppert's public show of support, would prove pivotal to the Yankees.

Huggins had an eye not just for the strike zone but also for talent. He had nurtured Rogers Hornsby as his replacement at second base for the Cardinals, and with the Yankees he swapped five players and cash for second baseman Del Pratt of the Browns. Then it was he who sold Ruppert on the idea of adding a game-changer like Ruth. Babe had become a two-way player in 1919 and crushed 29 homers to lead both leagues, impressing Huggins.

Ruppert brought Ed Barrow over from the Red Sox as his general manager, and charged him with the responsibility of acquiring good talent for Hug. Bob Meusel, Waite Hoyt, Carl Mays, Wally Schang . . . one after another came the talent wave. The Yankees won their first two pennants in 1921 and '22, losing both times to the Giants. Ruth led a state of unruliness off the field, carousing and flouting curfews, and players openly made light of their skipper. Huston was eager to capitalize on anything that might spell Huggins's demise, and he thought he found his eureka moment after the final game of the 1922 World Series.

Bullet Joe Bush was the Yankees' pitcher in that Game Five at the Polo Grounds. The righty from Minnesota was finishing a career year in which he went 26 – 7 before taking the Game One loss. The Yankees were on the brink of elimination and protecting a 3 – 2 lead in the eighth inning. With two out and Giants runners on second and third, Huggins ordered Bush to intentionally walk Ross Youngs, a left-handed batter, and take his chances with future Hall of Famer High Pockets Kelly, a right-handed batter who had batted .328 that season.

"What for, you stupid oaf?" Bush snapped back at Huggins on the bench. It was audible to many, including those in the ground-level press box and front-row boxes.

Bush reluctantly went through with the intentional walk to Youngs, and then grooved a gopher ball to Kelly. It was returned to center for a two-run single and the Giants added a third run in the inning for good measure. They took the game, 5-3, and the Yankee clubhouse was full of angry and griping players who were no longer just happy to reach the World Series. Those voices were emboldened by Huston's well-known hatred for Huggins. The manager closed the clubhouse door and lambasted Bush. Ruth angrily kicked a trunk, and then erupted when someone spoke to him: "Shut your trap before I put my fist in it!"

Huston hammered his point home that night at press head-quarters: "Miller Huggins has managed his last Yankee ball game. He's through! Through! Through!"

Ruppert refused to back him up, though, telling reporters: "I won't fire a man who has just brought the Yankees two pennants." That brought the dispute to a head, and Ruppert bought out Huston's interest that offseason. Barrow glee-fully told the manager: "Jake just bought out Til. We're home free now." And in a truly pivotal moment for the franchise, Ruppert, never one to set foot in the manager's clubhouse, walked into it the day after buying out his partner and said: "I am now the sole owner of this ball club. Miller Huggins is my manager."

Players had newfound respect for Huggins, and the team won its first title that subsequent season. "I would not go through those years again for all the money in the world," he said.

There was still the matter of his superstar, however. Ruth lived by his own set of rules, knowing full well who put fannies in the seats. Nearly a foot taller than Huggins and less than refined, Ruth had little respect for men of small stature.

"Hug's greatest problem was Babe Ruth, who for a time seemed to believe that his mere presence in the lineup was all he owed to the club," Waite Hoyt said. "The Babe paid no attention to curfew, never took the room assigned to him, and often trotted into the clubhouse just barely in time to make the game."

Miller Huggins in the Yankee dugout in 1922.

Huggins finally drew the line in 1925, the year the Yankees fell to 69 – 85. "Don't bother getting dressed," Miller told Ruth on August 29 in the visitor's clubhouse at St. Louis. He fined Ruth $5,000, withstood the loud response and held his ground. Ruth retaliated for Huggins's punishment and gave the manager an ultimatum: He goes or I go. Both men stayed, and Ruppert, despite knowing Ruth's turnstile value, was unequivocal again in his support for Huggins.

"Huggins will be manager as long as he wants to be manager," Ruppert said, "so you can see where we stand and where Ruth stands."

After the suspension reached nine games, a repentant Ruth conceded that Hug was boss. The fair treatment of individuals, the refusal to make exceptions, had served Huggins well. The Yankees proceeded to go to three straight World Series, losing in 1926 to St. Louis is seven as Pete Alexander struck out Tony

Lazzeri in the key seventh-inning at-bat, and then winning with the greatest team ever in 1927 and a repeat in 1928.

There was another very pivotal moment in the Huggins managerial term that is noted elsewhere in this book. On June 1, 1925, Ruth returned after his prolonged health issue—famously glossed over as "The Bellyache Heard 'Round The World." In that same home game against Washington, Huggins sent Lou Gehrig up to pinch-hit for Pee-Wee Wanninger against Walter Johnson in the eighth inning. That technically began Gehrig's historic streak of 2,130 consecutive games played, and the following day, Huggins wrote the names of Ruth and Gehrig into the same lineup card—beginning a fabled fact of life.

"He was more like a father to me than anything else," Gehrig said of Huggins. "He never became impatient when I made a mistake. He would take me aside and tell me he had confidence in me. I call him the squarest shooter in baseball."

In the new locker room immediately after the 1923 coronation, Huggins was given a diamond ring as a special gesture of Ruth. The manager was hoisted onto the shoulders of players and then gave a moving victory speech: "We have had our little arguments during the season, but they were not real hard feelings; they only appeared so at the time. Underneath it all and when it is all over there can't help but be a great friendship between all of us who have fought the greatest battle of all and come out on top."

John Kieran wrote in the *Times*: "In winning the first three pennants Huggins had shown that he knew how to buy [players]. In winning his last three he showed he knew how to build."

Huggins was finally inducted into the Hall of Fame in 1964, after enough people saw past the fact that he managed so many elite players. His forte was his ability to patiently and adroitly handle diverse personalities, and he was especially effective with pitchers. What he had learned from Taft in those law-school lectures would stick with him.

Huggins died from a blood infection at the age of 51 on September 25, 1929, having turned the team over to Art Fletcher with 11 games left that season, and every AL game was canceled on the day of his funeral back in Cincinnati. The Yankees' tradition of Monument Park began with the unveiling of a tablet near the center-field flagpole on Memorial Day in 1932.

"There never has been a better judge of raw baseball talent than Huggins," columnist Arthur Robinson wrote in February 1964. "And every manager of the Yankees since him—all of them—have benefited from the foundation of the dynasty he built."

Joe DiMaggio

Giuseppe Paolo DiMaggio was the eighth of nine children born to immigrants who had settled near San Francisco after leaving *Isola delle Femmine*, an islet off the coast of Sicily. Papa DiMaggio ran a fishing boat at a wharf and he believed his five boys should work the boat as well. They liked baseball. "Baseball, what is that?" he would shout. "A bum's game! A no good game! Whoever makes a living at baseball?"

Joe DiMaggio loved his bats in 1941, when he hit in a record fifty-six straight games.

"Joe" was good enough to sign a professional contract with his local team, the Double-A San Francisco Seals of the Pacific Coast League, but could his father have been right about making a living at it? That first year, after all, DiMaggio was not exactly pegged for the certain baseball immortality that would come a decade later. He tried every infield position, and in one single day while playing in an exhibition game for the Seals, he supposedly made 11 errors at shortstop. It is impossible to verify such futility, so let's just go with his description of "inauspicious."

"Every one of them was on a wild throw. I mean they were *wild* throws. They went clear into the stands," DiMaggio explained later. "It got so that every time a ball was hit to me the people sitting in the stands back of first base got up and ran, and when I say this I'm not kidding."

And yet the same Joe DiMaggio would become such a perfect ballplayer and idolized figure in the days and years ahead, Dodgers manager Tommy Lasorda would utter this upon a legend's passing in 1999: "If you said to God, 'Create someone who was what a baseball player should be,' God would have created Joe DiMaggio. And he did."

Back in the Great Depression, Seals manager Jim Caveney wisely moved his befuddling teenager to the outfield in desperation, and the result was history. In fact, it is hard to imagine a more pivotal moment in DiMaggio's own career. Now in his comfort zone, the outfielder flourished and put together a 61-game hitting streak in 1933, his first full year with the Seals.

Now there were only two issues. One was the spelling of his name. He had signed his first Seals contract "DeMaggio," but older brother Vince had signed his with two words: "Di Maggio". Seals vice president Charley Graham asked which way was correct, and Joe told him, "Spell it any old way." Graham decided on "DiMaggio", and so *The Sporting News* printed this headline: "It Should Be DiMaggio."

The other issue, of course, was more important for baseball decisions. DiMaggio's knee was "out of kilter," he said, after stepping out of a vehicle. There were torn tendons. Scouts scattered, but one was unbuoyed: Vinegar Bill Essick. He suggested to Barrow that the Yankees go for it. They sent him to a Dr. Spencer in Los Angeles for an exam, with Essick tagging along, and the prognosis was good enough for an acquisition. Colonel Ruppert, taking advantage of financial difficulties that had befallen Seals president Charlie Graham during the economic collapse, gave up just $25,000 and five nondescript prospects. Graham's only stipulation was that he stay with the Seals for 1935, moving to center, and the Yankees obliged. DiMaggio hit .398 with 34 homers and looked good in the outfield in 1935.

It would be one of the Yankees' defining moves.

DiMaggio would say later that he felt bad for Graham, and that he could have commanded three times that cash sum a year later. Veteran columnist Joe Williams would write in 1948 that he considered that "spectacular swindle" to be "the best deal the Yankees ever made"—Ruth included.

DiMaggio was a Yankee from 1936 – 51, excluding the 1943 – 45 seasons spent in military service during World War II. He wore number nine his first year, as Frankie Crosetti had number five. Starting in 1937, Crosetti was number one and the five jersey went to DiMaggio . . . and on into Monument Park.

In those 13 seasons, DiMaggio slashed .325/.398/.579; hit 361 homers; made the AL All-Star team every year; led the Yankees to an unbelievable 10 World Series and celebrated an even more unbelievable nine titles; covered center field with an easy and consistent grace; and won three MVP awards. The issue was no longer with how to spell his name, but with which nickname to apply: Joltin' Joe, the Yankee Clipper, DiMag, Joe D.

And then there was the ultimate compliment: "Hello, Joe." That is how the Bambino greeted him when they first met a couple years after Babe left the club. Anyone who knew Ruth would tell you that he never used a person's first name. "Hi-ya, keed" was standard. This was a show of respect that would prove remarkably prescient, a passing of the torch. So was this from Gehrig in early 1936: "He's all ball player. That boy is going far and should be one of the real greats of the game. I think he'll win the pennant for us this year."

And many more.

DiMaggio brought a uniquely batting wide stance, with feet about 36 inches apart, in the middle of the box. He would wait until the last possible moment to start his swing. "I look for his fastball," he said of the pitcher. "Then if he comes in with a curve, I still have time to swing." That helped ward off slumps, and it helped generate the second incredible hitting streak of his professional career—his most fabled one.

From May 15 through July 16 of 1941, DiMaggio hit safely in 56 consecutive games. It blew away Wee Willie Keeler's longstanding Major League record of 44 in a row. Today it is considered one of the "unbreakable" records in MLB, as no one has made it even to 40 since Pete Rose dramatically tied Keeler's old mark in 1978.

"I'm kind of proud of that record—not just because it's written down in the book with my name next to it, but because every one of the ninety-one hits I made during that cycle were clean, legitimate blows," DiMaggio said. "There were no infield hits among them, none made with the official scorer's pencil. It was just one big binge."

That fabled Summer of '41 was the showcase of both Joe and Ted, as Williams put his name into the history books for rival Boston with a .406 final batting average—one that would hold up to date as the last time a player hit .400. DiMaggio batted .357 with 30 homers and a league-leading 125 RBIs. In retrospect, Williams had the higher season WAR—10.6 to 9.1, according to baseballreference.com—but the Yankees finished 17 games ahead of the second-place Red Sox in the AL standings. Plus, DiMaggio typically got extra points for his defense.

He went into the war at age 28 and resumed play at 31. Imagine him batting in that prime!

"When you think of DiMaggio, the book on him was that he played defense effortlessly, not because of a lack of effort but because he was so smooth," Idelson said. "The hitting streak obviously is a big focal point of what people remember about DiMaggio, but also just the ease with which the game seemed to come to him."

In 1969, when baseball writers were surveyed on the sport's 100th anniversary, DiMaggio would be named the "greatest living player." By then, he had been through a whirlwind marriage with actress Marilyn Monroe and seen her tragic demise. He had left the game hobbled but on top in 1951, proudly responding to an 0-for-11 start (and much naysaying) in that last World Series against the Giants by putting he team on his back and going 6-for-12 with a homer, three doubles and two intentional walks to secure one final ring.

On March 8, 1999, after DiMaggio had left and gone away, Idelson spent all day at the Hall taking phone calls and conducting interviews. He told the nearby *Oneonta Star* back then that it was as "intense a day as anything outside of an induction weekend. We're talking about a man that was held in the highest esteem. . . he had a certain way of handling himself that exuded class and dignity. From that standpoint, he was someone that any young kid or adult could look up to."

DiMag had said he would mostly remember "the great loyalty of the fans." Today in Cooperstown, many of those fans gaze at DiMaggio's plaque, and they also reminisce over his number five jersey hanging in his actual locker. He was inducted there in 1955.

"They wonder about him and Marilyn," Idelson said. "Realize that it wasn't a comfortable relationship for him, but people are enamored by the center fielder from the Yankees and one of the great actors of the silver screen coming together in a union for a short period of time. There is still a lot of interest from a lot of fans about not only DiMaggio but also his relationship with Marilyn. This is a guy who had a song written about him, Joltin' Joe DiMaggio, married to Marilyn Monroe, shows up in a Simon & Garfunkel song; he's definitely someone in the game who has had an impact on various parts of American culture."

HOF ARTIFACT INVENTORY

Game-used equipment in the Baseball Hall of Fame:

JOE DIMAGGIO

B–428.56	Joe DiMaggio's locker from Yankee Stadium.
B–211.53	Yankees cap.
B–2763.63	Yankees cap.
B–49.52	Yankees shirt, 1951 home uniform.
B–2761.63	No. 5 Yankees jersey.
B–48.52	Yankees pants, 1951 home uniform.
B–2762.63	Yankees pants.
B–51.52	Uniform socks, 1951.
B–2764.63	Uniform socks.
B–2852.63	Shoes.
B–52.52	Glove.
B–2715.63	Glove from 1938–39 seasons and World Series.
B–2744.63	Glove, autographed.
B–2998.63	Bat.
B–139.75	Pen used to sign $100,000 contract prior to 1949 season, making him baseball's first six-figure player.
B–28.2002	1951 World Series ring, his ninth and final one with the Yankees.

And on the future tradition of the Yankees. "Joe, he win all the time," DiMaggio would remember his papa saying in broken English, explaining why father rooted for younger son Dom during Boston's failed 1948 pennant chase. *All the time.* Yankees like Derek Jeter have hoped it would literally rub off, as they reach up in the clubhouse tunnel before games and slap the sign bearing DiMaggio's quote from October 1949—"I want to thank the Good Lord for making me a Yankee." Then there is this story that Idelson shares, from his days in the club's front office:

"This was Opening Day in 1989 and Joe DiMaggio was there to throw out the first pitch at the Stadium. Joe comes into the locker room, and he says to Nick Priore, our clubhouse guy, 'I want to meet the Yankees' center fielder.' Roberto Kelly was our center fielder. Nick brings Joe over to meet Roberto, this young Panamian kid. Joe is talking to him and he looks into his locker, and he sees a Steve Balboni bat, a Tom Brookens bat, he sees three or four different bats, none that are his. He says, 'Where are your bats?' Roberto says, 'Well, this is my first year starting and I kind of burned through my supply, so I'm using some of my teammates' bats.' DiMaggio heads to Mr. Steinbrenner's suite after delivering the first pitch, and George sees him come in and grabs him by both shoulders, and says, 'Joe, it's so good to see you, it's so good to see you, how are you, Joe?' The first thing he says to George is: 'How can the Yankees' center fielder not have his own bats?' Within four or five days, Roberto had four dozen bats in his locker."

All ballplayer.

Don Mattingly

One could argue that the most pivotal thing about Don Mattingly's career was the impact of his congenital back issue in 1990, when he was 29 and in his prime and suddenly baseball's highest-paid player after a sixth straight All-Star season for the Yankees.

But enough already. Trust me, I have thought long and hard enough about all that. He became eligible for the Hall of Fame ballot at about the same time that I became eligible to vote for it, and I never checked the box beside his name from 2001 – 15. That is not easy to say when you are from his same hometown of Evansville, Indiana, where I played high school ball against him and we all took pride in watching him flourish into a superstar and role model on the biggest stage.

We got over it then, so let's just leave the Hall of Fame thing alone. For one thing, Mattingly has plenty of mementoes in the museum already, game-used items representing incredible feats such as the eight consecutive games with a home run to tie Dale Long's record. For another, his number 23 adorns Monument Park, a proper tribute among Yankee immortals.

"I've tried to give you all a hundred percent of myself every time I walked out on the field," the guest of honor told fans, family and ex-teammates who came to "Don Mattingly Day" at Yankee Stadium for that number retirement ceremony on August 31, 1997. "I tried to keep it pure, I tried to keep it simple, and just play great baseball for you over the years. I hope you appreciated it."

We still do, well into his coaching and managerial days.

Some things cannot be measured with championship rings or statistics. Things like building character in others, leading by example, giving a parent someone their children can look up to, playing the game the right way, showing up every single homestand in your glory years to sign autographs so kids have beautiful memories, or more recently sponsoring a team in the RBI (Reviving Baseball in Inner Cities) leagues. These are the kinds of things that made him Donnie Baseball.

"I learned to play baseball the way it's supposed to be played from the guys you grew up with," Mattingly said in accepting a Lifetime Achievement Award in 2011 at the MLB Players Alumni Association's Legends for Youth fundraising dinner. "The guys you watched play the game. It's the same thing I try to bring to our club . . . we play the game with respect. Not only for the fans who come to see you play, but also the people who played the game before you, and the way they played it."

In Spring Training of 1983, I was a sportswriter for the *Miami Herald* and Mattingly was battling for a roster spot. He had torn up the Minors and had a cup of coffee with the Yankees the previous season. I asked Billy Martin, who was beginning to manage the Yankees for a third go-round, what he thought of Mattingly and his chances of making the roster. "I really like this kid's swing" is all that I remember of the response, but I do remember rushing to a pay phone near the Yankees' Fort Lauderdale training facility and dictating those words back to the Evansville *Courier* sports desk for a headline the next morning: *Martin likes Mattingly's swing*. It might not have made the New York tabs, but I knew that people in our hometown, like me, were hanging on every word about the prospect.

Mattingly won a roster spot that year, and then split the season with the Yankees and Triple-A Columbus. He came back up when Bobby Murcer announced his retirement on June 12, opening a reserve outfield position. Mattingly was used in various roles, and even made the rare appearance as a left-handed fielding second baseman for the August 18 resumption of the famous "Pine Tar Game" against Kansas City. That was not a shocker to those of us from his hometown; he played shortstop one afternoon in 1977 for Memorial High School at my school, Central. He pitched, he could do it all. Mattingly had great hands, and that included both of them.

With the parent club in 1983, that kid's swing resulted in a .283 average with four homers and 32 RBIs in 279 at-bats. Then comes the pivotal moment for Donnie Baseball, if you want something other than the back problem. George Steinbrenner fired Martin again, this time replacing him with legend Yogi Berra that December. Yogi announced at the start of 1984 Spring Training that Mattingly would be with the Yankees all season, but that he would begin as a reserve. Roy Smalley was being groomed to start at first base. Yogi said he liked that Mattingly's stroke lent itself well to pinch-hitting duties because he could "sit for three weeks and still hit."

Mattingly's fate had been unclear a year earlier when I asked Martin that question, and now the good news was that Mattingly did not have to play for his job in the Grapefruit League. Still, he was not the type to accept being a bench jockey. He told reporters he would try to change management's mind and make it hard to follow through with the plan. And that is exactly what he did. Mattingly was in command at the plate and he was a natural at first base; Berra announced that he was his Opening Day first baseman, the beginning of a great era.

Mattingly got off to a hot start and not only hit but also hit for power. That was largely because of hitting coach Lou Piniella's influence. Piniella said he worked all that year with Mattingly to keep his weight back and hold his body in balance through the swing. In July, Mattingly was named to his first of six consecutive All-Star Games, and Steinbrenner took a jab at the city's other club by declaring Mattingly better than Mets sensation Darryl Strawberry. Mattingly was batting .339 by the Midsummer Classic, and he went on to overtake teammate Dave Winfield on the final day of the season to win a much-hyped batting race, .343 to .340.

HOF ARTIFACT INVENTORY

Game-used equipment in the Baseball Hall of Fame:

DON MATTINGLY

B-214.86	Bat used by Don Mattingly during the Yankees' 1986 season.
B-379.87	Bat used for home run off Jose Guzman at Texas on July 18, 1987, tying Dale Long's record of eight consecutive games with a homer.
B-380.87	Bat used to hit his sixth grand slam of the 1987 season, off Bruce Hurst of the Red Sox in the third inning on Sept. 29 at Yankee Stadium. It led Yanks to a 6-0 win and set the Major League record for most grand slams in a season.
B-178.2000	First baseman's mitt used by the Yankees' captain. He retired with the highest fielding percentage of any position player in history and was a nine-time Gold Glove winner.
B-154.2017	Rawlings Gold Glove Award in 1994, his ninth and last.
B-82.2014	Temporary locker room tag for Mattingly as Los Angeles Dodgers manager, used in the 2014 MLB Opening Series in Australia.

In addition to the batting title, Mattingly led the AL in hits with 207 and doubles with 44. He finished fifth in voting for MVP, but that award would come the following season, as Mattingly went on a three-year run in which he hit at least .320 with 30 homers and 110 RBIs while emerging as a perennial Gold Glover at first. Unfortunately, his run of dominance in the game coincided with one of the Yankees' worst dry spells overall, when you look at the big picture within this book's context of epochal success. Steinbrenner was never the type to settle for it, and Mattingly was not immune from the stress and tabloid quote wars.

"When I was there, the Yankees weren't very good, but Donnie was already an established superstar," Hall of Fame president Jeff Idelson said as we discussed Mattingly one day in the building where his plaque shoulda-woulda been. "He brought that Midwestern disposition to the Bronx, and it was impossible not to like him. He wore the Captain label, but it was a guy who led by example rather than words. Work ethic second to none. Just a quiet popularity, absolutely perfect for the Yankees.

"I remember one time, we were so bad, sky-high popup, he's chasing it, chasing it, to the stands it goes, kid in the front row is eating a bag of popcorn, he starts eating it, and the kid looks at Donnie and goes, 'Ohmygod, the Yankee first baseman is eating my bag of popcorn.' That's how he was; he treated everybody exactly the same."

Idelson knew about Mattingly's physical issue far more than most people, as a traveling member of the Yankees' public-relations team, and even tried his best to help the slugger cope with his back it in those days.

"He was having such back problems by the time I got there in eighty-nine," Idelson said. "I was a little younger, I asked him, 'Have you ever slept on a futon?' He had no idea what a futon was. So I explained it to him, and he said, 'That sounds cool.' I bought him a futon, and when we traveled, that is what he slept on while on the road the whole eighty-nine season . . . and he hit .303.

"You think about how bad the hotels were back then, you'd go to the Sheraton in Texas, you know. I had slept on futons in college because they're very firm. I bought a small single. The equipment guy [Nick Priore] hated me, putting them on planes. No frame. I got bungee cords for him, I said, 'Try it.' He loved it."

Nevertheless, Mattingly lost much of his power at the plate in 1990, appearing in only 102 games. His home run totals gradually increased from five that year to nine to fourteen to seventeen. He was never quite the same, but he was hardly a slouch in the final years, either. He might have even been a great story with a World Series stage in 1994, but so many possibilities vaporized when a labor stoppage stole the traditional finish from everyone.

Mattingly was the best player for a decent stretch in the game's history, and Stan Musial even said he reminded him of himself. At long last, Mattingly finally reached the postseason in his final season, emerging as a clutch hero before Edgar Martinez ended the brief run in that unforgettable 1995 AL Division Series. Fans got their chance to chant "Don-nie Base-Ball!" in an October setting at old Yankee Stadium. Mattingly knew the feeling of being selected as Captain, he had the respect of his peers and all fans, as someone who left it all on the field.

There was nothing like those days, when he was a Yankee first baseman and you could go into "Mattingly's 23" restaurant in Evansville and see the dazzling memorabilia on the wall, including some sweet items from his buddy Larry Bird up Highway 41 in Terre Haute. I was covering the Majors for the San Jose *Mercury News* and then *The Sporting News* in those days and I could often be found wearing a favorite white Mattingly's 23 T-shirt. Idelson told me he had one of those shirts, too. If you've ever had to share someone from your hometown with the world, then you know the feeling. Donnie Baseball was perfectly Evansville, and then suddenly he was perfectly New York, with a mustache and eye black.

"It's such a great place to play because it's so demanding, because every day is a new day and we needed to win the game," Mattingly said while talking about Steinbrenner in the 2011 biography *Donnie Baseball*. "That kind of mentality is, to me, the perfect baseball mentality. It pushes guys to be better, it forces them to concentrate on a daily basis. It doesn't allow you to rest on your laurels or get caught up in what you did in the past. I think it's the perfect atmosphere."

Here's another pivotal moment that helped make it possible for him to play in that atmosphere—and a little-known one that I saw while perusing Elston Howard's clip files at the Hall of Fame research library. The Yankees had taken a chance on Mattingly with a 19th-round selection in the 1979 draft after his Memorial High team had barely missed repeating as state champs. In 1980, his first full professional season, he batted .358 with 105 RBIs in 133 games for Greensboro of the Class A South Atlantic League. Howard had been on the Yankees' coaching staff when Steinbrenner bought the club in 1973, and he had retained Howard in the front office. Now the Yankees were sending Howard to Greensboro to give an evaluation on this surprising prospect from Evansville. Howard's judgment was that Mattingly "is a Major League prospect and it would be a mistake to trade him," and it was because of that input that Mattingly was not included in a deal being considered at the time.

That article by Phil Pepe appeared in the *Daily News* on April 15, 1982—when the buzz was starting to heat up about this prospect. Today, Mattingly is a part of Monument Park, and that 23 in a pinstriped circle beyond the Yankee Stadium center field wall is there for all to see year after year as a reminder. If you watched Mattingly play, you don't need a reminder, anyway. He was the Yankees' best first baseman other than Lou Gehrig, definitely the best defensive one, and one of their most beloved players overall. And he has continued to have a big impact in uniform long after retiring.

When I came home to Evansville to launch my book *Diamonds from the Dugout* at Barnes & Noble in October 2017, Donnie had just finished managing a Marlins season. He graciously emailed me a congrats and said he would be at the event near his home if he could, "but it overlaps with Little Louie's nap time, and ol' Dad needs his rest." Donnie Baseball took a rest and I was just fine with that. He is still bringing up ballplayers, still the pride of our town.

"I'm proud of what I did," Mattingly said. "I think more than anything I'm proud of the way I played the game and how I cared about it. I got myself ready to play. I mean, that's the biggest thing—I came to play every day. I didn't really want to sit out. I didn't like taking days off."

Earle Combs

History is filled with baseball legends who hoped for Hall of Fame induction one day only to be posthumously enshrined without that ultimate satisfaction. Think of people like Ron Santo of the Cubs, or maybe Josh Gibson, thought by some to be the best power hitter ever. So when viewed from that perspective, one could say that good fortune smiled upon Earle Combs. He was born in 1899, was finally voted in by the Veterans Committee in 1970, and for the final six years of his life he felt the same prestige accorded to so much of the fabled Murderers' Row.

In hindsight, Bernie Williams is more deserving than Combs in the Hall of Fame, as are many other center fielders not presently enshrined. Williams ranks 26th all-time among center fielders with a 43.6 JAWS (Jay Jaffe's key starting point in my own ballot-checking process), compared to Combs, who ranks 38th at 38.4. Williams won four rings and Combs three, and, in Williams's case, it was a harder path because of such a mine-filled postseason structure. But a Hall plaque is a Hall plaque, and Combs's visage appears on one in the ultimate gallery.

"It was the last thing I expected," Combs said upon learning of the Veterans Committee's decision. "I thought the game was for superstars, not just average players like me."

Combs was blessed with that kind of humility, a trademark of his life, so those words would not be so much a belittlement of himself as they would a pure example of his gentlemanly, modest manner. He made others feel at ease and was guided through life by the Bible. His straight-arrow and likeable character surely deserved credit, especially given some of his surrounding cast and the times in which he played, as baseball came back in the 1920s from gambling and roared through Prohibition. He was inducted as a "good guy," as the best leadoff hitter of his time, as the table setter for the greatest team in history. It was respect by association, in his case. So let's leave it at that, knowing he timed it right and felt peer-group satisfaction while he was alive, and knowing he started a long line of center field glory for the Yankees.

"They wouldn't pay baseball managers much a salary if they all presented as few problems as did Earle Combs," said Babe Ruth, the ultimate contrasting figure who played beside him in the outfield and drove him in for runs over so many summers. "[He] was more than a good ballplayer. He was always a first-class gentleman."

"If you had nine men like Combs on your ball club," added their manager, Joe McCarthy, "you could go to bed every night and sleep like a baby."

Combs was from Pebworth, Kentucky, one of six children from a hill-farming family. He desperately wanted to play baseball, but after attending Eastern Kentucky State Normal School (now Eastern Kentucky University), he taught instead in the tiny Kentucky hill town of Ida May. There were 40 students in his one-room schoolhouse, ages 6 – 16.

"It wasn't much of a school, and I wasn't such a hot teacher," Combs said. "But we had a swell ball team and I was an excellent player/manager. Those kids played ball morning, noon and night, whether they wanted to or not. . . . I had the whole class, including girls, shagging baseballs."

The teacher would soon become the student. Combs started playing for the local team in Harlan, Kentucky, batting .444. He caught the eye of the Louisville Colonels of the American Association and was signed, but he made several errors in his debut and the last one lost the game. McCarthy was managing that Louisville team and saw Combs's concern that he might not belong. "Look, if I didn't think you belong in center field on this club, I wouldn't put you there," McCarthy told him. "And I'm going to keep you there."

Combs responded the way his own students might have to such positive reinforcement, tracking fly balls with aplomb and batting .365 with 118 extra base hits across two seasons with Louisville. But he was not through being instructed by future Hall of Fame skippers. In 1924, the Yankees bought Combs for $50,000 and two players, and Miller Huggins had a long talk with him upon arrival at Spring Training. Combs had been called "The Mail Carrier" at Louisville because of his speed on the bases, but Huggins made it clear he wanted someone who could simply get on base and then wait for the sluggers to knock him in.

"Up here we will call you the Waiter," Huggins finished.

What little ego Combs might have brought with him was immediately set aside, and the rookie went on to fulfill Hug's request and then some. Sixteen would be his highest stolen-base total in any season after that, as Murderers' Row emerged and evolved. Combs walked 65 times his first full season (1925), and that would be about average for him. He also had 203 hits in his first full season, and scored 117 runs. It would be the first of eight consecutive seasons with triple-digit run production from him, and that was usually a formula for Yankee success. The lefty batter was quick down the line and often beat out infield hits or sprayed them around the outfield.

Leading off for the nonpareil 1927 Yankees, "The Kentucky Colonel" led the Majors in hits with 231, and that would remain the most by any Yankee until Don Mattingly broke his record in 1986 with 238. Combs also led everyone in 1927 with 23 triples, 726 plate appearances and 648 at-bats. In that year's World Series, he was 5-for-16 and scored six runs as that team swept the Pirates for his first ring. A typical example of his impact came in Game Three as the series shifted to Yankee Stadium; Combs led off the bottom of the first with a single off Lee Meadows, and scored with Mark Koenig as Lou Gehrig hit the decisive two-run triple right away.

NOTABLE HALL OF FAMERS WHO PLAYED FOR THE YANKEES

Tim Raines: Although he was no longer an everyday player for the Yankees following a trade from the White Sox in December of 1995, it was with the Yankees that he received his only two World Series rings as a player. Ask any Yankee from that era, and they'll tell you he was a key cog. As for Charlie Hayes catching the final out of the 1996 World Series: "In that moment, I went into another world where my baseball life flashed before me . . . it filled me with satisfaction to know that my wait was about to end."

Randy Johnson: Big Unit already was 41 when he was traded to the Yankees prior to the 2005 season, but he had finished either first or second in the NL Cy Young voting in five of past six seasons. He had a solid 2005 season (17-8, 3.79 ERA, 1.13 WHIP, 211 K in 225.2 innings), scuffled in 2006 and went back to Arizona. "I had no remorse coming here," he said of New York after being inducted. "I enjoyed every moment of it. I know it might be hard for people to believe that. I enjoyed the history of the game. I never imagined doing any of the things that I did."

Phil Niekro: Played two seasons in New York but had one of his greatest career moments in what would be his final game as a Yankee. At age 45, he tossed a four-hit shutout against the Blue Jays in Exhibition Stadium for his 300th career win. Interestingly, he didn't break out his signature knuckleball until the final batter of the game. "I figured if there's any way I'm going to win my 300th game by striking the guy out, I was going to do it with the pitch that won the first game for me."

Johnny Mize: Although he is better known for his years as a perennial All-Star slugger for the Cardinals and Giants, Mize won five straight World Series titles for the Yankees from 1949-53. He provided value as a part-time player, with his best year coming in 1950, when he hit 25 home runs with 72 RBIs in just 274 at bats. Mize retired after 1953 at age 40, saying "I'd rather quit when they're still applauding me than hang around until they start to boo." Upon his retirement, the *Eugene Register-Guard* credited Mize as "the Yankee hero of the 1952 World Series." In that series, he went 6-for-15 (.400) with three homers and six RBIs.

Dazzy Vance: One of the most interesting careers of any Hall of Famer, he went from minor league journeyman to one of the greatest strikeout artists. The Midwest-raised right-hander pitched just eight games for the Yankees in 1915 before injuries took over. He bounced around the minors for the next few years, returned briefly to New York in 1918 but was quickly sold to Sacramento. Vance would not win a big league game until age 31, but finished his career with 197 of them and led the NL in strikeouts and K/9 in each of his first seven years with Brooklyn. The Yankees had no idea what they were giving up at the time. He was the first real Hall of Fame campaign case, requiring 17 BBWAA ballots before finally being elected in 1955.

Wade Boggs/Rickey Henderson: Each of them made four All-Star teams in their five years in pinstripes, and Boggs famously rode horseback around the field after the 1996 title.

Combs batted leadoff in 1,059 of the 1,334 games he started as a Yankee, and he was such a mainstay at the top of the order that he was given jersey number one in 1929. Billy Martin would be honored with the number's retirement in Monument Park, yet here was a future Hall of Famer who was the first one to wear it and through considerable success.

As a matter of fact, Combs was officially the first Yankee to wear any uniform number, because that 1929 season was the first one that began with numbers on the back in baseball. Numbers were assigned in the order of the Yankees' usual batting order, helping radio broadcasters. New York's Opening Day game was rained out, and the Indians, who were also adopting the practice, played that day and thus became the first official team to open a season with numbers. The Yankees debuted numbers two days later, with Combs leading off for the Yankees and wearing number one.

Many people remembered Combs for the way his 12-year career with the Yankees came to a fateful end. In July of 1934, Harlond Clift of the St. Louis Browns drove a fly to the left-field bleacher wall at Sportsman's Park, and Combs was running at full speed to make the catch when he crashed violently into the green concrete. He collapsed unconscious, suffering a fractured skull. Combs spent more than two months in hospitals, and doctors feared he might not make it. He tried to come back in 1935 but broke his collarbone in the middle of the season.

That was the end of the road for Combs as a player, but it was hardly the end of his impact with the Yankees. His most pivotal role may have come right after that, as he joined the coaching staff of his two-time manager, McCarthy. The 1936 season marked the arrival of Joe DiMaggio, and Combs was there to mentor him starting at Spring Training and through his rookie year. "If this boy does as well as you," Yankees general manager Ed Barrow wrote in a letter to Combs, "I'll be satisfied."

It would start a wave of standout center fielders for the franchise. There was Combs, then DiMaggio, then Mickey Mantle, then Bobby Murcer on down the line to Bernie.

Combs was still teaching, after all. He coached for the Yankees from 1936 – 44. He won six more World Series as a coach, so that meant nine rings in all. Combs retired in March of 1953 after 32 years as a player and coach. The last position he held was as a coach for the 1952 Red Sox. Lou Boudreau, who was the manager on that coaching staff, said, "I am sorry to see him leave. There is no finer gentleman than Earle and we'll all miss him."

Ironically, the same Lou Boudreau would be elected by the BBWAA in 1970, and Combs would be one of three extras added by the Veterans Committee for that induction ceremony, along with Ford Frick and Jesse Haines. Combs never had received more than 16 percent of the Hall vote in any BBWAA election, but he had been an integral part of a Yankee team that epitomized winning, and as Pee Wee Reese would note after Combs's passing, "I never heard anyone say an unkind word about him."

Combs became the fifth and final member of those 1927 Yankees to be inducted. Many people felt it would be incomplete without him, although modern analysis would cause considerable second-guessing. Joe Cronin, president of the AL at the time of Combs's election, said it best:

"He was the table-setter for Ruth and Gehrig. He was always on base, it seemed, when they'd hit a homer."

Paul Krichell

There have been efforts in the past to have Paul Krichell inducted in the Hall of Fame, notably by Birdie Tebbetts in the 1980s. Scouts were considered ineligible, despite the presence of front-office execs in the plaque Gallery. Here's hoping someone will make another try for Krichell, a former St. Louis Browns catcher whom Ed Barrow brought with him when he came to the Yankees from Boston in the 1920s. Krichell played a pivotal role in Yankee success as chief scout until 1957, and here are notable figures who caught his attention:

Whitey Ford: He played a good amount of both first base and pitcher in his high school days, but it was Krichell who helped him develop into a Major League pitcher. Krichell believed Ford, five feet, six inches at the time, lacked the size to be a power-hitting slugger but helped him develop a curveball after recognizing his strong arm and urged him to focus on pitching.

Lou Gehrig: The first big prize Krichell earned the Yankees. "I saw another Ruth today," Krichell proclaimed after seeing Gehrig play for Columbia in a game against Rutgers in 1923. Already impressed with the young slugger, Krichell then saw Gehrig crush a mammoth homer against Penn, and the Yankees signed the Iron Horse that April.

Hank Greenberg: The greatest player that Krichell pursued but failed to sign. Interested in the idea of marketing a Jewish superstar, Krichell went as far as bringing Greenberg to watch a game at Yankee Stadium. "I was a slugging first baseman and the Yankees had the greatest in Lou Gehrig," Greenberg said. "So I chose Detroit."

Charlie Keller: Krichell is credited with inking him to a contract out of the University of Maryland. Keller, who played 11 years in pinstripes between 1939 and 1952 (with one year of military service and two years with the Tigers mixed in), was consistently overshadowed by the Yankees' parade of superstars, but his career certainly warrants strong appreciation. The left-handed-hitting outfielder slugged 189 homers in just 3,790 career at bats and authored a lifetime .286/.410/.518 slash line with an incredible 152 OPS+ that ranks 29th all-time and sixth among all eligible players not in the Hall of Fame.

Tony Lazzeri: He was the talk of Minor League baseball in 1925, hitting 60 homers and driving in 227 runs in 197 games for the Salt Lake Bees of the PCL. Bob Connery, president of the Yankees' St. Paul farm team, said of Lazzeri: "He's the greatest thing I've ever seen." Krichell shared the same sentiment, urging Barrow to sign the Italian-American second basemen despite his epilepsy.

Phil Rizzuto: Krichell first obtained a report on him when Scooter was still a high schooler in the early 1930s. Rizzuto later attended a one-week baseball school held by the prestigious scout at Yankee Stadium, and Rizzuto made the final cut from 60 to 20 players. Impressed with his speed, Krichell asked if Rizzuto wanted to play pro ball. "I said 'Sure, where are the papers?'" He was not old enough to sign, so his father signed for him.

Joe McCarthy: The legendary Yankee manager was out as Cubs skipper after the 1930 season, but while he was in Philadelphia watching that year's World Series between the A's and the Cardinals, McCarthy was approached in the grandstand by Krichell and told that Col. Jacob Ruppert wanted to see him the next day in his office. "That was the first inkling I had that the Yankees were interested," McCarthy would say later. Krichell was more a messenger in this instance, but another sign of his omnipresence.

Casey Stengel: The scout was not only a good talent evaluator, but an astute judge of managers as well. It was Krichell's recommendation to Barrow that led to the signing of Stengel to manage the club following the 1948 season. Barrow sang the praises of Krichell, declaring that Krichell was "the best judge of baseball players I ever saw."

Casey Stengel

American life was changing rapidly in the postwar days of 1948. Babe Ruth passed away on August 16 of that year, and many Yankee fans mourned the loss of a big part of their youth. New Yorkers gathered around their new RCA 630-TS, the first mass-produced television set that had been sold in the prior two years, to watch Milton Berle's *Texaco Star Theater* on NBC or Ed Sullivan's *Toast of the Town* on CBS or *Candid Microphone* (later *Candid Camera*) on ABC. Scrabble, the 33 rpm record and the transistor radio were new on the scene. People entrenched, built homes and families, bought appliances and welcomed a new normal.

Part of that "normal," of course, was the continued expectation that the New York Yankees would dominate Major League Baseball the way they had always known. The club won one title from 1944 – 48, and for any other franchise, that would have been cool beans. Not for the Yankees. They had returned to title form in 1947 under new manager Bucky Harris, but 1948 brought a third-place finish. Even though the Yankees were 94 – 60 and surged to finish only 2 ½ games behind the eventual champion Indians, third place was third place.

Harris was fired amid a reported rift with George Weiss, the Yankees' general manager who had been denied Harris's own home telephone number as a show of independence by the skipper. Imagine Billy Martin doing that to George Steinbrenner! Conversely, Weiss knew he had a good relationship with a journeyman Major League outfielder named Casey Stengel whose knowledge for the game he admired.

They went back to their days in the Eastern League, when Weiss ran the New Haven club and Casey managed Worcester for the Braves. In 1945, when he was vice president and head of the Yankees' farm system, Weiss had given Stengel the managing job of the Kansas City minor league club. They had stayed in touch as friends, and Weiss had lobbied each year for new Yankees owners Dan Topping and Del Webb to consider his unique candidate as the best person to continue Joe McCarthy's winning ways. Finally, as GM following the departure of Larry MacPhail, Weiss convinced them.

"Fly right to New York," Webb told Stengel over the phone in a call from the World Series in Cleveland. "We want you to manage the Yankees."

In California, Casey's wife Edna had just retired from her estate business. She hoped he wasn't serious about going through with the signing, and he promised that it would be for just "one year." He signed a two-year contract.

"Edna, I had to," he told her. "I owe it to myself to prove that I'm a better manager than they've given me credit for. I have to prove that I can win in the majors. I have that confidence in myself. But I have to prove it to others."

Boy, did he ever. On October 12, 1948, Stengel was announced as manager of the Bronx Bombers, and the move was met with mostly shock and skepticism—by fans, by the press, by the roster he would inherit. *Why Casey Stengel?* He had managed from 1934 – 43, and not once in those seven seasons had a team finished in the first division. The only team in that run that finished .500 or better was the 1938 Boston Bees with a 77 – 75 mark good for fifth place. Such a record would not normally lead to further consideration at *any* point in baseball history, much less by the franchise that was synonymous with world championships and first-division finishes. He was an NL lifer, he had a "clown" reputation, he seemed old (58), and so on. But, hey, his Oakland Oaks had just won the Pacific Coast League crown in 1948 and Weiss had his bosses on board.

Casey Stengel helping the Brooklyn Robins to the 1916 World Series.

On top of all that, Stengel arrived with a strategy of platooning players and matching up his starting pitchers against specific opponents instead of a normal rotation.

Five World Series championships in his first five years was pretty good proof. Stengel won 10 pennants and seven World Series with the Yankees. It didn't take long for the doubting Thomases to back down and hail his platooning system as revolutionary, even if he still had occasional detractors inside and outside the clubhouse.

"The pivotal thing about Casey is the very first year as manager of the Yankees," said Marty Appel, the longtime Yankee publicist who penned the bestselling biography of Stengel in 2017. "Because there had been so much talk about him being a clown and 'What were they thinking hiring this guy?' Then they won the pennant after the great 1949 race with Boston and they won that World Series and it just shut everyone up. All the critics said, 'I guess this guy is good after all.' For Casey, he had been happy managing in the Pacific Coast League and living in California, but I know he thought when given the chance to manage the Yankees: 'This is my chance to win with really good players.'"

Appel was strolling through a blossomy Central Park one

spring day when we spoke by phone about the subject of that latest book. He was right across from the Essex House, where Stengel lived for eight years. I asked him what it was like to approach a biography about such an iconic and complex figure whose baseball career spanned so many decades and touched so many.

"First of all, it was obvious to me that nobody under 40 had even heard of the guy, let alone tell you of his accomplishments," Appel said. "Attention spans aren't the same nowadays.

"The idea came from my editor at Doubleday, who saw on MLB Network that Casey was selected as the greatest character in MLB history when they used to do that Prime Nine ranking segment. So they called me and asked, 'Would you be interested in this book as a subject?' My first reaction was that Bob Creamer's book on Casey was one of my favorite books—how can I do better? My editor said to think about it, because it's been thirty years since his book and that's not unusual for an important subject to get refreshed. I figured Bob didn't have a lot of research material in the early eighties that was available online now. Then the family found out I was working on the project, and they gave me Edna Stengel's unpublished memoir from 1958, and that was a wealth of information. Bob was a good friend of mine, and I would say, 'Bob, I'm not going to try to better you now, I'm just going to try to supplement it.'"

Charles Dillon Stengel was born on July 30, 1890, in Kansas City, Mo. That was two summers after the publication of Ernest Thayer's immortal poem, "Casey at the Bat: A Ballad of the Republic Sung in the Year 1888." Stengel explained in his 1962 autobiography that his nickname of "Casey" was a result not only of his hometown initials, but also because of the popularization of Thayer's work and just how often Mighty Casey had struck out. He had been Charlie as a youth and through high school, and the two nicknames soon followed. Stengel said "K.C." evolved into "Casey" as writers began calling him "strikeout Casey" after the poem verse, citing his penchant for whiffs early in his career.

HOF ARTIFACT INVENTORY

Game-used equipment in the Baseball Hall of Fame:

CASEY STENGEL

B-124.64	Last baseball from the Polo Grounds, signed by Casey Stengel.
B-473.53	Yankees shirt, 1952.
B-475.53	Yankees cap worn as manager.
B-268.78	Shoes.
B-269.78	Mets road uniform shirt worn as manager in 1962.
B-271.78	Uniform shirt worn at Old-Timers' Day.
B-274.78	Navy blue cap worn with all the insignia of the ball clubs he was associated with during his career. Worn with Old-Timers' Day uniform.
B-275.78	New York Giants uniform from 1924 European Tour.
B-277.78	Mets blazer (sports coat) worn as manager in 1962.
B-278.78	Royal blue & orange Mets jacket.
B-279.78	Yankees jacket.
B-228.66	Shoes.
B-2846.63	Shoes.

In hindsight, he deserves more credit than that. His .404 on-base percentage for the 1914 Brooklyn Robins actually led the Majors. Stengel played his entire 14-year career (1912 – 25) in the National League, a left-handed hitter with a closed stance and some pop, and a good glove used primarily in right field by Brooklyn, Pittsburgh, Philadelphia, New York and Boston. While Joe McCarthy's absence of Major League playing was so glaring that it literally led the blurb on his Hall of Fame plaque, Stengel was more like old Miller Huggins, someone who had learned first-hand on the front lines and used the knowledge to his advantage as a manager.

Stengel's slash line was .284/.356/.410, and his WAR on Baseball Reference was 20.1, putting him at 117th all-time among right fielders as of 2018, around Nick Swisher and Andre Ethier territory. Stengel had a career 120 OPS+, 1,219 hits, 60 homers and 131 stolen bases—a good guy to have on your team. Now consider his postseason experience and the likely street cred that those three World Series would carry as a manager.

In 1916, Stengel appeared in four of the five games for Brooklyn, a bright spot (4-for-11 with two runs) as the Robins were beaten by the Red Sox; he sat out all 14 innings of Game Two as a Boston starter named Babe Ruth pitched all 14 innings for the win.

The Giants and Yankees met in the World Series each year from 1921 – 23. Stengel's postseason highlight—and maybe his ultimate highlight as a player—came in Game Three of the 1923 World Series, when he provided the only run with a homer off Sad Sam Jones that soared over Ruth's head in right. He thumbed his nose at the Yankees' bench as he rounded third, drawing a subsequent fine from Commissioner Kenesaw Mountain Landis.

"One of the things I learned in doing the book, he was a much better player than I had thought," Appel said. "If they had All-Star Games in his day, he would have been an All-Star two or three times. There was one time when Mickey Mantle looked at Casey, who taught him how to play balls off the Ebbets Field wall, and he said, 'You, old man, *you* were a player?' It was almost the same revelation to me too, because Casey was a good player. I put a picture in the book of him being escorted off the field by cops at the Polo Grounds, because it showed how athletic he looked, with his muscular upper body and a big chest. It wasn't at all what we remember of this crooked-shaped old man."

Stengel managed the Yankees until 1960, and Mantle was on his last 10 squads, overlapping with the great Joe DiMaggio at the start. Yogi Berra, Whitey Ford, Phil Rizzuto and Elston Howard were among the many legends who racked up one ring after another under The Old Perfessor's command. His cutting-edge style of platooning may not have been for everyone, but everyone who had an issue with it was either shipped out or forced to deal with it. Joe Maddon would be a strong modern-day comparison, with his revolutionary shifts and his entertaining and amusing interaction with insiders and outsiders. Stengel was a trend-setter.

When Stengel had played for the Boston Braves, he had grown familiar with the art of platooning—often being platooned himself. He brought the strategy, popular in the 19th century, back into the forefront of his managerial identity. Stengel often would deploy a right-handed hitter against a left-handed pitcher and vice-versa—standard practice today.

"I never saw a man who juggled his lineup so much and who played so many hunches so successfully," said Connie Mack, the all-time leader in managerial wins.

Stengel also took relief pitching to a next level and set a foundation for future specialists. He used Joe Page in 60 games and Page recorded 27 saves, five more than any previous hurler. Ford probably would have won many games had he started in a four-man rotation like so many other pitching staffs, but Stengel lined him up for just the right opponents, hence the pivotal moment in Ford's section of this book.

Unlike most managers, Stengel had no qualms about upsetting players. He went with the hot hand, and he could rely on the fact that the Yankees had a strong front office and were fully capable of finding adequate replacements whenever a particular player did not perform up to expectations.

"The secret of managing is to keep the five guys who hate you away from the guys who are undecided," Stengel said.

His best team was actually in 1954 when the Yankees went 103 – 51 (.669) but finished eight games behind a Cleveland powerhouse that folded in the World Series against the Giants. Stengel's Yankee teams won at least 92 games and finished a minimum of 30 games above .500 in 11 of 12 seasons at the helm. He won 1,149 games, a .623 clip. His number 37 would be retired by both the Yankees and Mets.

It took a long time for Appel, and probably many others, to get over Stengel's firing by the Yankees after the 1960 season, when his team finished 40 games over .500 and won another pennant, losing to Pittsburgh on Bill Mazeroski's freak Game Seven walk-off homer. Stengel liked to say that he made the mistake of turning 70, a point well made.

"Being a Baby Boomer myself, he was my childhood manager," said Appel, who was the youngest MLB public relations to date when George Steinbrenner elevated him to the post in 1973. "So when he got fired in 1960, it was really like losing a father figure. I remember my thoughts at age twelve. I thought, 'They are out of their mind. How are they ever going to win another game? Casey was genius of all this!' That was one of my first impactful moments as a baseball fan in a sad and negative way.

"Maybe somebody will write that about Joe Girardi one day. It was like, 'Welcome to real life, guys get fired.'"

Stengel and Weiss both have plaques in the Hall of Fame, and in both cases it was largely because of that pivotal stretch in 1948 – 49 when Weiss persuaded his bosses to take a chance on a man who "proved it to others," just as he had told Edna he would. Stengel remains the all-time leader in several managerial categories, including World Series appearances (10), World Series games managed (64), World Series victories (37) and World Series titles (10, tied with McCarthy). And, of course, Casey left us all of those great Stengelese gems.

Billy Martin

"**I may not have** been the greatest Yankee to ever put on the uniform," Billy Martin said on the day the team retired his number one jersey and unveiled his plaque in Monument Park, "but I was the proudest."

One could not analyze the most pivotal moments of Martin's Yankees career without dividing it between Billy the second baseman and Billy the manager. He played an instrumental role in multiple World Series titles while in both capacities, and in both cases his fervent pride and his fiery passion were a combustible combination that took him repeatedly up and down.

Billy the Player

Jerry Coleman went off to serve in Korea early in the 1952 season, opening the second base position for Martin. He had played for Casey Stengel in 1947 and '48 on the Oakland Oaks teams in the Pacific Coast League, and now that Stengel was managing the Yankees, he wanted his fiery infielder in the lineup. The next time you visit Monument Park, pay special attention to the big words "CASEY'S BOY" right under Martin's name on his plaque.

In parts of seven seasons with the Yankees, Martin batted .262 with 449 hits and 220 runs, earning one All-Star selection in 1956. He was an average player at best over that time, but Stengel loved Martin's makeup, whatever off-field bravado it carried with it. Most importantly, Martin was someone who rose to the occasion in October.

In the bottom of the seventh inning in Game Seven of the 1952 World Series, Jackie Robinson stepped to the plate with the bases loaded and two outs, Brooklyn down 4 – 2. Robinson skied a high popup on the infield that hung in the air a long time. The wind was blowing the ball back toward home plate and Yankees first baseman Joe Collins—just into the game for defense—appeared to lose the ball in the sun. Martin came all the way from second base to lunge and catch the ball in full sprint, saving Collins and allowing the Yankees to get out of the inning unscathed. Without Martin bailing out Collins, the game surely would have been tied and the Dodgers very well could have taken the lead in the inning. The Yankees held on by a score of 4 – 2 and clinched their 15th World Series title. Biographer David Falkner referred to Martin's hustling grab as "one of the great moments in World Series history."

BEST SECOND BASEMEN

Rankings of all-time Yankee second basemen are all over the place, so this top five is going to be very subjective. I put extra weight on modern analytics and less on mystique and rings.

1. Robinson Cano: He struggled through his first seven games in 2005 with a .087 average, and despite the small sample the press was ready to pounce. Harvey Araton wrote in the *Times*: "To the right (of shortstop Derek Jeter), uncertainty reigns in the presence of Cano, a rookie hitting .087." Cano not only proved that his slow start was a fluke, but also that he was one of the 10 best second basemen in Major League history.

Cano's fluid quickness on the field and his signature across-the-body throw to first on a grounder up the middle only complemented his powerful bat. He is one of only 16 players with a career .300 average, 2,000 hits, 1,000 runs, 500 doubles, 300 homers and 1,000 RBIs, joining an elite group that includes Babe Ruth, Lou Gehrig, Hank Aaron, Willie Mays and Stan Musial.

The Dominican was a fixture at second base in the Bronx for the next eight years. He was durable, playing in at least 159 games every Yankee season except his rookie year and 2006, when he missed more than a month on the DL. The perennial All-Star led the Yankees to a 2009 world championship and bolted for free agency after the 2013 season.

With a number seven all-time ranking among MLB second basemen according to JAWS—and probable top-five ranking before he's done—Cano's place in Cooperstown was secure going into 2018. Then he failed a drug test for steroids and was suspended for 80 games, a sign of the times in Hall voting stability. Just like that, he goes from a first-ballot selection to a probable no-way. My own voting policy clearly states that I will consider any deserving candidate before the MLB Joint Drug Prevention and Treatment Program (ie Barry Bonds and Roger Clemens) but not for those punished after it became institutionalized, so Cano, dontchaknow, sadly will be there beside Alex Rodriguez and Manny Ramirez watching year after year go by on the ballot.

Having said that, Cano is still head and shoulders above any second baseman in Yankees history and by all accounts passed a whole lot of drug tests before going to Seattle.

2. Joe Gordon: "Flash" was "renowned for superb defensive range" and combined "acrobatic" agility with "tremendous power," according to the Hall of Fame plaque. What more can you ask for in a second baseman? If only he had played longer with the Yankees, Gordon would top this list. He appeared on six All-Star teams as a Yankee before being traded to Cleveland for Allie Reynolds right after the 1946 season, then helped Cleveland to the 1948 title.

Gordon replaced another Hall of Famer, Tony Lazzeri, at second base and became one of the premiere offensive players at his position. He averaged 22 homers per season with the Yankees and won the 1942 AL MVP Award with a .322/.409/.491 slash line. He is still eighth all-time in homers as a second baseman despite missing two seasons serving in World War II and retiring at age 35. At the time of his retirement, only Rogers Hornsby was ahead of him.

3. Tony Lazzeri: Poosh 'Em Up spent 12 years with the Yankees in the Babe Ruth era and established himself as one of the best offensive second basemen in history up to that point. A five-time World Champion in New York, Lazzeri was a key part of the lineup in many of those series:

1932	.294 BA	2 HR	5 RBIs
1936	.250 BA	1 HR	7 RBIs
1937	.400 BA	1 HR	.526 OBP

As a Yankee, Lazzeri hit an impressive .292 with 169 homers and 1,157 runs. The first great Italian player in the Majors brought excellent leadership (mentoring key figures like Joe DiMaggio), and you can't argue with five rings. He played 1,457 games at second, 165 at third and 89 at short, often moving around. That's no knock on him (in fact more of a value), but if we're talking best second basemen in Yankee history, he's a few spots down.

4. Willie Randolph: I was tempted to bump up Randolph right behind Cano, citing his No. 13 all-time WAR among second basemen right behind Hall of Famer Roberto Alomar, but ultimately he just lacked enough pop for that lofty status. Fourth is still amazing for this nonpareil franchise. Randolph was a fixture in New York for 13 seasons, hitting .275 with a .373 on-base percentage, beloved by fans, and playing more games at second for the club than anyone on this list.

Randolph was more than a viable bat at the top of the order, and defense was his forte. His 143.9 defensive rating on FanGraphs is best among second basemen in franchise history—and his career DEF rating of 168.2 is ninth all-time among all second basemen. He was by far the best baserunner of the five on this list, with a 17.6 BsR and 251 steals.

Randolph represented the Yankees in five of his six All-Star Game selections, and won two rings and four pennants while with the club. He was a combined 3-for-35 in the 1976 postseason, but fared a little better the next October in scoring nine combined runs as the Bombers finally won another title. He was injured late in the 1978 season, so Brian Doyle heroically took his place. The Yankees honored Randolph with a Monument Park plaque in 2015, part of that due to his continued popularity as the team's longtime coach through dynasty years.

> **5. Bobby Richardson:** There is a big dropoff after the top four on this list, and I give the five-time All-Star a nod over Gil McDougald, simply because the latter played so many infield positions. Richardson won eight Gold Gloves, and though he was an ordinary offensive player, he unquestionably raised his game in the postseason. He is the only player in baseball history to win the World Series MVP award as a member of the losing team, as he did in 1960.
>
> Richardson might have finished higher on this list, but he retired in his prime at the age of 31, following a fifth straight All-Star season in 1966. On that September 17, before a meaningless home game against the Twins, the guest of honor told the crowd on Bobby Richardson Day: "How lucky it has been for me to have been a Yankee."

Martin had his best season as a player for the 1953 champions, appearing in 149 out of 151 games the Yankees played. The 25-year old slashed .257/.314/.395, good for a slightly below average 94 OPS+ (his career mark was a subpar 81) while scoring 72 runs. Martin also set career highs in hits (151), doubles (24), triples (6), home runs (15), runs batted in (75), and walks (43) in the 1953 season. Again, though, his World Series impact was the highlight.

Martin hit like a one-man wrecking crew in that Fall Classic, batting .500 (12 for 24) while slugging five extra base hits (including two homers), driving in eight and scoring five times. He also tied the record (since broken) with 12 hits in a single World Series. Of anybody to reach 12 hits in a single Fall Classic, he did so in the fewest plate appearances. The Yankees continued their mastery of Brooklyn by winning in six, and he almost surely would have been named World Series MVP if not for the fact that it was invented two years later.

Martin did, however, receive the equivalent at the time. It was the Babe Ruth Memorial Award, for the best player in the World Series. Also like the Bambino, Martin won a World Series four times as a player: 1951 – 53 and 1956. The commonality was apropos, inasmuch as they are literally beside one another for all eternity.

"Look at him. He doesn't look like a great player—but he is a helluva player," Stengel said of Martin. "Try to find something he can't do. You can't."

Billy the Manager

Martin was a manager for parts of 16 Major League seasons, including five stints with the Yankees. (See: George Steinbrenner.) His combined record was 556 – 385 (.591) in parts of eight seasons as Yankee manager, celebrating two AL pennants and the 1977 World Series title.

When Martin took over the Yankees job on August 2, 1975, the Yankees were a franchise desperate to get back to their glory days. It had been 13 years since their last World Series championship—an eternity for this franchise—and 11 seasons since their last postseason appearance, a Game Seven loss to the Cardinals in 1964. The Yankees had finished no higher than fifth in the AL for the next four seasons, and they finished above fourth place just twice in the divisional era, which began in 1969.

Martin and the Yankees finished just six games above .500 in 1975, but they jumped to 97 victories and a pennant in his first full season as manager of the club. The Bombers won their 21st World Series championship in 1977 under his leadership, complete with plenty of tabloid drama and one Fenway Park scuffle along the way (see: Reggie Jackson).

The Yankees repeated as champions in 1978, but Martin was not around to enjoy the celebration. He resigned under fire that July, thus ending his first of five terms as manager. Steinbrenner hired him a second time in June of 1979, but canned him a second time at the end of that season due to Martin's fight with a marshmallow salesman outside a hotel bar in Minnesota.

The third term was 1983, as Martin managed the Yankees the entire season but was then fired due to growing unrest among his players, not to mention a steady soap opera between Steinbrenner and the team's best player (see: Dave Winfield).

Martin managed a fourth time from April 1985 through the end of that season. He was deposed after another bar fight, this time with pitcher Ed Whitson, who sustained a broken rib and split lip. "We just can't have him getting into these things every two months," Steinbrenner said. "It's not good for organized baseball."

The fifth and final act of the Shakespeare tragedy lasted from Opening Day to June of the 1988 season. "All I know is [as Yankees manager], I pass people on the street these days, and they don't know whether to say hello or goodbye," Martin said.

Bucky Dent developed under Martin and called him "a true Yankee—one of the truest ever. He always said he wanted to die a Yankee. He was his own man. He was fiery and he could be charming. He was a great manager."

Martin is buried roughly a game of pepper away from Babe Ruth's grave at the Gate of Heaven cemetery in Westchester County. Not to compare them as players, but they both lived hard and by their own credo, and they are remembered for their success and excess.

Andy Pettitte

Andy Pettitte retired in 2013 as MLB's all-time postseason leader with 19 wins, 276 2/3 innings pitched and 44 games started. He was the definition of a postseason ace, and out of respect for every Whitey Ford fan out there we will just add the quick disclaimer that the postseason consisted only of a World Series for most of the game's history. The point is, Yankee fans came to rely on Pettitte for a generation as the one typically with the ball for a Game One.

That is how Joe Torre remembers him, and his best memory of the left-hander goes back to October of 1996. With Torre at the helm as manager for the first season, the Yankees were back in the Fall Classic for the first time in 15 years. Pettitte had busted out in his second season with a 21 – 8 record and 162 strikeouts, finishing just behind Toronto's Pat Hentgen in the AL Cy Young race. Pettitte was the natural choice to start the opener for Torre, and it was a jubilant scene at packed Yankee Stadium. It was new people but like old times.

Then Pettitte allowed Atlanta seven quick earned runs in just 2 1/3 innings of a 12 – 1 loss. I sat out in the auxiliary press box on those back-to-back nights as the Yankees fell behind 2 – 0 at home, hardly an indication of a dynasty to come.

"With Andy, I'll go right to the start, 1996," Torre said. "Game One, he gets murdered against the Braves. The fact of the matter is, he comes back in Game Five and pitches a one-oh gem, eight and a third innings. So when you consider it's the

World Series, you're going from your home field for Game One to the visiting ballpark in Game Five, he knew right away how he dealt with pressure."

Torre told me that while I was covering one of his annual Safe at Home Foundation gala red-carpet sessions in 2014. He happened to be honoring Pettitte that night. Andy was listening to Torre share that memory, and then he jumped in with his own version of it:

"I had just come off pitching against Baltimore and pitching real well for us to get to the World Series," Pettitte jumped in. "Then to lose Game One the way I did, it was just a major disappointment in my life. For Joe to handpick me when he could have picked any of the other four guys to start Game Five, and to be able to come back in Atlanta and throw a shutout, that was huge. I was able to fall back on that the whole rest of my career. Even when I struggled in the playoffs or had a bad game here and there, I was always able to look back and say, 'Hang on, you pitched horrible in Game One.'"

That was the pivotal moment in Pettitte's career, setting the stage for a long string of success. He finished 256 – 153 for a brilliant .626 winning percentage. He tied Ford for most games started by a Yankee pitcher with 438, and passed Ford at the end for most strikeouts by a Yankee pitcher with 2,020. Because he chose to return home to Houston for that 2004 – 06 stint to be near his family and reunite with fellow Texan Roger Clemens, Pettitte finished third instead of first on the Yankees' all-time win list, with 219 (Ford had 236 and Red Ruffing 231). Some of those aforementioned all-time postseason pitching records came with the Astros. But take away those three years in Houston, and one 18-win season would have ultimately resulted in a number one on the all-time Yankee wins list.

But make no mistake, when the Hall of Fame ballot discussion cranks up, Pettitte's case will center around his postseason glory. There were so many unforgettable moments. There was his near-shutout in Game Two of the 2003 World Series against the Marlins, temporarily righting a ship. There was his

MVP performance in the 2001 ALCS against a 116-win Seattle powerhouse, with two big victories to lead the way.

There also was his clinching win in Game Six of the 2009 World Series against Philadelphia, good for his fifth ring. That made him the first pitcher ever to win a clinching game in three series during the same postseason. He should not be penalized for the fact that he had more postseason opportunities than a Ford or a Ruffing; quite the opposite, in fact. He rose to the occasion and used the modern playoff structure to his advantage as the master of it.

"When you consider that he won his first world championship in ninety-six and just happened to be around in 2009 to win another one is pretty remarkable," Torre said. "I'm not sure how much consideration he'll get for the Hall of Fame, but if people pay attention to postseason performances, he can go to the top of the list. He's been remarkable in how he's handled the pressure of postseason, especially in the city of New York, which is not easy to do."

Pettitte will have my vote when he appears on the Hall of Fame ballot this winter. Obviously he is not a slam-dunk like Mo Rivera, but he is deserving. Not only do I feel he is deserving, but I also would simply want to do my part to help avoid what happened to Jorge Posada. It was a joke that the longtime Yankee catcher was a one-and-done in his first year of ballot eligibility, and they were both in the Core Four. I am sure Pettitte will become a yearly subject of debate who will gradually get in, especially when considering that he admitted to PED use and some voters will hold that against him early based on voting history. So writing this in the summer of 2018 my expectation is a check for Pettitte in his first year of eligibility and then a lot of talk.

Brian Cashman

There are five Yankee executives in the Hall of Fame: Ed Barrow (1953), Larry MacPhail (1978), George Weiss (1977), Lee MacPhail (1998) and Col. Jacob Ruppert (2013). The first step in making it a half-dozen is the obvious enshrinement of George Steinbrenner, whose contributions to the game and all the championships far outweigh the tabloid dramas. Then there is the case of Brian Cashman, especially considering the 2017 induction of his contemporary in Atlanta, John Schuerholz, whose teams always contended but won a title only once. Cashman has a strong case as well, and a title in the Aaron Judge era should clinch it for Cashman.

"Cash" started from humble beginnings. After other colleges rejected him, he was offered a starting position on Catholic University of America's Division III baseball team in Washington. At the time he enrolled, there were no beds left, and he slept in the dorm hallways. He would graduate as the school's single-season hits leader.

In 1986, Cashman's father had pull with Steinbrenner and got his son an internship with the Yankees. There he spent long hours doing everything from transcribing reports to running errands for The Boss and working stadium security, and he moved up to baseball operations in 1989 and assistant general manager in 1992. When Bob Watson stepped down from the GM position in 1998 and Cashman was recommended, Cashman allegedly spent "a half hour begging [Watson] to reconsider."

Cashman withstood an oft-tumultuous relationship with Steinbrenner, considering a departure but always staying. He has not always had full autonomy in making deals, but he has earned respect within the organization and is a rare long-term exec in this business now. Cashman became the first GM in history to win three World Series in his first three years. While the jury is out on his blockbuster acquisition of Giancarlo Stanton, here are some of Cashman's most pivotal moves:

June 29, 2000: David Justice Trade

Justice was already a well-established slugger who had extensive postseason experience with Atlanta and Cleveland. Although the Yankees would go on to win their third consecutive title, they were only three games over .500 on June 29 and sat three games behind the division-leading Blue Jays. Cashman traded three players to get Justice. Of the three, Jake Westbrook would become a mainstay in Cleveland's rotation, producing solid but unspectacular results. Justice, who already had 21 home runs on the season, hit another 20 with the Yankees and also was named ALCS MVP.

December 7, 2000: Yankees sign Mike Mussina

One of Cashman's most successful free agent signings was the hefty contract he gave to Mike Mussina. Although he was not always the flashiest pitcher in the rotation, he gave them eight solid seasons and his Hall of Fame stock keeps rising as people appreciate it more fully. He arrived in New York from Baltimore one year after the 2000 championship and retired a year before the Yankees' next title, retiring on top of his game with his first 20-win season in 2008.

February 16, 2004: A-Rod for Alfonso Soriano and Joaquin Arias

In 2004, Barry Bonds was the only better player in baseball than Alex Rodriguez. A-Rod's subsequent extension after the 2007 season produced a mix of good (2009 World Series) and bad (PED suspension), but it is hard to argue the initial trade was anything but brilliant. "Since Babe Ruth, probably the biggest move in franchise history," Cashman said. "The Boss was so proud of that one."

January 3, 2006—Yankees sign Johnny Damon

When the Yankees got Damon, it was especially sweet since they were taking him from their biggest rival, the Red Sox. With the Yankees, he had some of his best seasons and was an important part of the 2009 championship team. In four years, Damon hit .285 with 77 homers and 93 steals, while averaging more than 100 runs per season.

December 5, 2014—Didi Gregorius Trade

There were obviously big shoes to fill after Derek Jeter's retirement, and Cashman found a solid replacement. Gregorius had batted only .243 in 191 Major League games, but Cashman deserves considerable credit for rolling dice on a supposed "defense-first player". The only player New York gave up in a three-team deal with Detroit and Arizona was Shane Greene, and since the trade, Didi has filled the void and then some.

July 25, 2016—Aroldis Chapman traded for Gleyber Torres, Adam Warren and Billy McKinney

With the Yankees' playoff chances looking bleak, Cashman sold off key players at the trade deadline for the first time in his tenure. He sought to rebuild the young core and there was no better team to pull an elite prospect from than the Cubs, who were desperate for their first championship in 108 years. It worked out for the Cubs of course, but the Yankees got the best of the long-term benefit, even re-obtaining Chapman the next season, anyway.

Mickey Mantle

Phenomenon. Derived from Greek *phainomenon*, "that which appears or is seen."

At the start of the 1967 season, when he already had filled the dreams of countless young baseball fans, Mickey Mantle was asked by *Sport* magazine to choose "My Ten Greatest Baseball Memories." Number one on the list was on September 17, 1950, when an 18-year-old, fleet-footed, power-hitting, starry-eyed, All-American shortstop out of Commerce, Okla., was called up by the Yankees late in the season and greeted by Joe DiMaggio.

The Yankees had brought Mantle to St. Louis for their series against the Browns, so he could see what the big leagues were like and take pregame workouts with the Bombers. The shy teenager was ushered into the visiting clubhouse. "Mantle put on a uniform and was told to take batting practice with us," DiMaggio recalled later. "It was an unfortunate situation. Tommy Byrne was throwing. He wouldn't give his *brother* anything good to hit whether it was a game or batting practice." So Mantle was never connected with those BP pitches, even after DiMag yelled to him to "take a couple more" . . . but Joe and others could see an electric swing anyway.

"I still get a thrill every time I see Joe D," Mantle said in that *Sport* interview, during his second-to-last season, "but the first time I ever did see him and shake hands with him was a great one. It was my first big thrill with the Yankees."

Those 10 memories were presented chronologically, yet the first one also happens to be the most important one for the purposes of a book about pivotal Yankee moments. That metaphorical passing of the torch was the point at which Casey Stengel's phenomenon, or "phenom", appeared or was seen. It was the detour from a certain future in lead and zinc mines back home to the brightest lights and to mythical status. A tradition of dominance had its newest face and Mount Olympus another god. Ruth, Gehrig, DiMaggio, Mantle.

The latest legend in the line hit 536 home runs when the 500-homer club was tight, plus another 18 in the World Series to pass the Bambino for a Fall Classic record that still stands majestically today. Mantle was a three-time AL MVP, a 20-time All-Star, a Triple Crown winner in 1956. He played in pain virtually his entire 18-year career, his legs forever wrapped in bulky tape and bandage under the number seven uniform. He was a defining face of a new TV generation, from hayseed to hallelujah, and most importantly to Yankee fans he was a winner.

Led by Mantle, the Yankees secured seven more World Series titles—numbers 14 through 20 in their ever-growing and unmatched collection—and 12 pennants.

When Mantle got that close-up sense of Clipper awe late in the 1950 season, the Yankees were in the process of repeating as world champs. Upon adding him, they would turn it into a five-year title run, the only time it has happened in Major League Baseball history. The only question back then, though, was whether the time was now to unleash the "whizbang."

Yankee scout Tom Greenwade, who covered Missouri, Kansas and Oklahoma, had been tipped off in 1948 about this fleet prep athlete by Joplin firefighter Kay Magness. A year later Greenwade had gone back to Commerce to see him again, and found that a rival Cardinals scout was also hot on his heels. Mantle wanted to be a Yankee, though, and Greenwade clinched it when Mutt told him the club would have to at least match how much his son could make by working in the mines all summer and playing ball on Sundays. Greenwade calculated it to be worth $1,500 and that meager sum was enough to land a legend.

MICKEY MANTLE'S
10 GREATEST MEMORIES

When *SPORT* magazine hit newsstands with this list on April 18, 1967, Mickey Mantle was sitting on 496 homers. He would become only the sixth player to reach 500 a month later, and that impending milestone was covered by number 10 in this personal ranking. Note that it was only presented *chronologically* by SPORT, leaving readers to decide their own order.

1. September 17, 1950. The 18-year-old shortstop is awed at his first meeting with Joe DiMaggio.

2. April 17, 1953. Batting righty, the switch-hitting slugger bashes a 565-foot homer over the left-centerfield bleachers and into history at Griffith Stadium in Washington. The ball from that shot, which was thought at the time to be the longest home run ever, is in Cooperstown and the resulting distance-measurement theatrics led to the term "tape-measure" homer.

3. October 4, 1953. Becomes fourth player to hit a grand slam in the World Series. It goes to the upper deck in left-center at Ebbets Field despite batting lefty.

4. June 21, 1955. Mantle swings from the right side and sends one 486 feet to dead-center at Yankee Stadium—the longest hit to that area of the park.

5. October 3, 1956. After giving Don Larsen all the run support he needs with a homer, the center fielder preserves the historic World Series perfect game by making a backhanded grab of Gil Hodges's low liner to left-center.

6. May 22, 1963. The closest anyone came to officially hitting a ball out of Yankee Stadium (Negro Leaguers claimed Josh Gibson once did), at least at that point. "The hardest ball I ever hit," he says of the rising liner into the third deck in right.

7. August 4, 1963. "If I had to pick one as the greatest of all ten memories, this might be it," Mantle says of his return from a 61-

game absence (broken left foot) with a loud ovation and a game-tying pinch homer against Baltimore. Again, he said that before number 500, though.

8. September 17, 1964. Mantle singles for his 2,000th hit, then swats his 450th homer the next time up.

9. October 10, 1964. As Bob Costas recalls in the Mick's essay here, you have to include the walk-off blast against Barney Schultz of the Cardinals. It was Mantle's 16th homer in the World Series, breaking Babe Ruth's record.

10. 1967. As *SPORT* wrote: "The 10th great moment has not yet been realized by Mantle." He was looking forward to surpassing Lou Gehrig's record of 2,164 games as a Yankee (done) and reaching the 500 milestone (done). "These thrills may be the last," said Mantle, who called it a day after the 1968 season.

"This kid is the kind of juvenile ball player you might not see in a lifetime of major league experience," Yankees manager Casey Stengel said in the spring of 1951. One newspaper headline summarized that this way: "Stengel Drapes Mantle of Greatness on Boy." The great Mel Ott, then managing in the minors for Oakland, agreed: "this boy couldn't miss." Yankees general manager George Weiss was taking the contrarian view, in favor of sending Mantle out for more seasoning—in Kansas City. Writers were divided, and skeptics were usually the ones who hadn't seen him yet.

That spring, Frank Graham wrote about "The Case of Mickey Mantle." Given the surge of Mantle headlines, he believed that the phenom could go one of three ways:

1. "It can bolster his confidence, knowing that older hands agree he is as good as he thinks he is, for there never was a ball-player worth his pay check who didn't think he was good, because if he didn't think so he wouldn't be in there trying."

2. "It can scare the wits out of him and set him back three or four years."
3. "Or it can bring on a swelling of his noggin that will render him useless and, at the same time, obnoxious. [This] seems the least likeliest of all. Everything written about him indicates strongly that he is a level minded kid who can hit the ball and take the headlines in his stride."

Confident and "level minded" are hallmarks of the Yankee greats, and that included Mantle.

"The Switcher" still ranks as the all-time leader for home runs by a switch-hitter, and he had power to all fields. It was a skill he learned early, when his father, Mutt (who named him after Hall of Famer Mickey Cochrane) would throw to him right-handed and his grandfather Charles, a left-hander on the local sandlots, would throw to him from the opposite side. Mutt believed that hitting from both sides would increase his son's chances of a baseball career.

Many of Mantle's blasts were prodigious, resulting in lore handed down for generation. He literally invented the term "tape-measure homer" while he was at it, thanks to his number two entry on that list of his own greatest memories, while batting righty.

That was a 565-foot homer, according to Yankees PR director Red Patterson, who raced out of the Washington ballpark's press box to measure the ball's apparent landing spot after it cleared the left-field bleachers—the first time it ever happened there. It came off left-hander Chuck Stobbs on April 17, 1953. Mantle's teammate Billy Martin was a baserunner on third when the ball soared out, and as a gag he had stayed on third as long as possible, pretending that he was tagging up. Mantle, who almost ran into Martin on the trot, had not seen the gag, because, as he later said, "I used to keep my head down as I rounded the bases after a home run. I didn't want to show up the pitcher. I figured he felt bad enough already." Mantle agreed to post for a picture after the game with Patterson, holding up a tape measure—hence the new baseball term.

HOF ARTIFACT INVENTORY

Game-used equipment in the Baseball Hall of Fame:

MICKEY MANTLE

B-198.95	Baseball autographed and hit by Mickey Mantle for his 52nd home run against Boston on Sept. 28, 1956.
B-184.68	Baseball hit for his 522nd homer on May 6, 1968.
B-228.53	Ball hit for 565-foot "tape measure" homer off Senators pitcher Chuck Stobbs in the fifth inning at Griffith Stadium on April 17, 1953.
B-229.53	Bat used to hit that homer off Stobbs.
B-68.67	Joe Pepitone-model bat used to hit his 500th career homer on May 14, 1967.
B-247.69	No. 7 uniform shirt.
B-23.2005	Official American League baseball signed by Mantle and Roger Maris.
B-132.85	AL baseball signed by Mantle.
B-389.70	Baseball signed by Mantle and the Yankees.
B-2991.63	Bat used during his 1956 Triple Crown season.

Mantle teamed with Roger Maris in the magical 1961 season as the "M&M boys," each going after Ruth's single-season record of 60 homers set in 1927. Maris eventually broke the record with number 61, while Mantle still wound up with a career-best 54.

"Mickey Mantle was my guy," acting legend James Caan said to me during the 2012 season. "Mel Allen used to be the announcer, and a beer company sponsored the Yankees games. At the end of the game, he'd be drunk and would almost fall out of the press box, so they stopped that. I remember one year, one shot. Mickey twice, he hit two into the bleachers. Only like ten guys had ever hit into the bleachers, and Mickey went back-to-back into the bleachers. It was great, because the ball went straight up into the air, and the center fielder started running in, the second baseman started running back, and the thing dropped into the bleachers."

When Mantle retired, Ruth (714) and Willie Mays (587 at the time) were the only players who hit more home runs than him. "I've seen ballplayers do the job on just guts, but I've never known a guy do it over so long a time," Mays said of Mantle. Mantle said upon retiring that he "felt bad" that he did not maintain a lifetime average of .300, but .298 was just fine. No one ever cared after that. Sometimes round numbers just don't matter. These do matter: 110.3 WAR and 87.6 JAWS.

Those are two metrics that did not exist when he played but are of critical importance today in measuring performance. Both lofty stats rank Mantle fourth all-time among center fielders, behind Willie Mays, Ty Cobb and Tris Speaker. Then comes DiMaggio and Duke Snider, in order. Mantle led the Yankees in WAR every season from 1952 – 62, with the exception of 1960 (Roger Maris), a reign of excellence you knew with your eyes back then.

"A lot of people are still in awe of him," Hall of Fame president Jeff Idelson said, as we sat in his office at the hallowed institution. "In fact, over your left shoulder if you're curious, in the black framed photo, that's his house where he grew up, and the barn where his dad used to throw him against. I just love that. He would stand with a bat and his dad would use that as a catcher. It just shows what humble beginnings he came from."

I got up to look closer, and framed in black on Jeff's wall is a magnificent painting of an impoverished rural scene in an extraordinary Okie story. It is a small white house with a dilapidated, tin, red-roof shed off to the right. The two structures are separated by just enough distance for a dad to throw to a son, which was the space where it all happened for Mutt and Mick after the former got out of the mines each day.

They moved into this house when Mickey was three years old, and motorists along Route 66 stop by regularly to visit it today. This image on Idelson's wall freezes it in time, along with its overarching message: Anything is possible. A fan from Oklahoma sent it to him in the mail about 20 years ago, and Idelson made a copy for this wall and then gave the original to the Hall library.

"Mickey Mantle is an example of a guy who came from nothing and had a phenomenal career," he said. "A lot of fans are enamored by the legend of this kid from Oklahoma who became the, or one of the, most prolific switch-hitters in history. What he represents is baseball in its heyday in the Fifties with his style and pizzazz and ability. There seems to be a romanticism about him as a player, among fans, maybe moreso than others. Probably because of the era he played in. He was a good-looking farmboy who came to New York and made it big, and always responded in a very direct and simple way."

Idelson said one thing that stuck out to him about Mantle was the fact that he earned seven World Series rings, yet "the only ring he ever wore, at least in the years where I overlapped with him here, was his Hall of Fame ring. I think he just felt incredibly proud about being in the Hall of Fame." Idelson said the Hall's ring tradition dates back at least to the 1950s, and the ring they get today is the same ring they got then.

"At one point around 2012 – 13, we talked to the entire membership about whether they wanted it to change, and if anybody is traditionalist, it's the guys who get in here," Idelson said. "The answer was a resounding number. It's very understated, black onyx, not quartz-y."

In the spring of '53, *The Saturday Evening Post* opined that Mantle "could become the successor to Ruth, Gehrig and DiMaggio. Mickey can be as great as he wants to be. The only question is: Does he want it enough?"

To me, the answer to that question could be found in 1991 when I sat in a movie theater watching "City Slickers" at a theater in San Diego, while I was in town on a road trip covering a Giants-Padres series for the San Jose *Mercury News*. It was my second year as a BBWAA member, and coincidentally I would pay $50 for Mick's utterly perfect autograph at an Atlantic City card show later that season while driving from a Philly series up to Shea Stadium with legendary baseball writer Nick Peters. So there I sat in San Diego, watching Billy Crystal's Mitch Robbins character as he and his two buddies rode horseback on a therapeutic cattle drive out West, each taking turns telling about their best and worst day.

Crystal could be completely himself in this character, because here is how a Yankee fan remembered his best day:

"I'm seven years old and my dad takes me to Yankee Stadium. My first game. I'm going in this long dark tunnel underneath the stands, I'm holding his hand, and we come up out of the tunnel into the light. It was huge. How green the grass was, brown dirt, and that great green copper roof, remember? And we had a black-and-white TV, so this was the first game I ever saw and color. Sat there the whole game next to my dad. He taught me how to keep score.

"Mickey hit one out."

George Steinbrenner

On George Steinbrenner's desk during the 1983 Yankee season, next to a gold numeral 1 and a glass apple, was a small blue sign with white lettering. It read: "Lead, Follow, or Get The Hell out of The Way."

That is how "The Boss" lived his life and how he ran the Yankees during his tenure from 1973 – 2010, the longest ownership of the club. They won seven World Series titles (1977 – 78, 1996, 1998 – 2000, and 2009) during that time, and lost in four other Fall Classics (1976, 1981, 2001, and 2003). His election to the Hall of Fame is necessary soon, regardless of his headlines.

Steinbrenner's signature bravado and unabashed George Patton leadership style made him a cultural figure as well, complete with a recurring faceless character on *Seinfeld* and Miller Lite commercials as the alpha to Billy Martin's omega. The Boss's oversized plaque beyond the right field bleachers at the new Yankee Stadium says it all: A towering, endlessly looming figure whose legacy as a leader and key baseball figure goes on through time, no matter what anyone else thought while it all happened. There can never be another George Steinbrenner.

"Winning is second, right behind breathing," he once said. "I don't like it when people talk about winning and make it a bad word. Some people are taught that winning is not right or is a bad thing. I like to talk about the pursuit of excellence, which is one of the most important things there is to learn."

Bottom line, those are the words of success, a tradition carried on by his family. Steinbrenner bought the Yankees from CBS on January 3, 1973, and famously said that he would be a quiet executive behind the scenes. "We plan absentee ownership as far as running the Yankees is concerned. We're not going to pretend we're something we aren't. I'll stick to building ships."

Champion-ships, he meant.

Steinbrenner was a competitor from Cleveland's shipbuilding industry who bent or broke rules in baseball and prompted new ones. He built a massive payroll that made Yankee fans happy but outraged most every other fan base, and was the first to create a regional TV revenue stream. Bud Selig's big changes in his Commissioner tenure included a luxury tax, so that small-market clubs could stay competitive while the Yankees would have to lower payroll or pay opponents. They often warranted special treatment as a "premium" club at MLB Advanced Media, even though we literally worked for all 30 franchises—a fact of life.

The Yankees *always* led the way throughout the heady MLBAM days, including the historic day game on August 26, 2002, when MLB.TV was born with a live video stream in the Bronx for 30,000 daytime computer users mainly at the office. Steinbrenner's club always stayed in the vanguard as the tech driver, still does, benefiting 29 other clubs. His legacy goes on.

Of course, a day spent poring over several of his overstuffed clip files in the Hall of Fame's Bart Giammati Research Center means wading through mostly New York tabloid headlines still sizzling with controversy. The Yankees' longtime owner was a media magnet, the back page king, and someone who usually found a way to stay involved even if forced to sit it out.

In the "Bronx Zoo" days, Steinbrenner fired Martin four times as manager. It was such a revolving door that the duo appeared on a Miller Lite commercial in which ones says "Taste Great" and the other says "Less Filling." Steinbrenner told him he was fired, and Martin replied, "Oh, no, not again." The fact that they were able to make "Lite" of the situation spoke volumes about its drama series reality.

Steinbrenner often went out of his way to pressure members of his team, and one notable example was when he called out Winfield while ripping multiple veterans on his club during the infamous September 1985 tirade. Future Hall of Famer Phil Niekro, a member of that club that went on a losing streak after the tirade, would write later in his book "Knuckleballs":

"Every man has his right to his opinion, but I wish he would have remained silent for a little while longer. The last thing we needed was him puttin' more pressure on us. . . . I'm not one to tell George how to run his ballclub, but we really don't need this criticism from him right now."

Ron Guidry, who recently shared more insights in his new autobiography *Gator*, said back then that such motivational ploys were often successful even if reviled. "No matter what George's bad habits are, he wants to win," Guidry said in 1986. "Whatever he does, he tries to benefit the team. George has a funny way of lighting a fire."

"Let me say this for him," said 1977 Cy Young winner Sparky Lyle. "I got three World Series rings with the Yankees, and I wouldn't have had one of them, I don't think, if it wasn't for George Steinbrenner. He paid the freight to assemble some very good Yankee teams. And when it wasn't going right, it must have been very frustrating from his side to sit up there and not be able to do anything."

Steinbrenner said it was more difficult to play in New York than anywhere else, and more difficult to play for a club that had won far more championships than any other in baseball. He explained his "motivational" attacks on his players this way: "In many instances I do it to have guys fight back and go like hell. But if I see they can't take it, I back off. But it also tells me something about that player. He only wants the sweet and can't face up to the bitter. Life is full of sweet and bitter."

His run-ins with baseball personnel went well beyond his own payroll. A disciplinary sampling:

On August 23, 1973, Steinbrenner pled guilty to authorizing $25,000 of illegal campaign contributions to the Nixon reelection campaign. Money had been filtered through American Ship Building employees as bogus bonuses so that he could exceed the contribution limit. Steinbrenner also pled guilty to being an accessory after the fact by trying to cover up the crime, an obstruction of justice. Two months after the pleas, Commissioner Bowie Kuhn suspended him for two years, reduced on appeal to 15 months.

White Sox owner Jerry Reinsdorf—irked by how much Steinbrenner had paid for free agent Steve Kemp after the outfielder spent the 1982 season with Chicago—began a feud by suggesting it was time for new Yankees ownership. Steinbrenner, then infuriated that Reinsdorf and co-owner Eddie Einhorn outbid him and all MLB for Floyd Bannister, called the pair "Abbott and Costello." Steinbrenner was fined $5,000 by Kuhn on the same day that he made Martin baseball's richest manager.

On July 30, 1990, Commissioner Fay Vincent ruled that Steinbrenner permanently yield his title of managing general partner and cease all on-field business activities, based on an investigation of the owner's payoff of $40,000 to admitted gambler Howie Spira (for damaging information on Yankees outfielder Dave Winfield, whom he had dubbed "Mr. May" in September of 1985) and his long working relationship with Spira. Steinbrenner accepted the ruling and considered it an "agreement" rather than a punishment. Vincent lifted the ban after a couple of years, and Steinbrenner came back into his role a generally more mild-mannered Boss.

The 1980s had slipped past without a single Yankee title, but it was an aberration. Under his leadership, a new Yankee dynasty emerged, resulting in four titles in a five-year span, and then one for good measure in 2009. It was a championship opening of a new Yankee Stadium, just as it had been in 1923, and in both cases it was inside a ballpark that a George had built.

Once again, Steinbrenner's name appeared as a candidate for a special Hall of Fame election, making him eligible for 2019 induction. Would this time be any different than the snubs of the past decade? Now that Colonel Ruppert is in Cooperstown, circa 2013, it is time for another boss of the Bronx Bombers to find his way into the Gallery.

"I can't stump for him either way," said Idelson, who joined the Hall as president in 1994, when Steinbrenner was on its board. "When you talk about the history of the New York Yankees, George Steinbrenner is a *big* piece of that. He dramatically changed the paradigm to assure that the Yankees were always competitive. That was his goal. Every offseason, he wanted to make sure his team was competitive. He was part of great teams in New York. He helped part of the dynasty of the 1990s into the early 2000s. And he helped elevate the game in many, many ways: Regional television networks, to making sure he took care of the players."

Idelson knows firsthand what it was like to work for Steinbrenner. He was one of his publicists. "Marty Appel and I were pre-, during and post-suspensions," Idelson told me. "So we have that distinction." I hope he one day has the pleasure of seeing a plaque request.

"What's unknown about George is how committed he was to doing the right thing," Idelson said. "Often that gets lost in the bluster of how loud he was, but he was as big for affirmative action, giving second chances to those who needed them, and being inclusive, as anyone I worked with.

"While most of the attention usually was on Steinbrenner's signature style of leadership, behind the scenes was a quiet giver who left a large legacy of helping others."

Idelson came to the Yankees from the Red Sox in the 1980s, seeing both sides of The Rivalry and what it meant to The Boss to be on the "right" side of it.

"Nothing exceeded winning in George's mind, even if it was the opening day of Spring Training," he said. "He didn't like to lose, but he *really* hated to lose to the Red Sox. It may not have played out in the media when we did lose, but you knew when we lost to Boston, there was going to be a certain tension within the front office that you knew was coming. So you really wanted to beat the Red Sox as often as possible.

"Honestly, I really liked working for him. I learned a great deal working for him. I learned to always be prepared, I learned to always be ahead, I learned to anticipate, I learned to grow thick skin. At the end of the day, I enjoyed working for him, because he demanded perfection, which is something I always strived for. It was challenging, but I did enjoy it."

On the morning of the 2010 All-Star Game, I was at our MLB headquarters hotel in Anaheim and was about to head out to cover the events when suddenly I saw the announcement that The Boss was gone. It ripped across the sport, a sad reality and a reminder of a winner.

"George was 'The Boss,' make no mistake," said Yogi Berra, who was on the outs for years after a Steinbrenner dismissal but ultimately back in the fold with him. "He built the Yankees into champions, and that's something nobody can ever deny. He was a very generous, caring, passionate man. George and I had our differences, but who didn't? We became great friends over the last decade and I will miss him very much."

Ron Guidry

Louisiana Lightning was an electric left-handed pitcher who has a case as the best pitcher in Yankees history, factoring in modern metrics. His Hall of Fame support topped out at 8.8 percent on nine ballot appearances, but it often takes time to truly appreciate one's career. He would be a fine candidate to consider for the Veterans Committee on Modern Baseball when they meet in December of 2019 to vote on the credentials of 10 overlooked legends.

That would be a long way to Cooperstown from his first glimpse of Yankee Stadium. Here is what Guidry said in 2018 while speaking at the Yogi Berra Museum amid his *Gator* book tour:

> *"You see the blue seats. I remember I had goosebumps that were the size of golf balls. That's the best feeling. The most amazing thing is, that was probably the only time that I ever walked in that spot and looked in the field, but I know I got the same goosebumps when I walked in and I walked down the runway going into the locker room, because when you walk down there, you think about all the great guys that came before you."*

Guidry was selected by the Yankees in the third round of the 1971 draft out of the University of Louisiana at Lafayette, and he made his Major League debut four years later. Between

1975 and '76, he pitched sparingly, appearing in only 17 games, making a single start, and pitching a total of just 31 2/3 innings. Despite spending the majority of those two seasons in the minors, Guidry immediately burst onto the scene as a force to be reckoned with during the 1977 campaign and quickly became the anchor of a staff that already had Ed Figueroa, Mike Torrez and Catfish Hunter. Guidry posted a 2.82 ERA over 210 2/3 innings and finished third in the AL with 7.52 strikeouts per nine innings.

The most pivotal moment in his career probably was Game Four of the 1977 World Series, because that complete-game victory not only gave the Yankees a 3 – 1 Series lead on their way to a clinch in six, but the dominant form also would carry over into a 1978 season for the ages.

Guidry won the 1978 Cy Young Award with a 25-3 record, and the Yankees were an astounding 30 – 5 in his 35 starts. He completed 16 of his starts and authored an incredible nine shutouts, still a franchise record. Guidry completed at least eight innings in 23 of his starts and failed to complete six innings just twice, and 29 out of his 35 starts met the requirements for a quality start (at least six innings with three or fewer earned runs allowed).

Guidry had 10 double-digit strikeout performances on his way to a Yankee-record 248 K's on the season. His 1.74 ERA, 0.95 WHIP and 208 ERA+ all led the Major Leagues. Guidry finished second behind Jim Rice in the AL MVP race, although it was frequently mentioned that Rice was only 2-for-13 against him and Guidry led the Yankees' surge past Boston for the AL East title.

The highlight of that season came on June 17. After allowing an Angel to reach second base in each of the first three innings, Guidry was staked to a 4 – 0 lead in the bottom of the third inning. Guidry, already with six punch-outs on the day, settled in after being handed a comfortable lead and proceeded to strike out the side in the fourth, giving him a total of nine at that point.

"My fastball was zipping along the back of home plate. My

slider bit hard and in the right spots against lefties and righties," Guidry writes in *Gator*. He was on cruise control the rest of the game after that, fanning two Angels in the fifth and striking out the side for the second time in the game in the sixth inning. He finished the day with 18 strikeouts.

This was before Roger Clemens would come along to strike out 20 for Boston eight years later, so it was over the top. Guidry became the first Major Leaguer to record a nine-inning shutout while striking out at least 18. Phil Rizzuto said during his broadcast: "What an exhibition by the Louisiana Lightning man."

Over his 14-year career in pinstripes, Guidry completed 2,392 innings across 368 games (323 starts). He had a 3.29 ERA and 1.18 WHIP and prevented runs at a rate about 20 percent better than the league average (119 career ERA+). Guidry won two ERA titles, finished in the top five in WHIP six times, and five times ranked in the top three in the AL in strikeouts per nine innings (striking out 1,778 batters at rate of 6.69 per nine innings). He performed well in the postseason during the Yankees' back-back championships in 1977 – 78, won the Cy, and finished in the top three in Cy voting three times and the top seven six times. Remember also that people will increasingly pay less attention to the old 300-win benchmark as the years pass.

So, yes, the Veterans Committee needs to put this one on the list. Does Guidry truly belong in the Hall? It is borderline, but it at least requires a major discussion. You can't compare him to his teammate Don Mattingly as just another player whose career was too short to be considered for induction. As former Yankee catcher Rick Cerone said at the time of Guidry's Monument Park ceremony, "Every day he went out there, he had no-hit stuff."

Goose Gossage

One of the most infuriating things about seeing a longtime elite player like Jorge Posada fall off the Hall of Fame ballot after the first year of eligibility due to an antiquated five-percent rule is the history of Hall debate and trend-watching that often leads to an election. Goose Gossage was one of the most classic examples during my own decades as a voter.

"It's a crime that he's not in the Hall of Fame," former baseball executive Roland Hemond said of Gossage in a *New York Post* interview back when we received the annual ballot by mail in December of 2005. "I talk to the hitters from that era who are in the Hall and they all say they were overmatched by Goose."

Gossage had debuted on the ballot in 2000 with 33.3 percent of the vote, needing 75 percent for enshrinement. He jumped to 44.3 percent the next year, but then steadily trickled down to 43.0 in 2002, 42.1 in 2003 and 40.7 in 2004. It was not looking good. But one versatile reliever (Dennis Eckersley) had just been enshrined in 2004, and another (Bruce Sutter) was coming in 2006. It was a time when one-inning closers like Mariano Rivera and Trevor Hoffman were the new rule but voters were starting to re-examine the evolution of late relief.

"This is no knock against Mariano Rivera—he's currently the greatest closer pitching on the planet—but have him do what we did," Gossage said in that same 2005 *Post* article. "We'd come into a game for two or three innings, sometimes in the fifth inning, and we were always brought into the middle of jams. This was all season, not just late in the season."

As that debate grew louder, Gossage's vote totals grew by about 10 percentage points a year until he was enshrined in Cooperstown with 85.8 percent of the vote in 2008. It was his ninth year on the ballot, and a tribute to a big right-hander who was pivotal in both the evolution of the closer role in baseball and to the Yankees' title repeat in 1978.

The Yankees were one of the first teams to employ the modern setup man/closer format in their bullpen. In his first year with the team, the fireball-throwing Gossage paired with the crafty, slider-throwing left-hander Sparky Lyle, and, later, with Ron Davis. Still, relievers of that era often handled much larger workloads than today's relievers. In almost two-thirds of Gossage's career saves, he pitched two or more innings.

The Yankees signed him to a six-year deal in 1978, a highly unconventional move considering that Lyle had just won the AL Cy Young Award in 1977 and had been the winning pitcher in three consecutive postseason games on the way to a title. Gossage was optimistic about the idea of partnering with Lyle in the bullpen, while Lyle figured it would mean less innings for both and therefore less effectiveness.

"I knew I wouldn't be as good a pitcher being in fewer games," Lyle said. "The more I pitched, the better I got. That's what hurt me." Yankees third baseman Graig Nettles said that Lyle went "from Cy Young to Sayonara." That is exactly what happened.

Gossage pitched for nine different teams over two decades, and that included parts of seven seasons with the Yankees (1978 – 83 and 1989). He threw the final pitch of the 1978 season as catcher Thurman Munson caught the popup behind home plate to secure the repeat.

Gossage was a nine-time All-Star, compiling a 42 – 28 record with a 2.14 ERA with the Yankees, including 151 saves and 512 strikeouts in 319 games. He allowed just 390 hits in 533 innings pitched during his time in pinstripes, and he trails only Mariano

Rivera (652) and Dave Righetti (224) on the Yankees' all-time saves list.

When he finally did go into the Hall of Fame, Gossage went in with a Yankees cap on his plaque. Included are the words: "A DOMINANT RELIEF PITCHER WITH A TRADEMARK MOUSTACHE, WHOSE MENACING GLARE AND EXPLODING FASTBALL INTIMIDATED BATTERS FOR MORE THAN TWO DECADES."

"Playing with the Yankees was unlike anything else I've ever done in my life, and winning a world championship there, just being part of that great seventy-eight team, that was the best team I ever had the privilege of playing on," Gossage said. "Playing for The Boss was never a dull moment. It was absolutely as competitive as any of us. I think he's the greatest owner and has done more for the game. In terms of free agency, he was not afraid to go out. He wanted to put the absolute best-quality product out on that field. I *hated* losing, and I guess that's why Mr. Steinbrenner and I got along so well. He did *not* like to lose."

Steinbrenner's controversial signing was not immediately successful. The first five games in which Gossage appeared for the Yankees were all losses. Against Boston at home on June 27 of that year, with the Yankees 9 ½ games behind their rivals, he relieved starter Ron Guidry in the seventh with a 3 – 2 lead, the bases loaded and no outs . . . and promptly surrendered a two-run single to Rick Burleson, blowing the save. Gossage eventually got out of the jam with a double play, worked through the 11th inning, and turned it over to Lyle, who got the win on Nettles's walk-off homer in the 14th. The thought of overcoming Boston in the standings at that point was remote, but of course, they would do it after Bucky Dent's legendary homer at Fenway in a one-game playoff.

"It would have never been the greatest comeback in history if I hadn't dug us that deep hole," Gossage recalled. "When I joined the Yankees, I had put so much pressure on myself of putting on the pinstripes. I proceeded to stink the joint up. I had just reached rock bottom. I had lost the ballgame every way possible, and then worked my way out of that. Then we ended up catching the Red Sox to set the stage for probably the greatest game, I think. I don't think there's ever been a bigger game or a better game. You couldn't write a better script. The Yankees-Red Sox at Fenway Park, that great rivalry. They hated us, we hated them. The fans hated us.

"I had my work cut out for me. I came in that ballgame with one out in the seventh inning, I was on the mound, I had a couple runners on, two outs, and this is it. I had gone to bed the night before thinking, 'I'll be facing Yaz for the final out.' Sure enough, I got to that point. Yaz came to the plate. I had a conversation, I started asking questions and answering them, on the mound, this conversation just with myself. I said, 'Why are you so nervous? You've always played the game for the love of it and the fun of it. What's the worst thing that can happen to you?'

"Yaz stepped in the box, I stepped on the rubber, and the first pitch to him was down in the zone. I got two runners on, the game's on the line, five-four, one-run lead at Fenway with Yaz up. The next pitch was pretty much down the middle of the plate, it tailed in on his hands, and he popped it up to Nettles. We ended up winning that ballgame and then going through the Kansas City Royals in the playoffs and beating the Dodgers in the World Series and repeating as world champions."

Gossage remembered how little patience Yankee fans had for his early struggles, as he would be driven in from the bullpen in those days by a pinstriped car.

"The doors in center field used to open up from the bullpen and they'd drive us in," he said. "Through that really tough stretch, when I joined the Yankees for the first couple of months I really struggled. . . . When that car would come in, the grounds crew would fight over who was gonna bring me in. Because nobody wanted to bring me in. It was a dangerous job. When it came around the warning track, whatever people were eating, they were throwing on that car, so we had to turn the windshield wipers on to see where the hell we were going."

THE USE OF GOOSE

Hall of Famer Goose Gossage pitched out of the Yankees' bullpen from 1978 – 83, and this chart shows how different his role at the end of games was from that of a great closer like Mariano Rivera in later years. The "outs" columns refer to how many games Gossage pitched where he recorded at least that number of outs. "Runners on" refers to how many games Gossage entered with inherited runners already on base.

GOOSE GOSSAGE WITH YANKEES								
Year	Games	3+ outs	6+ outs	9+ outs	12+ outs	Runners on	ERA	Saves
1978	63	56	35	16	7	35	2.01	27
1979	36	32	12	4	1	22	2.62	18
1980	64	50	27	6	1	35	2.27	33
1981	32	30	9	1	0	18	0.77	20
1982	56	50	25	4	0	30	2.23	30
1983	57	45	17	5	2	49	2.27	22

For Gossage, perhaps the most pivotal moment in his Yankee days was when they no longer had to use the windshield wipers.

"I worked my way out of that, but it was the toughest stretch of my career that I'd ever gone through," he said. "I put so much pressure on myself being with the Yankees. Coming over, Sparky Lyle had won the Cy Young Award. I came over to work with Sparky. I had envisioned that we would be the best lefty-righty combination ever. And it didn't work out that way. They gave me his job on a silver platter and I proceeded to stink the joint up."

Lyle had been right about pitching in lower-leverage situations. In 1978, Gossage pitched 134 1/3 innings and led the AL with 27 saves. Although Lyle pitched in 111 2/3 innings, that was down from the year before. He only saved nine games and was traded to Texas after the season.

Gossage played through the evolution of the back-end bullpen. One of his finest performances was the 1981 postseason.

In the AL Division Series, Gossage saved all three Yankees victories, pitching at least two innings in each one. In the ALCS, he saved one more, and pitched another 2 2/3 scoreless innings over two outings. Finally, in the World Series, Gossage saved Games One and Two. In Game Five, he threw a scoreless ninth, but the Yankees lost, 2 – 1, and eventually lost the series. Overall, he saved six of eight games that postseason and did not allow a run.

"I love the feeling of coming to the ballpark every day and knowing I've got a chance to work," Gossage said. "I'd go crazy as a starter. Imagine having a bad game and then having to sit around four or five days before you pitch again. You'd be thinking about it all the time. That would be terrible."

Bernie Williams

On July 7, 1991, Bernie Williams was called up by the Yankees, soon to become the regular center fielder by bumping Roberto Kelly over to left and displacing Hensley Meulens from the lineup. "He was real quiet and shy," recalled Don Mattingly, who had to intervene when Mel Hall took advantage of that low-key demeanor and overdid the rookie ribbing. "I thought he lacked a little confidence. You could see he had the talent, but you could see the insecurities, too. I think confidence was the big key for Bernie. You have to believe you can play here. . . . Once you get that, you can do some things."

Williams did a lot over 16 seasons in the Bronx, where he became a fixture in the lineup through glory days. Consider Williams's *lowest* numbers in the following categories during his best seven-year stretch from 1996 to 2002: 101 runs, 19 homers, 94 RBIs, .305 batting average, .391 on-base percentage, .493 slugging percentage and 131 OPS+. Not many players would be disappointed to put up those numbers for a season, let alone have that be their *worst* season in a seven-year run. The Yankees retired his number 51 jersey and dedicated his plaque, honoring his continuation of a great tradition of center fielders in pinstripes.

That tradition is often said to begin with Earle Combs, but it is worth reiterating what I mentioned in the Combs section of this book. Williams is a more deserving Hall of Fame center field candidate than the leadoff man who was elected in 1970 by the Veterans Committee. Neither of them is actually deserving of Cooperstown, but just for the sake of argument, Williams brought more to the table than did the table-setter of Murderers' Row.

From an individual perspective, Williams (43.6) ranks 26th in JAWS among all-time centerfielders and Combs (38.4) is 37th. In WAR, Bernie (49.6) is 29th and Combs (42.5) 44th. Williams was arguably the best hitter on the Yankees from 1996 – 2003, with a .929 OPS compared to Derek Jeter's .853 and Jorge Posada's .849. Exclusion from the "Core Four" actually slighted Williams's perception, whereas Combs overdrew from his cohorts.

"To set the record straight, Bernie is a member of the 'Fab Five,'" Yankees general manager Brian Cashman said after Williams retired, trying to rectify that perception, to little avail. "He is a member of that fabulous five that got produced from our system that led to many of these championships."

From a team perspective, Williams won four rings (1996, 1998 – 2000) and played in six World Series. Combs won three rings (1927 – 28 and 1932) and played in four World Series. That was an incredibly harder feat in the Williams era, as the 1996 title came in only the second year that the postseason was expanded to include Wild Cards and many more obstacles.

Combs was a teetotaling, Bible-reading gentleman who had good friends, and he was inducted in part merely by riding the lore associated with Ruth and Gehrig and that era. Bernie is beloved by fans and liked by media, and he went on to play the guitar and make people happy. So the character aspect certainly would carry no more weight for Combs than for Williams.

I did not vote for Williams, but like Posada, he should not have been quickly bumped off the ballot without further conversation.

As good of a player Williams was, he will be remembered more for his consistently strong postseason play than anything else. In roughly three quarters of a season's worth of postseason play (121 postseason games with the Yankees), Bernie put up numbers (.275/.371/ .480) that strongly mirrored his career regular season averages (.297/.381/.477)—although his performance was stronger in the AL playoffs than it was in his Fall Classics. Overall in postseason play, Williams scored 83 runs, hit 22 homers, drove in 80 runs and drew 71 walks. When he retired, he ranked behind only Jeter is career postseason plate appearances (545), runs, hits (128), doubles (29) and total bases (223). Williams holds the all-time record for postseason RBIs, and only Manny Ramirez (29) has hit more home runs than Williams's 22.

"I think he was as important as anyone in the success the Yankees had because of his presence in our lineup being a switch-hitter and breaking up the left-handers, his ability to run and his ability to play defense," said Joe Girardi, his former teammate. "He was as important as any of those guys."

The Yankees celebrate Bernie Williams Day in 2015. From left to right: Andy Pettitte, Jorge Posada, Mariano Rivera, Bernie Williams, and Derek Jeter.
Courtesy of Arturo Pardavila III

Roger Maris

"**It was you, Rog.** You did it, you son of a bitch. And nobody can ever take that away from you, neither. No matter what bullshit they try to tell you, that record's yours."

When Thomas Jane's Mickey Mantle character says that in the hospital to Barry Pepper's Roger Maris at the end of Billy Crystal's vastly underrated film *61**, I am the quintessential guy who cries at movies, every time. (I should note that Crystal also got me in the movie *City Slickers*, when he learns about "that one thing.") I'm not sure exactly how Mantle's words came out in real life back in 1961, but he was right about his partner in the M&M Boys.

Nobody can ever take away what Maris did in 1961. It will last forever. And this is coming from someone who was at Mark McGwire's 62-homer game in 1998 with my son Matt. I list that among my own greatest thrills in baseball, along with being at Cal Ripken's 2,131st consecutive game played, and seeing Joe Carter's 1993 homer drop in front of me in Toronto. I was one of Big Mac's few Hall of Fame voters until his case was a lost cause, and I included him in my book *Diamonds from the Dugout* as he chose 61 over 62 as his own favorite hit.

So when I say the Maris record will last forever, I don't mean in a sense that subsequent seasons of 60-plus homers are diminished or tarnished due to an era of widespread PED abuse. I mean it in the way Maris used to ask the question himself: *Why can't people have room in their hearts for more than one person?*

Sadly, he went to his grave in 1985 assured that his was not the single-season home run record, but one with an asterisk thanks to former Ruth biographer Ford Frick, baseball's commissioner in 1961. Absolution, like Roger's homers, are out of reach for those who made him miserable. I can't put myself in the shoes of someone who lived during Babe Ruth's time and then witnessed Maris and Mantle pursue his 1927 record of 60, but if Maris taught us anything, it should be that times change and hearts have room.

Judge your success by what you had to give up
in order to get it.

- DALAI LAMA

Maris never even wanted a life in baseball, but he would help lead the Yankees to five consecutive pennants and World Series title Nos. 19 and 20. He would go to two more Fall Classics with St. Louis, finishing with three rings and retiring after his final World Series at-bat in 1968. He would hit six homers in seven total World Series. Over a dozen years in the big leagues, Maris would hit 275 homers, score 826 runs, drive in 851 and bat .260 with a 127 OPS+. He would win the AL MVP in back-to-back seasons, 1960 – 61, and he was an All-Star in four years, with seven total selections given the brief experiment of two games per year.

His older brother Rudy was the one who had a future in the game, they thought. But the Indians signed Roger, and it was with their Keokuk (Iowa) Three-I League affiliate in the mid-Fifties that he learned to pull the ball and develop the power that would create a legend. Maris debuted with Cleveland in 1957 and was traded to the Kansas City A's during the following season. He was hitting .328/.384/.624 with 10 homers and 26 RBIs on May 21, 1959, before missing the next month of the season due to a bout with appendicitis. His numbers tailed off significantly and Kansas City traded him to the Yankees after that season along with Joe DeMaestri and Kent Hadley for Hank Bauer, Don Larsen, Norm Siebern and Marv Throneberry.

FAMOUS LAST WORDS

Here was Phil Rizzuto's TV broadcast call of Roger Maris's historic 61st and final home run of the 1961 season:

"Here comes Roger Maris, they're standing up, waiting to see if Roger is going to hit number sixty-one, here's the windup, the pitch to Roger, WAY outside, ball one. The fans are starting to boo; low, ball two. That one was in the dirt and the boos get louder. Two balls, no strikes on Roger Maris, here's the windup, fastball, HIT DEEP TO RIGHT, THIS COULD BE IT, WAY BACK THERE, HOLY COW HE DID IT, SIXTY-ONE FOR MARIS!"

With Bauer jettisoned, the truly pivotal moment for Maris was Spring Training of 1960, when Casey Stengel made him his everyday right fielder as one of his last key moves as Yankee manager. Maris was an All-Star for the second year in a row, and that was just a start. He led the league with a .581 slugging average, batted .283, hit 39 homers, drove in 112 runs, scored 98 times, and posted a 160 OPS+. After that 1960 World Series, which the Yankees lost on Bill Mazeroski's historic walk-off homer in Game Seven for Pittsburgh, Maris was a Gold Glover and he won his first of two straight AL MVP awards.

For this one, Maris drew 225 voting points, edging out Mantle (222) and Brooks Robinson (211). Mantle received more first place votes (10) than Maris (8), and that fact fed a narrative among fans and media that would become a trend. Media made up false stories that Maris and Mantle had a rivalry with one another. They were good friends and wound up sharing an apartment with teammate Bob Cerv. Fans loved Mantle, and media could not understand the introverted Maris's reticence. It all fed into a 1961 machine that would stress Maris out so badly that he began losing hair while fighting his way through hatred and death threats.

Then came the season to remember, if only he could have remembered it fondly.

MLB expanded for the first time since 1901, with the Los Angeles Angels and Washington Senators joining the American League. Eight games were added to the regular schedule, going from 154 to 162 games. While it meant watered-down rosters and theoretically more mediocre pitchers to face, one could argue that 162 was harder because of more travel.

Maris got off to a slow start. In the first eight games, he batted in the 5-7 slots in the order while Mantle hit cleanup each time. New Yankees manager Ralph Houk bumped Maris up to the three hole for the first time that season in the ninth game, a 4 – 3 loss at Detroit. Stengel, ever the lineup alchemist, had tinkered with that combination the previous year as well and made it a fact of life down the stretch and through the 1960 World Series.

In the 10th game of 1961, Maris was back down to the seven hole, but he hit his first homer of the year. It was a solo shot off of Paul Foytack in the fifth inning. It was also the first time Maris finished a game in 1961 at .200 or better. Meanwhile, Maris slugged two more homers for seven on the year. Maris continued to move around in the order, scuffling.

Then came the most pivotal moment of the Roger Maris era with the Yankees.

It was in games 29 – 32, spanning three cities and five days. On May 17 at Yankee Stadium, Maris batted seventh and hit his fourth homer, a two-run clout in the eighth off Pete Burnside of the Senators. Then the Yankees went to Cleveland for two games, and Maris was moved back up to the three hole for both of them. He responded with a solo homer off Jim Perry in the first inning of the first game, and then came a solo blast off Gary Bell the next day. New York returned home to open against Baltimore, and Maris was in his now-familiar three spot in the order. He was 3-for-4 and banged another solo shot, this one off Chuck Estrada.

That was four homers in four straight games for Maris, and his average was up to .252 in the process. The 3 – 4 combination of M&M Boys was fixed. The race was on.

On July 25 at Yankee Stadium, Maris hit two homers in each end of a doubleheader against the White Sox. His final homer of the day was already his 40th of 1961. Maris was almost one full month ahead of Ruth's 1927 pace, and Mantle was right there with him. Maris actually hit his *50th* homer 34 years to the day that Ruth reached 40, and Mantle was at 46 on that date. The Yankees were in their usual pennant race, but all the attention was on the M&M Boys and the possibility of history. They were a couple of sluggers from small-town middle America, but Mantle was their celebrated hero and the other their ill-adjusting, loathe-to-smile interloper. At least that was the common perception via the press.

"He was not only fighting the memory of a dead hero, but also . . . trying to beat out a current hero," Maury Allen wrote in his 1986 biography *Roger Maris: A Man for All Seasons.*

After a doubleheader on September 10, Maris was at 56 homers and Mantle at 53—with 18 games remaining in the season. Mantle hit his 54th and final homer on September 23, but he came down with flu-like symptoms and went in for a supposedly magical shot—as given to other celebrities—that created a nasty abscess on his hip. Mantle was a hospital spectator as Maris finished the chase virtually alone, with Ruth's widow Claire and Frick tactlessly rooting against him.

"When I got hurt late in the season and knew I no longer had a shot at the record," Mantle said in Phil Pepe's book *1961**, "I was pulling for Roger to do it as much as anybody."

Frick had proclaimed that Maris would have to reach 60 homers through 154 games, just like Ruth had done, if he wanted to be the new single-season record holder. Maris was sitting on 58 entering that September 20 night game at Baltimore—boyhood home of the Bambino—and that was game Number 154 for the Yankees. He would need to homer twice that night. Him against the world, and Maris proceeded to knock one out and make Frick and Claire sweat. Then there was widespread relief as Maris finished the game at 59. Technically, traditionalists felt, Babe Ruth's hallowed record was safe from this pretender.

Maris was homerless in the remaining three games of the road trip, leaving five final games at Yankee Stadium to play out the now-unofficial string. Meanwhile, the Yankees were 105-52 with another pennant already in the bag. That was the focus all along for Maris, and he was castigated for being so dull and refusing to join in the hype. He crushed his 60th homer on September 26 against Jack Fisher of Baltimore, tying Ruth. Four games remained.

"I told people all season in '61 that I didn't care if I broke the record or not, that all I was interested in was helping the Yankees get into the World Series," Maris said in 1981. "A lot of [reporters] interpreted that as being surly. But it was the truth. I didn't give a damn if I broke it or not. And I proved that by taking a day off the day after I hit the sixtieth."

Indeed, Maris sat out game 159. On October 1, 1961, the final day of the season, there were only 23,154 fans at Yankee Stadium—about a third of capacity. The Bombers were already headed to the World Series, Mantle was out, and Frick had assured them that Babe's precious record was safe. Why watch? Sal Durante, a 19 – year-old truck driver from Brooklyn, had the answer. He had bought tickets for himself and fiancée Rosemarie Calabrese in the right field bleachers, and he had watched where Maris was hitting them in batting practice. Sam Gordon, a restaurateur in Sacramento, Calif., had been offering $5,000 for a 61 ball.

Facing Boston rookie righty Tracy Sallard in the fourth inning with one out and no score, Maris pulled a 2 – 0 pitch down the right-field line. He had 61 homers in 161 games in '61. Durante caught the ball and Maris urged him to keep the $5,000 souvenir. Maris was forced to come out for curtain calls by his teammates, many of whom had rooted for Mantle.

Perhaps Fay Vincent's utmost contribution during his brief run as commissioner was the rightful removal of Frick's asterisk. That was in 1991, six years after Maris died at the age of 51 due to cancer. McGwire and Barry Bonds still faced the asterisk in subsequent years, but there was no comparison. Their public jurors came *after* the chases, after the overflow crowds saw them push the record into the 70s. Maris faced his resistance *during* his pursuit. It was not Maris's fault that he became a North Dakotan in New York. The Yankees traded for him. It is no American's duty to fit into a new town's culture, large or small. He was entitled to be himself, just as the Babe had ignored rules and took over the town as a lost boy from Baltimore.

"As a ballplayer, I would be delighted to do it again," Maris said in the 61 postgame press conference. "As an individual, I doubt if I could possibly go through it again."

Whitey Ford

The most pivotal moment in Whitey Ford's Hall of Fame career happened just before his 32nd birthday, or past the peak of what is considered a Major League player's prime. It was after the shocking ending to the 1960 World Series on Bill Mazeroski's walk-off homer. Ford already had won 143 decisions and four rings by then, but a changing of the guard in the Yankees' coaching staff would have a twofold impact on a big surge in his performance:

- Casey Stengel, the only manager Ford had known with the club, was discharged and replaced by Ralph Houk. "You're gonna pitch every three days," Houk told Ford. Stengel had routinely rested Ford to have him ready for big games, and so the pitcher's starts soared from 29 in 1960 to 39 in 1961, while his innings shot up to 283.
- Johnny Sain became the Yankees' new pitching coach as a result of that shakeup as well, and Ford credited the former Yankee and Red Sox All-Star right-hander with perfecting his slider as a new out pitch. "He noticed I was throwing it with a violent, jerky motion. . . . Sometimes it nearly tore my arm right off. It felt that bad," Ford said. "Sain showed me how to take the long follow through. It was more gentle that way and a lot less strain on my arm. That really was the beginning of me and the slider and I think the beginning of a lot longer career."

Both adjustments made a big difference in Ford's career, and in hindsight they contributed to an extension of the Yankees' championship tradition in the process. Ford not only became a 20-game winner for the first time, but he also finished with a dazzling 25-4 record and kept going right through a World Series MVP trophy. He received his only Cy Young award. The Chairman of the Board finished his 16-year Yankee career with a 236 – 106 record for a .690 percentage, best of any twentieth-century pitcher with more than 200 wins and good for 10 All-Star selections over his 16-year career. His ERA was a svelte 2.74 and he led the AL twice in that category. Ford was 10 – 8 in the World Series from 1950 – 64, earning six titles and four pennants, and setting the record for most Fall Classic wins that stands today.

He was a combined 4 – 0—all shutouts!—in the 1960 – 61 Fall Classics, earning MVP honors in the latter. Two years after that 1961 breakthrough, his 24-7 season got him third place in the overall AL MVP voting, behind batterymate Elston Howard and Al Kaline.

On August 21, 2000, Ford would come back to the Stadium for a celebration of his 50 years with the Yankees. He said on that memorable afternoon that what made him proudest was that "the first fourteen or fifteen years that I was here, we only missed being in the World Series twice, 1954 and 1959." The fact that he even became a Yankee certainly must be considered as a pivotal moment in franchise history as well.

Edward Charles Ford, son of a bar owner, was born October 21, 1928, on 66th Street in Manhattan and grew up in Astoria. The bigger and stronger kids pitched when he played for the 34th Avenue Boys, and since he didn't want to play the outfield, the tow-head, street-tough and cocky player settled in at first base.

"Baseball was my favorite game," he told Roger Kahn in 1958, "but I never thought much about it as a career." He entered Manhattan High School of Aviation Trades, where he and friend Johnny Martin were set to become airplane mechanics while they played on the school's team. In 1946, after he finished high school, Ford wrote to the Yankees and requested a tryout. He applied as a first baseman, although he had pitched some at Manhattan Aviation.

"Stop thinking about first base," said Yankees scout Paul Krichell, who had spotted Lou Gehrig in school, among many others. "Think about pitching."

"You've only seen me for a couple of minutes," Ford said. "How can you decide on that?"

"Well, you're not big enough for a first baseman and you can't hit," Krichell replied.

"Who says I can't hit?"

"I just said it. You can't hit good enough for a first baseman. Besides, even when you're just throwing the ball around, you're pitching curves. Go over there and warm up."

The Yankees gave Ford a $7,000 signing bonus. It was in two payments, and he took the first one for $3,500 and cashed the check so it would be a thick roll of $50 bills. He and his friend Dom hopped the subway to Times Square, where he went in a store to buy his mother a radio-phonograph console. The salesman took a suspicious look at his overalls and old jacket, and went in the back to talk to the manager, who asked him where he got the money. "He's Whitey Ford," Dom shouted at them. "He just signed with the Yankees."

Imagine if the store owner had kept those fifties. Ford produced a 1.137 WHIP in those 10 World Series. Although his WAR (78th all-time) and JAWS (99th) both would have ranked him far down the list of all-time starting pitchers by modern analytics—and thus a knock on his Hall of Fame case—his World Series credentials were indisputable.

Now that I have dutifully just mentioned WAR, JAWS and WHIP all in the same paragraph, you might be wondering what in the world Ford himself would have thought about all that stuff. I can give you a pretty good idea.

On the day of the 2008 All-Star Game in the final year of old Yankee Stadium, Whitey and Yogi were riding side-by-side as grand marshals for the annual red-carpet parade. The parade route traversed Avenue of the Americas, giving lunchtime fans a chance to see their heroes up-close behind barricades as that night's uniformed personnel rode in the back of pickup trucks. Just before the lead vehicle pulled out of Bryant Park, I got up alongside the flatbed and interviewed the legendary grand marshals, and somehow Whitey got on the subject of modern stats.

"It was so simple in those days," he told me. "Now it's too much. I guess people have a job to do. What's a WHIP? [I explained.] I see. So if I pitch a five-hitter and walk five, that's a what, ten WHIP?"

As I look at that standard-issue steno notebook now, the more enjoyable thing about it now is simply that the top of the first page says: WHITEY. It wasn't his first parade, not hardly. Like his fellow grand marshal and longtime batterymate, Ford was a winner, period. If not on a Cy Young victory-total scale, then at least per team and fan request.

"If you had one game to win and your life depended on it," Casey Stengel said, "you'd want him to pitch it."

Ford's impact on the Yankees was immediate. Brought up to the parent club in June of 1950, he went 9 – 1 with a 2.81 ERA over 20 games, including 12 starts. If not for left fielder Gene Woodling's error on a fly ball in the late-afternoon shadows with two out in the ninth inning of Game Four against the Phillies, he would have perfectly clinched the world championship as a rookie with a complete game; that two-run error was followed by a single, and Allie Reynolds came on for the triumphant save. Ford would always remember that as a disappointment, but it was still a win for him, the first of 10 on the biggest stage.

No other pitcher has more than seven World Series wins, no active player is anywhere close, a likely unbreakable mark. There certainly might have been more, considering that he missed 1951 – 52 due to service in the Army. When he was inducted into the Hall of Fame in 1974 along with his longtime teammate and roommate Mickey Mantle, the Cooperstown crowd was predictably enormous. Just as it will be for Mariano Rivera and then for Derek Jeter.

"Whitey's a great representative of the franchise, not only because of his incredible ability to win and be successful, but also because he's a New Yorker," Hall president Jeff Idelson said. "There aren't too many New Yorkers who started for the Yankees. So for Yankee fans from New York, that was their guy. Just a fan favorite. A diminutive [five-foot, ten inch] guy who was larger than life on the mound."

Ford has been widely respected by the other greats who would return to Cooperstown each summer. Idelson said the southpaw loved to come up early, Wednesday or Thursday, with Joan, and sometimes they'd come up with the Berras.

"I remember once I was talking to him, we were putting together a ballot of retired players we thought needed to be considered," Idelson said. "We had maybe five or six Hall of Famers in the room, including me. We get to Spud Chandler. He had a .717 winning percentage, a shorter career, but it was even better than Whitey's. So they're talking about Chandler and I said to Whitey, 'How is it possible that Spud Chandler had a better winning percentage than you?' He said, 'You didn't have to go out drinking with Billy and Mickey every night.'"

Even Mickey described Whitey as "crafty," so I reluctantly use that horrible cliché in this section on the Chairman, just as infinite people before me. I would argue that Ford was simply a dominant pitcher and that the word "crafty" is defined as *deceitful*, *cunning* or *sly*, as if he had to rely on sneaky tricks to overcome an overall weakness. Maybe that was applicable toward the end of his career, when he admittedly mixed in an occasional illegal pitch. Honestly, Ford simply had a lot of arrows in one of the best quills ever, and he knew how to use them all.

"He was an artist," Joe Torre said. "He wasn't overpowering, but he was still intimidating."

Hideki Matsui

True confession: In the second inning on the night of November 4, 2009, I was carrying an irresistible tray of garlic fries through the muffled center-field tunnel past the museum to make my way to the left-field bleachers where my wife and stepdaughter Rachel were sitting among a sellout crowd. It was Game Six, Phillies at Yankees. I have always prided myself on witnessing big sports moments, but I was stuck in that long walk while the place began vibrating. The tunnel opened up and I arrived with the garlic fries just in time to see that the Yankees had taken a 2 – 0 lead on a Hideki Matsui homer.

It was not just any Hideki Matsui homer. It was a blast off Pedro Martinez that struck an advertisement on the facing of the second deck in right, ending an eight-pitch at-bat. The Yankees were Pedro's "Daddy" once again. This homer on a three-hit night for Matsui would give them a 2 – 0 lead on their way to their 27th Yankees world championship that night. He was World Series MVP. Then he was a parade hero up Broadway as Jay-Z and Alicia Keys delivered *Empire State of Mind* nonstop on the radio and all over the city:

> *I'm the new Sinatra, and, since I made it here*
> *I can make it anywhere, yea, they love me everywhere*

Matsui was 8-for-13 (.615) in the 2009 World Series. He was used exclusively as a DH that year, and therefore his overall impact was minimized against the Phillies. That made the fact that he won a World Series MVP trophy even more impressive. He started only three games, relegated to pinch-hitting duty in Philadelphia's home games where no DH was used. Matsui made the most of his playing time, becoming the first player to drive in six runs in a World Series clincher.

"It's awesome. Unbelievable. I'm surprised myself," he said through a translator.

Hey, at least I had seen his first homer at the old Yankee Stadium—a grand slam the day after a snow-out in the home opener. That was 2003, his introduction to new fans. He really was Godzilla. Matsui had come to the Yankees as a free agent from Japan's Central League after the 2002 season. In his final season with the Yomiuri Giants, he clobbered 50 home runs, just five shy of legendary Sadaharu Oh, who held the record at the time.

"I hope it works out," Matsui said of his future with the Yankees back then. "I love New York, I love the Yankees, and I love the fans here."

Matsui was one of the first Asian-born offensive stars in the U.S. and was immediately a favorite of the Yankee fan base. He finished that first season with 16 homers and 106 RBIs, chosen for his first of two straight All-Star Games and finishing second in AL Rookie of the Year balloting. This was definitely *not* Hideki Irabu, in case you were wondering. Not a Fat Toad.

Matsui was a happening in New York, and his massive Japanese media entourage suddenly was a fact of life. He became the only rookie ever to appear in 163 games, and he batted .261 with a homer and four RBIs in the 2003 World Series as the Yankees fell to the Marlins in six games. The 2004 season opened with two games in Tokyo against the Rays as a nod to this star's presence, and that same fall he went on an absolute tear. Matsui had a phenomenal 2004 postseason: a combined 21-for-51 against Minnesota and then Boston. But he was denied a Fall Classic after the team's meltdown against the Red Sox.

YANKEE WORLD SERIES MVPS

The World Series Most Valuable Player award was first handed out in 1955, when Johnny Podres won it after Brooklyn finally beat the Yankees in seven games. Any of the 16 Yankee World Series championships prior to 1955 are not included below as no MVP award was given. Bobby Richardson was the only Yankee to win one in a losing cause.

YEAR	OPPONENT	RESULT	MVP	STATISTICS
1956	Brooklyn Dodgers	Won 4 – 3	Don Larsen	Pitched first WS perfect game
1958	Milwaukee Braves	Won 4 – 3	Bob Turley	2 – 1 record, 1 save, 16.1 IP
1960	Pittsburgh Pirates	Lost 4 – 3	Bobby Richardson	11-for-30, 8 runs, 1 HR, 12 RBIs
1961	Cincinnati Reds	Won 4 – 1	Whitey Ford	2 – 0 record, 14 scoreless IP
1962	San Francisco Giants	Won 4 – 3	Ralph Terry	2 – 1 record, 1.80 ERA in 25 IP
1977	Los Angeles Dodgers	Won 4 – 2	Reggie Jackson	5 HR in Series (3 in Game Six)
1978	Los Angeles Dodgers	Won 4 – 2	Bucky Dent	10-for-24, 7 RBIs
1996	Atlanta Braves	Won 4 – 2	John Wetteland	Recorded save in all 4 victories
1998	San Diego Padres	Won 4 – 0	Scott Brosius	8-for-17, 2 HR, 6 RBIs
1999	Atlanta Braves	Won 4 – 0	Mariano Rivera	4.2 IP, 0 runs, 1 win, 2 saves
2000	New York Mets	Won 4 – 1	Derek Jeter	9-for-22, 6 runs, 2 HR
2009	Philadelphia Phillies	Won 4 – 2	Hideki Matsui	8-for-13, 3 HR, 8 RBIs

Matsui was a productive player in the middle of the Yankees' lineup for his seven-year tenure with New York. He slashed .292/.370/.482 with a 123 OPS+, and amassed 140 home runs. Godzilla provided the Yankees with three seasons of 100 or more runs scored, and four years driving in more than 100 runs. He lived up to the hype and remains a popular legend to New York fans.

Between his 332 longballs in Japan and 175 more in the U.S., Matsui totaled 507 homers in his career. With so much fuss being made about Ichiro Suzuki's combined hit total in Japan and the U.S., it is surprising that not more noise has been made about this fact. His 500th overall career homer came on July 20, 2011, as a member of the Oakland Athletics. Matsui's 175 Major League home runs were the most ever by an Asian-born player until Shin-Soo Choo—born in South Korea—belted Number 176 on May 26, 2018.

Matsui was inducted into the Japanese Baseball Hall of Fame in 2018 in his first year of eligibility. "I played as a professional baseball player for twenty years, but I only played in NPB for half of the time, ten years," he said in a statement. "I was given the honor of being selected for the Baseball Hall of Fame, nevertheless. And I would like to express my appreciation to those concerned."

None of his home runs was bigger, or more pivotal in his Yankee career, then the one that finally ended that at-bat against Pedro. I wish I had waited on the garlic fries.

"Ichiro Suzuki has had many accomplishments, but they've all been in the regular season," said Masanori Murakami, who was the first Japanese-born player to reach the Majors, in 1964. "As the first Japanese to win an MVP in the World Series, this is a great accomplishment for Matsui and will have a huge impact."

Matsui said it was hard to make a comparison between lofty achievements in Japan and MLB.

"When I was in Japan, that was the ultimate goal," he said right after winning World Series MVP. "Being here, winning the World Series, becoming world champions, that's what you strive for here. . . . You could say that I guess this is the best moment of my life right now."

George Weiss

The Yankees hired George Weiss in 1932 as farm system director with the task of building a pipeline to the Majors and perfecting the developmental concept that Branch Rickey had established first for the St. Louis Cardinals. Mission accomplished, according to these words on his Baseball Hall of Fame plaque: ". . . developed best minor league chain in game."

Weiss served under Col. Jacob Ruppert and Ed Barrow as farm director for 15 years, helping to feed the roster with thoughtful signings and minor league development throughout the Joe McCarthy era. But Weiss is probably best-known for being the general manager half of the super-success tandem with manager Casey Stengel—with whom he later went on to build a Mets franchise from ground up. Weiss measured his success by a slew of World Series trophies.

"There is no such thing as second place," he said. "You're either first or you're nothing."

Weiss was known to have a keen eye for amateur talent. To wit, consider this in the September 20, 1954 issue of *Sports Illustrated*:

"Weiss has always had plenty of cash behind him, but it is to his credit that he has gathered his greatest players for very little. Phil Rizzuto cost pennies, Yogi Berra came off the sandlots for $500 and Gil McDougald was signed for $1,500. What Weiss considers his greatest outfield represented an investment of $31,000. He got Joe DiMaggio for $25,000 when no one would take a chance on Joe's trick leg; he signed Charley Keller at the University of Maryland for $5,000; Mickey Mantle got an initial bonus of $1,000. A fourth great Yankee outfielder, Tommy Henrich, cost $20,000."

After serving as the Yankees' farm director for 15 years, Weiss was suddenly fired in 1947 following another World Series championship. The club had been sold two years earlier by Ruppert's estate to the trio of Larry MacPhail, Dan Topping and Del Webb, but during a celebration of the '47 title, a drunk and emotional MacPhail, who had announced his resignation shorty after the game, infamously and aggressively approached Weiss and abruptly fired him. The next day, Topping and Webb bought out MacPhail's shares of the team and reinstated Weiss as the new GM. Topping, Webb and Weiss would stay together for another 13 years.

During Weiss's tenure as GM (1948 – 60), the Yankees won 10 AL pennants and seven World Series titles. The 1959 season was the only one in which his team won fewer than 92 games during that stretch. After Weiss left, the Yankees won four more pennants in a row from 1960 – 64, with many of the players having been acquired by him.

Key position players purchased or acquired in trades included Roger Maris, Johnny Mize and Johnny Sain. Weiss also had a penchant for acquiring pitchers like Bob Turley and Eddie Lopat whose true talent was being masked by their mediocre won-lost records on poor teams.

Backing up his reputation as a brilliant farm director, the Yankees' minor league affiliates were extremely successful during Weiss's tenure. Newark won seven pennants in 12 seasons, and Kansas City won three pennants in four years after becoming a Yankees' affiliate.

Jackie Robinson broke baseball's color barrier in 1947, and not until an embarrassing eight years later did the Yankees finally follow suit with Elston Howard. They were one of the last teams to include a black player on their roster, and yet it was all happening in New York City, where integration was pioneered.

Eight years was an eternity under such circumstances, and there is no question that the Yankees were bottom-dwellers in this department.

Weiss was not the only influential voice in the organization on this important front, but he was in the decision-making chair during that long wait. It is not even worth bringing up excuses here, because doing so would absolve him. In fact, it is troubling how many words have been written by pundits who have tried to reason the lack of leadership in integration. It was indefensible, as any of Roger Kahn's readers well know, and that mark goes on Weiss's record along with the titles he was able to celebrate. "You're either first or you're nothing" should not have applied.

In the end, though, Weiss was named Executive of the Year by *The Sporting News* four times, more than anyone in MLB history. His plaque is on the wall in Cooperstown, certainly not the only one from Yankees management over the years.

Babe Ruth

We saved the best for last. The Sultan of Swat. The Wizard of Whack. The King of Clout. The Behemoth of Biff. The Big Bambino. Those are the nicknames, in order, that Claire Ruth mentioned in a 1974 remembrance called "My Husband Babe" amid renewed interest in the greatest sports icon ever as Hank Aaron inevitably passed his all-time record of 714 home runs.

I think about those nicknames, and the rush there must have been to outcoin one another on press box typewriters and New York City street corners, as I stand in the solemn Rotunda of the National Baseball Hall of Fame and Museum's gallery gazing at the center wall and the quintet of bronze plaques honoring "1936: THE FIRST CLASS". The plaque on the bottom left is Babe Ruth's, alongside those of Christy Mathewson, Ty Cobb, Honus Wagner and Walter Johnson.

"GREATEST DRAWING CARD IN HISTORY OF BASEBALL."

Those are the first seven words on Ruth's plaque inscription and that may be the most apt surviving label of them all. It should have been just six words, "GREATEST DRAWING CARD IN BASEBALL HISTORY," and the more I think about it, they really could have cut it to three words by eliminating the whole qualifier. GREATEST DRAWING CARD. After all, who in history was a better draw, in terms of actual volume of humans to *willfully* follow along? Confucius? Augustus? Washington? A religious figure, perhaps. So my only quibble is that the first sentence of his plaque should have had the same number of words as the number on his back, but the overall intent of the phrase remains magically relevant.

PLAYERS INDUCTED INTO HALL OF FAME AS YANKEES

PLAYER	POSITION	ELECTION YEAR	YEARS WITH YANKEES
Babe Ruth	RF	1936	1920-34
Lou Gehrig	1B	1939	1923-39
Jack Chesbro*	SP	1946	1903-09
Herb Pennock	SP	1948	1923-33
Bill Dickey	C	1954	1928-43; 1946
Joe DiMaggio	CF	1955	1936-1942; 1946-51
Red Ruffing	SP	1967	1930-42; 1945-46
Waite Hoyt	SP	1969	1921-30
Earle Combs	CF	1970	1924-35
Yogi Berra	C	1972	1946-64
Lefty Gomez	SP	1972	1930-42
Whitey Ford	SP	1974	1950; 1953-67
Mickey Mantle	CF	1974	1951-68
Catfish Hunter**	SP	1987	1975-79
Tony Lazzeri	2B	1991	1926-37
Reggie Jackson	RF	1993	1977-81
Phil Rizzuto	SS	1994	1941-42; 1946-56
Rich Gossage	RP	2008	1978-83
Joe Gordon	2B	2009	1938-46

* Chesbro played for the New York Highlanders

** Hunter opted for a blank cap on his plaque

Babe Ruth did not invent the home run nor the New York Yankees franchise, but he gave both their power and their stardust. No matter who makes news with home runs in the future, no matter how many more titles come the Yankees' way, history will still note that Babe Ruth: hit 60 homers one year for the best team ever— one-seventh of all 16 Major League teams' total longballs in that 1927 season; finished with 714 homers, the most famous American sports stat ever known; led the Yankees to seven World Series and their first four of 27 titles; topped U.S. President Herbert Hoover with an $80,000 salary; slugged .690; set 54 records; made possible the construction of not one but two stadiums in the Bronx; made the autograph a modern way of life; put the roar in the Roaring Twenties; saved the national pastime after a scandal; lived famously large; and put smiles on the faces of kids everywhere.

Babe Ruth in the Yankee dugout in 1921.

Any listing of the most pivotal moments in Yankees history begins in January of 1920, when the club announced it had bought Ruth from Red Sox owner Harry Frazee for an unprecedented $125,000, and paid him a $20,000 salary. Frazee called it "an amount the club could not afford to refuse" and claimed the Yankees were "taking a gamble." James O'Leary, writing for the *Boston Globe* on January 6, 1920, evoked a homer journalist's echo of Frazee with this gem: "Cy Young, Tris Speaker and other stars were let go and the Red Sox still won championships." O'Leary added: "It looks as if [Frazee] had made a good bargain." Those words, readily available down the coast in New York, may have sealed what for nearly a century was known as the "Curse of the Bambino."

The Red Sox were not only crazy enough to part with Babe Ruth, but they also had the gall to publicize their reason for it. Not until 2004 would Boston win another title. Meanwhile, the Yankees would average a few per decade over that time—26 of them before the Red Sox finally broke through. Frazee's club would become synonymous with heartbreak over an epoch and Ruth's new club would become the gold standard of sports.

Ruth had emerged as an elite lefthanded pitcher with Boston, but in 1918 his then-manager Ed Barrow persuaded Ruth to play the outfield and bat on days when he was not pitching. After Ruth hit 11 homers in 1918, Barrow asked him, "Babe, what do you really want to do, pitch or play the outfield?" Ruth replied: "Well, I certainly like to hit." The slugger was reduced to 15 mound starts in 1919 while otherwise starting in left. Given that extra time at bat, he led the AL with 29 homers, 113 RBIs, 103 runs and a 217 OPS+. It was not hard for Yankees owner Jacob Ruppert to project the possibility of a complete year as a position player—or the headlines from a Gotham press already eager to extol the virtues of big-bang baseball.

The Babe delivered. He moved to right field and bashed 54 homers, five more than his combined Boston total from 1914 – 19. In 1921, Ruth walloped an unthinkable 59—at least half of them "smacked off bad balls, pitches I had to reach for. Nobody gave me a good ball to hit," he later said. The Yankees reached the World Series for the first time that season, but they were promptly eliminated by the Giants—not once but in consecutive autumns. In 1923, after being "deeply humiliated," Ruth came back on a mission. On the first game at brand-new, $2.5 million Yankee Stadium in the Bronx, a cool and cloudy Wednesday in mid-April, more than 74,000 watched as the Bambino crushed a changeup from Howard Ehmke of the Red Sox far into the right field seats. Fred Lieb called it "The House That Ruth Built" that day in his New York *Evening Telegram* story, and other scribes picked up on it. That year, Ruth earned his only Most Valuable Player Award—joining Ty Cobb (1911) as the only unanimous picks—with a superhuman 14.1 WAR. There was a new World Series champion and it would become a habit.

In 1927, Ruth teamed with Gehrig to lead the vaunted "Murderers' Row" lineup. With the AL pennant already well in hand, Ruth went into the final three-game series at home against Washington sitting on 57 homers. His second homer that day, off Paul Hopkins, was a grand slam and matched his 1923 total of 59. Then the next day, Ruth took Tom Zachary deep for a two-run, game-winning homer in the eighth inning. Ruth had made good on his spring promise to the New York *Sun* of "sixty homers for Jake." After doing it, Ruth bellowed: "Sixty, count 'em, sixty! Let's see some son-of-a-bitch match that!" That team won the World Series and would be generally regarded as the greatest ever.

From 1910 – 18, baseball attendance failed to increase as quickly as the U.S. population. From 1919 – 30, however, it increased far faster than the population. One person was mostly responsible. GREATEST DRAWING CARD, indeed.

The late Hall of Fame baseball writer Leonard Koppett wrote in 1973 that Ruth's fame "was based on two numbers." One was that single-season record of 60 homers: "a feat whose significance needed no explanation to most of the 125,000,000 Americans then living. And in 1930, he attained an annual salary of $80,000, a figure whose significance was awesomely clear wherever people could read."

HOF ARTIFACT INVENTORY

Game-used equipment in the Baseball Hall of Fame:

BABE RUTH

B-13.48	Yankees uniform (with cap) issued to Babe Ruth, possibly between 1929 and 1934.
B-1.39	Game shoes.
B-2787.63	Bustin' Babes uniform shirt worn in 1927 and 1928.
B-22.49	Single gilded shoe worn by Ruth.
B-113.49	Babe's fountain pen used to sign autographs and contract.
B-26.59	Schaeffer Lifetime pen used by Ruth and Jacob Ruppert to sign $75,000 1932 contract with the Yankees.
B-2854.63	Game shoes.
B-351.69	Ruth's locker from Yankee Stadium.
B-488.84	No. 3 jersey worn by Ruth. It is believed that this dates from the 1930s and then was sent to the Yankees' farm team in Butler, Pa., where it was worn by minor league players into the 1940. Donor was a batboy for Butler team and retained possession of the shirt after the club folded with the onset of World War II. "Health" patch was added about 1942.
B-21.49	Bronzed fielder's glove, c. 1930s.
B-562.75	Shaving brush.
B-2740.63	Baseman's mitt used (unsure when) and signed on May 6, 1947.
B-2717.63	Fielder's glove used in 1927.
B-261.69	Game shoes.
B-15.49a	Fielder's glove used in 1926 World Series.
B-253.39	Glove used in 1928.
B-2777.63	Cap that belonged to Ruth.
B-254.39	Bat with 28 notches around trademark on barrel, each representing a home run.
B-90.39	Bat used to hit 60th HR on Sept. 30, 1927.

B-138.60	Bat used to hit 57th and 58th homers at Polo Grounds, Sept. 26, 1921.
B-2993.63	Bat.
B-44.72	Bat used to hit last 3 career HRs at Pittsburgh, May 25, 1935, with Boston Braves.
B-43.62	Bat used early in 1919 season while with the Red Sox.
B-16.48	According to the ledger: Last baseball with which Ruth hit a homer in aforementioned Braves-Pirates game.
B-248.59	Baseball from Red Sox vs. Tigers, Ruth pitching.
B-538.75	Home Run 500 ft. Lighthouse 1915, and signed by Babe Ruth. It should be "1918". The ball is from an exhibition game at New Haven, Aug. 18, 1918. Handwritten on the baseball is "Home Run 550 Ft. Lighthouse 1917." However, the estimated distance of Ruth's home run at the time was 500 feet and the year was 1918, not 1917. For this reason, the Hall believes that the written information was added to the ball well after the event occurred.
B-15.49	According to handwritten inscription and signature on bat: To E.C. Bostick I got three home runs with this bat at St. Louis. Keep it with my best wishes. "Babe" Ruth (signature) World Series 1926.
B-457.52	Pair of bowling shoes.

That point is well-taken, but Ruth's fame was definitely based on more than two numbers. It was also based on his natural attention to the happiness of children everywhere. Sure, the idolatry stemmed from his power and showmanship in uniform, but the interaction with youth was a direct result of his own path as a boy. Young George was declared an "incorrigible" as a boy, taken off the streets of Baltimore and placed in the St. Mary's Industrial School. He tried to run, but Brother Matthias took him back to teach the young rebel a shirtmaker's trade. Brother Gilbert was the school's baseball coach and discovered George's natural athleticism, clearing a path to a professional career. Through all of his own admitted mistakes and all of his glories, Ruth never lost sight of his past. Even incorrigibles can amount to something.

Consider his own final words for proof of this, for confirmation of his sincerity. The last message he ever composed was written with the help of a few friends, including Joe L. Brown of the same MGM Studios that produced *The Babe Ruth Story*, and it was received on the day Ruth died by the offices of *Guideposts*, the publication then run by editor-in-chief and renowned positive thinker Norman Vincent Peale.

"I never forgot where I came from," Ruth wrote. "Every dirty-faced kid I see is another useful citizen. No one knew better than I what it meant not to have your own home, a backyard, your own kitchen and icebox. That's why all through the years, even when the big money was rolling in, I'd never forget St. Mary's, Brother Matthias and the boys I left behind. I kept going back."

It has been more than 70 years since George Herman Ruth Jr. "died a beautiful death," in the words of the catholic priest who administered last rites at what is now Memorial Sloan Kettering Cancer Center in Manhattan. In examining a copy of death certificate number 18226, amongst myriad papers within one of the many fat and oft-handled Ruth clip files inside the Hall of Fame's research center, I cannot imagine the dread finality felt by those around him. According to a science story in *The New York Times* 50 years after his death, what almost no one knew at the time—maybe not even Ruth—was that he had contributed in a big way to society at the end of his life, as one of the first examples of a cancer patient receiving a consecutive treatment of chemotherapy and radiation.

"Few men in American history have been a greater inspiration to the youth of our land," said Earl Warren, speaking after Ruth's passing as New York governor and also vice presidential running mate for Thomas Dewey. "Throughout his life he played the game fair and hard and never gave up to the very end."

The measure of a man, in Ruth's case, was not just in his extreme 53 years of life but also after he fell asleep for the last time on that evening of August 16, 1948. Not surprising were headlines of enormous point size covering New York tabs in subsequent late-PM and morning editions. But consider the *Los Angeles Times* treatment:

SPORTS-LOVING NATION MOURNS
DEATH OF HOMER KING BABE RUTH
Dream Malady Takes Life
Of Beloved Baseball Player

"No other sports figure ever challenged him closely for our affection and adoration. No one probably ever will," Al Wolf wrote for that paper in his obit column.

It would not have seemed like an outlandish statement of hyperbole back then, yet it is remarkable that words like those were so prophetic. No one ever has. Today, Hall of Fame visitors look for his plaque, see his statue in the Rotunda and his special exhibit complete with his actual locker and other items. I have walked with new Hall electees many times in their orientation tours of the museum, and one of the highlights is always when they don white gloves and then hold up Babe's actual uniform. The jersey is square and unfitted, giant, just like his bat that they then handle.

"When you think about Hall of Famers, you think in many ways if they are heroes to different people," Hall of Fame president Jeff Idelson said. "Babe Ruth and Jackie Robinson stand at the top for very different reasons, but both were heroes to many. Ruth was so much better than so much of the competition when he played. You talk about accessibility; the joke is that there are fewer baseballs *unsigned* from the 1920s by Babe Ruth than there are *signed* by Babe Ruth. Which shows you how accessible and how much he enjoyed the social part of the game. You wonder how he would have survived in a social media community, given his larger-than-life status, but that's another topic for another day."

Idelson said the fans' two most-asked questions about players when visiting the Hall of Fame are: "What do you have on Jackie Robinson, and what do you have on Babe Ruth? The home runs, the ability to set the table for Shohei Ohtani as a hitter and a pitcher, and his personality all combines to make sure that he is still remembered as a fan favorite almost a century after he finished playing."

Before completing this part of the book in early March, I drive with my wife to the expansive Gate of Heaven Cemetery north of New York City, up the Saw Mill Parkway. We eventually find the home plate-shaped Section 25, where Billy Martin also rests. I park and trudge up the snowy hill, following the myriad footsteps.

The "RUTH" tombstone is surrounded by evergreens and overlooking a sublime vista punctuated by the distant sight of an MTA train silently inching like a caterplillar left-to-right on its way toward Yankee Stadium. The marker depicts Jesus with a young baseball player. Six baseball bats, many baseballs (some autographed to him), a photo of Babe and Lou, and a bottle of Budweiser are at the base of the marker. There is a Red Sox cap and a snow-covered pinstripe cap, and I reach down and chip away the snow with my hand to reveal the famous Yankee logo on the latter. I say a prayer aloud and a thanks. There are so many ways to look back upon Ruth, yet no way to be here yourself.

Suddenly I envied people of the 1920s and '30s. We have modern medicine, longer lifespans, mobile devices and so forth. But they had Babe Ruth.

Looking at the sculptural design of this marker and turning away, I think again of his Cooperstown plaque likeness, the funny face photographed by everyone. I reflect on a passage from Homer's *Iliad* that had inspired the sculptor Pheidias in his creation of the Statue of Zeus at Olympia, one of the seven wonders of the ancient world:

ἦ καὶ κυανέῃσιν ἐπ᾽ ὀφρύσι νεῦσε Κρονίων
ἀμβρόσιαι δ᾽ ἄρα χαῖται ἐπερρώσαντο ἄνακτος
κρατὸς ἀπ᾽ ἀθανάτοιο μέγαν δ᾽ ἐλέλιξεν Ὄλυμπον.

He spoke, the son of Cronos, and nodded his head with the dark brows,
and the immortally anointed hair of the great god
swept from his divine head, and all Olympos was shaken.

References

"Lou Gehrig: A Quiet Hero", by Frank Graham, 1942
"The Joe DiMaggio Story, True, 1954
"The Yankee Encyclopedia", 2003
Appel, Marty. Casey Stengel: Baseball's Greatest Character (p. 150). Knopf Doubleday Publishing Group
Baseball Almanac
Baseball Hall of Fame
Baseball Hall of Fame, oral history interview, April 27, 1987
Baseball Hall of Fame, oral history interview, Oct. 11, 1981
Baseball Reference
Boston Globe, June 19, 1977
Boston Globe, Oct. 2, 1978
Brooklyn Eagle, Jan. 13, 1939
Casey Stengel: Baseball's Greatest Character, 2017
CBS New York, Sept. 22, 2014
CBS News, Sept. 29, 2014
Chris Jaffe, Evaluating Baseball's Managers, 2010
Clyde Partin, Emory University, LA84 Foundation, http://library.la84.org/SportsLibrary/NASSH_Proceedings/NP1985/NP1985zt.pdf
ESPN Sport Science, 2011
ESPN, Jan. 24, 2010
ESPN.com, March 11, 2015
Eugene Register-Guard, April 20, 1976
Eugene Register-Guard, May 9, 1968
Falkner, David, The Last Yankee: The Turbulent Life of Billy Martin. 1992, Simon & Schuster

Frank Graham, New York Journal American, Oct. 7, 1964
https://sabr.org/research/
new-york-yankees-team-ownership-history
https://www.bostonglobe.com/sports/1920/01/06/red-sox-sell-
babe-ruth-for-cash/muYGoMdAzCl8WlRHK2LumI/story.
html
https://www.snopes.com/fact-check/
wally-pipp39s-career-ending-39headache39
Hudson Valley Journal News, Dec. 7, 2010
James and Neyer, The Neyer/James Guide to Pitchers, p. 367
Jane Gross, "Yanks Won't Start Mattingly," New York Times,
March 13, 1984.
Jim Kaat, If These Walls Could Talk
Jimmy Wood, Brooklyn Eagle, Sept. 5, 1941
Joe King, New York World Telegram, Feb. 3, 1959
Joe McCarthy, New York Times, Sept. 25, 1977
Joe Torre and Tom Verducci, "The Yankee Years," Doubleday,
2009
Joe Williams, The Sporting News, May 12, 1939
John Tullius, "I'd Rather Be a Yankee," 1986
Jorge Posada, "The Journey Home: My Life in Pinstripes,"
2015
Lefty: An American Odyssey, 2012
Los Angeles Times, June 2, 1986
MacLennan, Society for American Baseball Research
Mark Gallagher, The Yankee Encyclopedia, 2003
Marty Appel, "Pinstripe Empire," 2011
Mike Shalin, "Donnie Baseball", 2011
Milton Richman, The Sporting News, 1973
Montreal Gazette, Jan. 2, 1975
New York Daily News, April 16, 2009
New York Daily News, Jan. 13, 1939
New York Daily News, Sept. 21, 2011
New York Herald-Tribune, Oct. 11, 1950
New York Herald-Tribune, October 1930
New York Journal-American, Dec. 16, 1953
New York Journal-American, March 28, 1951
New York Post, April 10, 2018
New York Post, Dec. 17, 1980

New York Post, Feb. 15, 2014
New York Sun, Jan. 13, 1939
New York Times, Aug. 1, 1993
New York Times, Dec. 28, 1994
New York Times, Feb. 22, 1981
New York Times, Jack Curry, 2009
New York Times, July 18, 2008
New York Times, July 22, 1976
New York Times, June 4, 2003
New York Times, Nov. 13, 1933
New York Times, Nov. 28, 1972
New York Times, Oct. 14, 1921
New York Times, Sept. 25, 1977
New York Times, Sept. 5, 1986
New York World-Telegram, May 22, 1951
Newsday, March 9, 2013
Newsday, May 20, 2009
Paul Votano, Tony Lazzeri: A Baseball Biography, McFarland
    & Co. Inc, April 15, 2005
Phil Pepe, Talkin' Baseball, p. 298, 299.
Pinstripe Empire, 2012
Pittsburgh Post-Gazette, Sept. 10, 1999
Providence News, Nov. 2, 1923
Ray Robinson, "Lou Gehrig: Iron Horse in His Time"
Reading-Eagle, Sept. 13, 1942
River Ave. Blues, Jan. 30, 2018
Robert Cutter, "Joe DiMaggio and Ted Williams" book, 1964
SABR, http://sabr.org/bioproj/person/25ce33d8
Sam Walker, The Captain Class
San Francisco Examiner, 1991
Sarasota Journal, March 30, 1953
Scott Miller, CBSSports.com, July 13, 2013
Sid C. Keener, "Huggins, Manager of a Million-Dollar Fran-
    chise," St. Louis Times, May 17, 1919
Society for American Baseball Research
Sparky Lyle, The Bronx Zoo
Sport, April 18, 1967
Sporting News, May 1, 1941
Sports Illustrated, Aug. 24, 2014

Springfield, Mass., Union, Sept. 29, 1951
The Joe DiMaggio Story, True magazine, 1954
The National Pastime Museum, http://www.
    thenationalpastimemuseum.com/article/
    there-was-yogi-berra-there-was-bill-dickey
The Oklahoman, Dec. 28, 1994
The Saturday Evening Post, April 18, 1953
The Saturday Evening Post, April 24, 1937
The Sporting News, 1933
The Sporting News, Aug. 17, 1933
The Sporting News, Dec. 10, 1948
The Sporting News, Jan. 4, 1964
The Sporting News, Feb. 13, 1957
The Sporting News, Feb. 19, 1972
The Sporting News, March 22, 1961
The Sporting News, May 1, 1941
The Sporting News, Oct. 23, 1930
The Sporting News, October 19, 1963
The Telegraph-Herald, Oct. 9, 1927
TIME, Oct. 4, 1948
Tom Meany, "The Merry Mortician on the Mound," Baseball
    Digest, March 1952
Tom Verducci, Sports Illustrated, May 7, 2001
USA Today, https://www.usatoday.com/story/sports/
    mlb/2016/08/13/yanks-honor-1996-world-series-champi-
    ons-in-pregame-ceremony/88693202
Vecsey, The New York Yankees Illustrated History, pg. 3
Washington Post, Aug. 3, 1979
Washington Post, Oct. 29, 1979
William A. Cook, "Waite Hoyt: A Biography of the Yankees'
    Schoolboy Wonder", McFarland, 2012
Yankee Magazine, July 21, 1983
Yankees Magazine, August 2015
Yankees.com, Feb. 25, 2018
YES Network, "Kids on Deck", 2004

Acknowledgements

Adam Dore and Jason Dore were my remarkable research assistants for this book and it would not have all come together without their invaluable work.

Cooperstown was the beginning point for this book, if not literally for baseball as a whole. I thank the entire staff at the National Baseball Hall of Fame & Museum. Jeff Idelson sat with me for multiple interviews and I was additionally inspired by the books and art in his office. Craig Muder, Jon Shestakofsky, Erik Strohl, Jim Gates, Bruce Markusen and Cassidy in the library are among the many there who helped me so much.

Thanks to the whole team at Cardinal Publishers Group and its Blue River Press imprint. We plotted this quick-turn-around work while I was in Indy for a *Diamonds from the Dugout* national book tour stop, and I especially appreciate the way they made my faithful and odiferous English Bulldog travel companion Bingley feel at home under the conference table.

Yogi Berra, Aaron Boone, Robinson Cano, Chris Chambliss, David Cone, Bucky Dent, Whitey Ford, Goose Gossage, Derek Jeter, Aaron Judge, Billy Martin, Tino Martinez, Don Mattingly, Graig Nettles, Paul O'Neill, Andy Pettitte, Jorge Posada, Willie Randolph, Bobby Richardson, Mariano Rivera, Alex Rodriguez, Gary Sanchez, Mark Teixeira, Joe Torre, Roy White, Bernie Williams and Dave Winfield were among Yankees I interviewed leading to this. Thanks to Diana Munson and Lindsay Berra for loving legacies you carry on with such pride and passion.

Marty Appel was walking through Central Park and talking to me on his phone about Torre and other subjects when suddenly he was interrupted by a pedestrian who recognized him and asked him for his thoughts on the Yankees. That said it all. Marty is a Yankee legend himself and was a valuable resource.

I am also thankful to another author, Lou Gehrig biographer Ray Robinson, who passed away before I started this book yet filled me with fun stories about the Iron Horse and the Bambino during my decades as a baseball writer.

Nikki Warner and the staff at the Major League Baseball Players Alumni Association are always helpful to me in my pursuit of books about former players. One of those players, fellow author and longtime pitcher Mark Littell, was always a Facebook message away.

Bob Costas and James Caan are beloved by masses and I loved the stories they shared with me about Mickey Mantle.

The New York Public Library on Fifth Avenue was always there when you needed it with its wondrous reading room for manuscript work. The cornerstone for that edifice was laid at about the same time the Yankee franchise laid its own, and these two magnificent New York institutions have gone hand-in-hand ever since.

Thanks to Arturo Pardavila III for your pics and longtime teamwork.

Baseball Reference, Yankees.com and the Society for Baseball Research were routine go-to sources for player, team, league and game data. Thanks to my longtime colleague Barry Bloom for some early oversight of the topic list and beers in Cooperstown.

Nothing is possible without the love and support of my wife Lisa and our combined crew of Matthew, Benjamin, Joshua and Rachel. Sure, I'm lucky – just like Lou said.

About the Author

Mark Newman is author of the No. 1 bestseller *Diamonds from the Dugout* (featuring Derek Jeter on the cover) and is now based with wife Lisa in St. Petersburg, Fla., after a nearly two-decade run with MLB.com and Yankees.com in Major League Baseball's Chelsea Market office. The Indiana University graduate is a Hall of Fame voting member of the Baseball Writers' Association of America and a baseball writer since 1990, covering twenty-five World Series. He was an award-winning pro sports beat writer for *The Miami Herald*, *Fort Worth Star-Telegram*, and *San Jose Mercury News*, and while with *The Sporting News* accepted the prestigious National Magazine Award for General Excellence. For updates, including book tour information, visit marknewmanbooks.com and facebook.com/MarkNewmanAuthor.